Cartelization, Antitrust and Globalization in the US and Europe

The uncovering of a great number of cartels in the industrialized world has left an unfortunate, yet significant, mark on global economic developments in recent years. Globalization has forced firms into more direct competition, and the result has been global price-fixing. This situation has challenged antitrust authorities, as competition policy is regional or national, not international, in scope. This work examines the history of cartelization to demonstrate this transformation, and provides an overview of existing and proposed reforms in antitrust that seek to address the cartel problem.

Taking a broad yet detailed approach, this work sets a practical explanation of the history of cartels and antitrust law in a sound theoretical framework, as well as providing suggestions as to how potential reforms of antitrust laws could improve the situation going forward. The book includes a comprehensive analysis of the motivations behind and perceived necessity for organizations to enter into cartels, and the success (or otherwise) of legislatures' attempts to both uncover and prevent such cartels from taking place. A total of 24 price-fixing conspiracies uncovered in the US and Europe are examined as part of the analysis to demonstrate the globalization of collusion.

Several critical questions are raised regarding price-fixing and the antitrust response. Does stricter enforcement and higher penalties guarantee greater competition, or does the double-bind of strict anti-cartel and anti-merger policy cause firms to exit an industry? Can soaring fines jeopardize the health of firms and force them into financial difficulty that ultimately lessens competition? Should competition authorities regard markets experiencing tough competitive pressures—a situation primed for collusion—as needing regulatory oversight instead of prosecution? This makes for a comprehensive study that will be of great use to postgraduates, academics and researchers alike.

Mark S. LeClair received his PhD in Economics from Rutgers University in 1987. He is currently a professor of economics at Fairfield University in Fairfield, Connecticut, USA.

Routledge Studies in the Modern World Economy

1 **Interest Rates and Budget Deficits**
A study of the advanced economies
Kanhaya L. Gupta and Bakhtiar Moazzami

2 **World Trade after the Uruguay Round**
Prospects and policy options for the twenty-first century
Edited by Harald Sander and András Inotai

3 **The Flow Analysis of Labour Markets**
Edited by Ronald Schettkat

4 **Inflation and Unemployment**
Contributions to a new macroeconomic approach
Edited by Alvaro Cencini and Mauro Baranzini

5 **Macroeconomic Dimensions of Public Finance**
Essays in honour of Vito Tanzi
Edited by Mario I. Blejer and Teresa M. Ter-Minassian

6 **Fiscal Policy and Economic Reforms**
Essays in honour of Vito Tanzi
Edited by Mario I. Blejer and Teresa M. Ter-Minassian

7 **Competition Policy in the Global Economy**
Modalities for co-operation
Edited by Leonard Waverman, William S. Comanor and Akira Goto

8 **Working in the Macro Economy**
A study of the US labor market
Martin F. J. Prachowny

9 **How Does Privatization Work?**
Edited by Anthony Bennett

10 **The Economics and Politics of International Trade**
Freedom and trade: Volume II
Edited by Gary Cook

11 **The Legal and Moral Aspects of International Trade**
Freedom and trade: Volume III
Edited by Asif Qureshi, Hillel Steiner and Geraint Parry

12 **Capital Markets and Corporate Governance in Japan, Germany and the United States**
Organizational response to market inefficiencies
Helmut M. Dietl

13 **Competition and Trade Policies**
Coherence or conflict
Edited by Einar Hope

14 **Rice**
The primary commodity
A. J. H. Latham

15 **Trade, Theory and Econometrics**
Essays in honour of
John S. Chipman
Edited by James C. Moore, Raymond Riezman and James R. Melvin

16 **Who Benefits from Privatisation?**
Edited by Moazzem Hossain and Justin Malbon

17 **Towards a Fair Global Labour Market**
Avoiding the new slave trade
Ozay Mehmet, Errol Mendes and Robert Sinding

18 **Models of Futures Markets**
Edited by Barry Goss

19 **Venture Capital Investment**
An agency analysis of UK practice
Gavin C. Reid

20 **Macroeconomic Forecasting**
A sociological appraisal
Robert Evans

21 **Multimedia and Regional Economic Restructuring**
Edited by Hans-Joachim Braczyk, Gerhard Fuchs and Hans-Georg Wolf

22 **The New Industrial Geography**
Regions, regulation and institutions
Edited by Trevor J. Barnes and Meric S. Gertler

23 **The Employment Impact of Innovation**
Evidence and policy
Edited by Marco Vivarelli and Mario Pianta

24 **International Health Care Reform**
A legal, economic and political analysis
Colleen Flood

25 **Competition Policy Analysis**
Edited by Einar Hope

26 **Culture and Enterprise**
The development, representation and morality of business
Don Lavoie and Emily Chamlee-Wright

27 **Global Financial Crises and Reforms**
Cases and caveats
B. N. Ghosh

28 **Geography of Production and Economic Integration**
Miroslav N. Jovanović

29 **Technology, Trade and Growth in OECD Countries**
Does specialisation matter?
Valentina Meliciani

30 **Post-Industrial Labour Markets**
Profiles of North America and Scandinavia
Edited by Thomas P. Boje and Bengt Furaker

31 **Capital Flows without Crisis**
Reconciling capital mobility and economic stability
Edited by Dipak Dasgupta, Marc Uzan and Dominic Wilson

32 **International Trade and National Welfare**
Murray C. Kemp

33 **Global Trading Systems at Crossroads**
A post-Seattle perspective
Dilip K. Das

34 **The Economics and Management of Technological Diversification**
Edited by John Cantwell, Alfonso Gambardella and Ove Granstrand

35 **Before and Beyond EMU**
Historical lessons and future prospects
Edited by Patrick Crowley

36 **Fiscal Decentralization**
Ehtisham Ahmad and Vito Tanzi

37 **Regionalisation of Globalised Innovation**
Locations for advanced industrial development and disparities in participation
Edited by Ulrich Hilpert

38 **Gold and the Modern World Economy**
Edited by MoonJoong Tcha

39 **Global Economic Institutions**
Willem Molle

40 **Global Governance and Financial Crises**
Edited by Meghnad Desai and Yahia Said

41 **Linking Local and Global Economies**
The ties that bind
Edited by Carlo Pietrobelli and Arni Sverrisson

42 **Tax Systems and Tax Reforms in Europe**
Edited by Luigi Bernardi and Paola Profeta

43 **Trade Liberalization and APEC**
Edited by Jiro Okamoto

44 **Fiscal Deficits in the Pacific Region**
Edited by Akira Kohsaka

45 **Financial Globalization and the Emerging Market Economies**
Dilip K. Das

46 **International Labor Mobility**
Unemployment and increasing returns to scale
Bharati Basu

47 **Good Governance in the Era of Global Neoliberalism**
Conflict and depolitization in Latin America, Eastern Europe, Asia and Africa
Edited by Jolle Demmers, Alex E. Fernández Jilberto and Barbara Hogenboom

48 **The International Trade System**
Alice Landau

49 **International Perspectives on Temporary Work and Workers**
Edited by John Burgess and Julia Connell

50 **Working Time and Workers' Preferences in Industrialized Countries**
Finding the balance
Edited by Jon C. Messenger

51 **Tax Systems and Tax Reforms in New EU Members**
Edited by Luigi Bernardi, Mark Chandler and Luca Gandullia

52 **Globalization and the Nation State**
The impact of the IMF and the World Bank
Edited by Gustav Ranis, James Vreeland and Stephen Kosak

53 **Macroeconomic Policies and Poverty Reduction**
Edited by Ashoka Mody and Catherine Pattillo

54 **Regional Monetary Policy**
Carlos J. Rodríguez-Fuentez

55 **Trade and Migration in the Modern World**
Carl Mosk

56 **Globalisation and the Labour Market**
Trade, technology and less-skilled workers in Europe and the United States
Edited by Robert Anderton, Paul Brenton and John Whalley

57 **Financial Crises**
Socio-economic causes and institutional context
Brenda Spotton Visano

58 **Globalization and Self Determination**
Is the nation-state under siege?
Edited by David R. Cameron, Gustav Ranis and Annalisa Zinn

59 **Developing Countries and the Doha Development Round of the WTO**
Edited by Pitou van Dijck and Gerrit Faber

60 **Immigrant Enterprise in Europe and the USA**
Prodromos Panayiotopoulos

61 **Solving the Riddle of Globalization and Development**
Edited by Manuel Agosín, David Bloom, George Chapelier and Jagdish Saigal

62 **Foreign Direct Investment and the World Economy**
Ashoka Mody

63 **The World Economy**
A global analysis
Horst Siebert

64 **Production Organizations in Japanese Economic Development**
Edited by Tetsuji Okazaki

65 **The Economics of Language**
International analyses
Edited by Barry R. Chiswick and Paul W. Miller

66 **Street Entrepreneurs**
People, place and politics in local and global perspective
Edited by John Cross and Alfonso Morales

67 **Global Challenges and Local Responses**
The East Asian experience
Edited by Jang-Sup Shin

68 **Globalization and Regional Integration**
The origins, development and impact of the single European aviation market
Alan Dobson

69 **Russia Moves into the Global Economy**
Breaking out
John M. Letiche

70 **The European Economy in an American Mirror**
Barry Eichengreen, Michael Landesmann and Dieter Stiefel

71 **Working Time Around the World**
Trends in working hours, laws, and policies in a global comparative perspective
Jon C. Messenger, Sangheon Lee and Deidre McCann

72 **International Water Treaties**
Negotiation and cooperation along transboundary rivers
Shlomi Dinar

73 **Economic Integration in the Americas**
Edited by Joseph A. McKinney and H. Stephen Gardner

74 **Expanding Frontiers of Global Trade Rules**
The political economy dynamics of the international trading system
Nitya Nanda

75 **The Macroeconomics of Global Imbalances**
European and Asian perspectives
Edited by Marc Uzan

76 **China and Asia**
Economic and financial interactions
Edited by Yin-Wong Cheung and Kar-Yiu Wong

77 **Regional Inequality in China**
Trends, explanations and policy responses
Edited by Shenggen Fan, Ravi Kanbur and Xiaobo Zhang

78 **Governing Rapid Growth in China**
Equity and institutions
Edited by Ravi Kanbur and Xiaobo Zhang

79 **The Indonesian Labour Market**
Shafiq Dhanani, Iyanatul Islam and Anis Chowdhury

80 **Cost-Benefit Analysis in Multi-level Government in Europe and the USA**
The case of EU cohesion policy and of US federal investment policies
Alessandro Ferrara

81 **The Economic Geography of Air Transportation**
Space, time, and the freedom of the sky
John Bowen

82 **Cartelization, Antitrust and Globalization in the US and Europe**
Mark S. LeClair

Cartelization, Antitrust and Globalization in the US and Europe

Mark S. LeClair

Routledge
Taylor & Francis Group
LONDON AND NEW YORK

First published 2011
by Routledge
2 Park Square, Milton Park, Abingdon, Oxon OX14 4RN

Simultaneously published in the USA and Canada
by Routledge
711 Third Avenue, New York, NY 10017, USA

Routledge is an imprint of the Taylor & Francis Group, an informa business

Typeset in Times New Roman by
RefineCatch Limited, Bungay, Suffolk

British Library Cataloguing in Publication Data
A catalogue record for this book is available from the British Library

Library of Congress Cataloging in Publication Data
A catalog record for this book has been requested

ISBN 978-0-415-57343-6 (hbk)
ISBN 978-0-2038-4736-7 (ebk)

Dedicated to Gail Meyers and
in memory of Dolores Doornbosch

Contents

Illustrations

Figure

Tables

Abbreviations

ADM	Archer Daniels Midland
CSO	Central Selling Organization
CSP	Central Selling Point
CVA	Capper-Volstead Act
DOJ	Department of Justice
DRAM	Dynamic Random Access Memory
ECSC	European Coal and Steel Community
EEC	European Economic Community
FCO	Federal Cartel Office (Germany)
FTC	Federal Trade Commission
GATT	General Agreement on Tariffs and Trade
GIS	Gas Insulated Switchgear
HHI	Herfindahl–Hirschman Index
IBA	International Bauxite Association
ICA	International Coffee Agreement(s)
ICCA	International Cocoa Agreement(s)
IPC	Integrated Programme for Commodities
IRA	International Rubber Association
ISA	International Sugar Association
ITA	International Tin Agreement(s)
JFTC	Japan Fair Trade Commission
LCD	Liquid Crystal Display
MITI	Ministry of International Trade and Industry
NAFTA	North American Free Trade Agreement
NIRA	National Industrial Recovery Act
NRA	Natural Rubber Agreement(s)
OECD	Organization for Economic Cooperation and Development
OPEC	Organization of Petroleum Exporting Countries
PFMA	Plumbing Fixtures Manufacturers Association
STABEX	Stabilization of Export Earnings
SYSMIN	System of Stabilization for Export Earnings from Mining Products

TFT	Thin Film Transistor
TVA	Tennessee Valley Authority
UNCTAD	United Nations Commission on Trade and Development
WTO	World Trade Organization

Acknowledgments

I would like to express my appreciation to the Research Committee at Fairfield University for funding the fall 2008 sabbatical that enabled me to begin this work. An expression of deep gratitude goes to my wife, Kathy Doornbosch, for her painstaking work in preparing the final manuscript. The many hours she devoted to reading, commenting on, and helping me revise the text produced a clearer, more concise manuscript. To my sons Ryan and Evan (my technical support person) for their moral support and patience during the months leading up to the completion of this work.

To my ever-helpful colleagues in the Department of Economics at Fairfield University. I have had the opportunity to work with the most supportive department a person could hope for. I appreciate their time, insights and unending encouragement through all my endeavors at Fairfield University.

Preface

In 1999, it was revealed that a conspiracy had, for nearly a decade, manipulated global prices for bulk vitamins. The longevity of this cartel, coupled with the relatively large number of firms involved (nearly 20), made it one of the most significant antitrust enforcement cases of recent years. In the subsequent prosecution of the participants, it was revealed that the cartel members had conducted secret meetings to discuss falling market prices, and agreed to coordinated price increases that would return the market to profitability. It was a truly global endeavor, with firms from Europe, Canada and Japan all conspiring to raise prices. To escape detection, the members agreed to slow and methodical price increases; a process that led eventually to high double-digit increases in the prices of vitamins. By the time the cartel was uncovered, it had done inestimable damage to end-users (in particular, farmers). This was taken into account by the US Department of Justice and the European Commission in pursuing penalties against the participants, which included significant fines levied against the firms, and jail time for key executives. The bulk vitamin agreement was but one of a lengthy list of cartels that have been uncovered within the industrialized world since 1990. This can be partly explained by enhanced antitrust enforcement that forced more cartels to the surface. It is also due, however, to the sheer number of collusive accords that have been formed in response to increasingly competitive markets.

Cartelization is almost exclusively confined to industries that are oligopolistic in structure: a reality that creates significant problems for antitrust authorities. As demonstrated in Chapter 2, tacit cooperation is the expected outcome in such industries, with competitors essentially matching each other's prices. While such an outcome may appear collusive, it is simply profit-maximizing behavior, since competition on price would be destructive. A major part of the antitrust "problem" is determining a means by which to uncover cartels if cooperative pricing is the norm. Game theory is applied to demonstrate how newer enforcement tools, such as leniency policy, alter the firm's decision process and may expose more violations. Finally, Chapter 2 also examines the problem of industrial societies (trade associations) that on the surface appear to be legitimate organizations.

Conversations about marketing techniques and new product lines may eventually veer into (unlawful) discussions of pricing policies, and contribute to the development of collusive agreements. Key executives, particularly those from smaller firms, may be unaware of what constitutes illegal cooperation, and this may result in collaboration that extends beyond what is permitted.

This text will place a historical emphasis on the role of collusion, assuming that each period has something to reveal about how firms (countries) form, manage, and benefit from cartels. The period prior to the passage of the Sherman Antitrust Act in 1891 illustrates firm behavior in the absence of any regulatory restraints; collusion is commonplace and visible. As detailed in Chapter 3, the US railroad industry routinely harmonized tariffs as a means of preventing undue competition. Once antitrust legislation is in place, a half-century of tentative enforcement ensues. During this period firms managed to circumvent the law through less obvious means of collusion, such as interlocking boards or agreements that allocated sales regions to each firm. General Electric, in its role as the primary light bulb producer in the 1920s, controlled the bulb market in Europe through participation in the management of nearly every competitor; a tactic that worked until low-cost Japanese producers entered the European market. It was not until the 1950s, with the compulsory breakup of Alcoa into two firms, that antitrust policy was strictly enforced.

The advent of the 1950s saw the rise of the international commodity cartels, supported both by the developing nations and the United Nations Commission on Trade and Development (beginning with the International Sugar Agreement of 1954). No longer were antitrust concerns a constraint and this freed up participants to try a variety of means of stabilizing prices, including buffer stocks and export controls. Although cartelization appeared to offer great promise to struggling developing nations, many of the commodities involved were simply not conformable to the cartel model. Consequently, most of these efforts were either never implemented, or eventually collapsed under the weight of excess production. As described in Chapter 3, these experiences demonstrate the difficulty of maintaining a cartel, even in the absence of a regulatory threat.

As the international cartel period faded into history in the late 1980s, cartelization was reborn in the industrialized world. Antitrust enforcement was strengthened and new tools were employed to uncover collusive accords. This resulted in an alarming number of cartels being brought to the surface in Europe and the United States. What were assumed to be functioning markets had, in fact, been transformed into alliances of firms that carefully segmented demand and managed prices. Not surprisingly, most of these cartels arose in markets for intermediate products; those that were traded from one firm to another and not to the end-user of the good. Active manipulation of prices to consumers raises significantly the probability of detection. Thus, in the food industry, products such as lysine, food dyes, bulk vitamins, sorbates and citric acid were all subject to price manipulation, yet the price of the goods these raw materials were used to produce rose only as consequence of the now higher input costs. Similarly, patients in Europe facing a medical procedure would have little reason to expect that the cost of the treatment was higher partly due to a cartel in the medical gases sector. As will be detailed in Chapter 5, the overwhelming majority of cases of collusion uncovered over the past two decades have involved inputs on their way to becoming other products.

The contrast between the commodity cartel period and that currently prevailing in Europe and the US illustrates the impact of antitrust enforcement on cartel formation and structure. Once collusive behavior had to be hidden, participants resorted to bid-rigging, market segmentation and price minimums to "manage" the market. Gone were buffer stocks, sales (export) constraints and central selling points. The lower visibility of these latter measures made them ideal for avoiding detection and prosecution, but made cartel enforcement more challenging. The monitoring of price minimums in a market for intermediate products (without market prices) is particularly problematic. Firms engaged in the cartels recently uncovered in the industrialized world had to be concerned about whether their partners were actually complying with agreed pricing arrangements.

A complete examination of contemporary antitrust policy, enforcement and collusive behavior across the world would be an impossibly complex task. The focus of this narrative will be on the US and Europe, with particular attention to cartel enforcement within the European Union. While US antitrust legislation and guidelines predate those of most of the industrialized world, there has been a significant convergence of policies in the last two decades. In Chapter 1, where antitrust legislation and case law is examined, some attention will be paid to the Japanese experience, given that it provides an enlightening contrast to the experiences in the rest of the industrialized world. Cartelization was encouraged in pre-war Japan—the government believed that consortiums of firms would raise efficiency during the economic crisis of the 1930s. At the end of World War II, with the nation in ruins, a similar policy was adopted. Consequently, in contrast to Europe and the US, the "antitrust" authority in Japan was, at least for a while, an enforcer of cartel agreements. It was not until the economic ascendancy of Japan in the 1970s that competition policy took on any real meaning.

The last two decades have witnessed rising investigative activity against cartels in both Europe and the US, coupled with an increasing willingness to utilize harsh penalties (including jail time for executives) against violators. It was assumed that this ratcheting up of enforcement would result in a rethinking on the part of executives about the wisdom of collusion. Yet, as illustrated in Chapter 5, the sheer number of cartels uncovered in recent years makes this assumption questionable. This may be partly attributable to the difficulty of measuring unobservables using only what has been revealed.

As most cartels are never uncovered, competition authorities are forced to draw inferences about the prevalence of cartelization. Harsher enforcement may, in fact, have reduced the prevalence of collusive accords, and driven more of those that exist to the surface through generous leniency provisions. Even if this is the case, it cannot be argued that aggressive antitrust activity has solved the cartel problem when so many new violations of competition law are uncovered.

Chapter 6 examines some potential reforms of antitrust legislation that may improve the odds of uncovering and dismantling cartels. The issue of economic incentives facing firms is examined, particularly under those circumstances where market conditions have substantially eroded. A business facing declining prices, possibly due to the entry of new competitors, may be placed in a "double bind." As profitability declines, the business may merge with a competitor, collude, or exit the industry. If the first is blocked by competition authorities and the second by the legal system, then the firm's only real choice is to cease activity in that industry. All three outcomes are likely to be equally bad for consumers, a reality that does not seem to be fully recognized by antitrust agencies. This raises the issue of whether merger and anti-collusion enforcement need to be more closely coordinated.

1 The regulatory environment—antitrust law and enforcement in the US and the EU

The plethora of collusive agreements uncovered in recent years in the United States and the European Union suggests that antitrust enforcement is not providing sufficient deterrence to the formation of cartels. Some colluders have been prosecuted for their roles in multiple price-fixing schemes. Even with penalties imposed on the conspirators increasing with each offense, some corporations still find collusion attractive.

This chapter examines the antitrust environment in the industrialized world, with a focus on the US and the EU. Connor's seminal study focused on three cartels active in the US—citric acid, lysine, and bulk vitamins—as the means of understanding both how collusion develops and how antitrust agencies can best respond to price-fixing schemes (Connor, 2007). This study uses a wider lens to consider numerous corporate and commodity cartels that have operated in both the US and Europe; it examines both similarities and also fundamental differences in the American and European enforcement systems in order to assess the strengths and weaknesses of current antitrust initiatives.

Despite the legal reach of the Sherman Antitrust Act and the European Union's Articles 81 and 82, in practice the existing legislation does not provide sufficient deterrence. The inability of international bodies to rout out collusion can be explained by a combination of factors, including the widespread perception that cartels can outmaneuver competition policy, that penalties are more a nuisance than a deterrence, and that amnesty programs do not offer sufficient incentives for transgressors. The latter part of this chapter compares antitrust legislation and enforcement in Japan, which until recently has been lax, to the legal environments in the US and Europe.

The framework of antitrust law

Nearly all developed nations have developed competition policies that include antitrust provisions for thwarting collusion. As will be demonstrated in Chapter 2, businesses that pursued price-fixing and thereby jettison competitive markets in favor of higher monopolistic price structures inflict considerable harm upon consumers. Prior to the passage of the

Sherman Antitrust Act in 1890, corporations (most notably, the railroads) openly colluded in the US, and prices for end-users rose. Strict antitrust enforcement against price-fixing, which began in the US in the 1950s, is credited with producing substantially more competitive markets. The stridency of anti-cartel policy and enforcement in Europe, beginning in the late 1950s, now rivals that of the US.

The most commonly used measure of the damages arising from price-fixing is the price-premium (i.e. overcharge) that consumers ultimately pay as a result of the cartel's manipulation of the market. In his extensive study of cartel overcharges, Connor (2005) demonstrated the significant economic damage that collusion causes consumers (for an analysis of the far-reaching consequences of overcharging, see also Han et al., 2008). Connor found that the average surcharge was 25 per cent domestically, and rose to 32 per cent for international cartels (Connor, 2005: 1). His figures significantly exceed the 10 percent rule commonly used in sentencing guidelines in the US and Europe. Connor's later studies (Connor and Lande, 2007; Connor 2007) confirmed the magnitude of overcharges arising from collusion. Bolotova (2009) estimated that the average worldwide price markup from collusion was 20 percent—a figure derived from an examination of 406 instances of price-fixing. The author found that collusion produced higher premiums in Asia than in either the US or Europe. Bolotova et al. (2009) estimated cartel overcharges in the US at approximately 18 percent, and argued that premiums declined as stricter antitrust enforcement was put into place. Nieberding (2006) provided an analysis of the methodologies used to determine overcharges, particularly the proper use of reduced-form equations.

The widespread abuse of consumers through concentrated market power in the petroleum, railroad, and steel industries prompted the adoption of the first antitrust legislation in the US in the late 1800s. To ensure the free and unobstructed operation of markets, the Sherman Antitrust Act was adopted to regulate oligopolistic industries, and its regulatory power remains intact today.

The Sherman and Clayton anti-trust acts

The Sherman Anti-Trust Act was approved in July 1890, amid growing public frustration with the railroad and petroleum trusts in the United States (see Appendix 1.1 for the text of the Act). All contracts "in restraint of trade"—that is, those fostering anti-competitive practices—were declared illegal. Persons enforcing or attempting to enforce such contracts were found guilty of a misdemeanor. The Act specifically bans agreements made with overseas corporations that restrain trade. The more strident provisions of the Sherman Act can be used by the courts to punish US firms that engage in illegal contracts with foreign firms operating largely outside US jurisdiction. Section 6 of the Act allows US circuit courts to seize property that has been acquired through collusion, a provision that has since become the basis for highly punitive fines in antitrust cases. Finally, Section 7 supports civil litigation by parties injured as a result of collusion.

A relatively short and simple document, the Sherman Act constituted at the time of its passage the first real deterrence to the formation of monopolies in the US. Twenty years or so after the passage of this legislation, however, it had become clear that the Department of Justice needed additional ammunition in its efforts to ensure competitive markets, and in 1914, the Clayton Antitrust Act was signed into law.

Whereas the provisions of the Sherman Act are very broad, leaving it to the courts to interpret and define what constitutes illegal behavior, the Clayton Act (see Appendix 1.2) outlines specific behaviors that constitute collusion and monopolization (see Appendix 1.2). With the Clayton Act, price discrimination that contributes to a substantial lessening of competition, or tends toward the creation of monopolies, is ruled illegal (see Section 2). Section 3 of the Clayton Act bans the use of contingent contracts, whereby a colluding firm uses as a condition of sale the prohibition of its clients to trade with competing firms. Had the De Beers Diamond Syndicate been operating within US jurisdiction, for example, it would have been forbidden from using disadvantageous contracts to punish firms that strayed from the cartel (see Chapter 2). Section 7 of the Clayton Act forbids acquisitions and mergers that substantially reduce competition, a provision that has resulted in the Federal Trade Commission (FTC) examining most large corporate consolidations.

Applying the Sherman and Clayton acts: case histories

This section focuses on landmark cases that were critical in the development of antitrust law. Some of these prosecutions involved relatively small markets and therefore impacted few consumers and yet they formed the basis of case law. In other cases, the charges of collusion remained unproven but the legal precedents that were established impacted later antitrust cases. These various legal precedents bolstered the impact of the Sherman Act as it has been applied in the US court system over the last half century. Determining when the Sherman Act can be invoked has been a contentious issue in the courts, and these ancillary cases have provided prosecutorial authorities with precedents for defining what constitutes interstate commerce. Other cases reviewed here helped to clarify the degree to which firms can utilize professional associations to conduct business without crossing the line to collusion.

Some of the early applications of the Sherman Act were only tangentially related to price-fixing. These cases demonstrate the difficulties the Department of Justice had in successfully pursuing restraints of trade. In 1892, the DOJ charged the E.C. Knight Company with monopolization of the sugar industry after it merged with American Sugar Refining

Company to gain control of 98 percent of the US market (156 U.S. 1 (1895). This prosecution of a monopolizing firm impacted the merger provisions of the antitrust law. Further guidance to emerging anti-collusion legislation was provided by the prosecution in 1904 of the Northern Securities Company, which had used interlocking boards to end its competition with Northern Pacific Railway, Great Northern Railway, and the Chicago, Burlington and Quincy Railroads (Sup. Ct. 193 US 197). In a case from 1902, the DOJ filed charges of restraint of trade against Swift & Company for using artificial bids to inflate meat prices (*Swift & Co. v. U.S.*, Sup. Ct. 196 U.S. 375). Swift's representatives countered that the company's plants operated wholly within certain states (Missouri, Nebraska, and Minnesota), and as such their operations were not subject to the Sherman Act. The DOJ's victory in this case introduced the notion that a company's physical location in one state does not exempt it from the provisions of the Sherman Act if its products are shipped across state lines.

It was left for the DOJ to raise antitrust cases that would elicit federal rulings with broader implications than the narrow language of the Sherman Act suggested. The DOJ's first "experiment" with antitrust enforcement concerning cartels occurred in 1897 with its prosecution of the Trans-Missouri Freight Association (*U.S. v. Trans-Missouri Freight Association,* 166 U.S. 290 (1897)). In a practice common prior to the Sherman Act, a consortium of railroads had formed to regulate prices charged for the movement of freight. Arguing before the US Supreme Court, lawyers for the railroads asserted that the consortium's goal was to keep prices low, a somewhat dubious argument that was rejected as irrelevant. It was also argued that the railroads should not be subject to the Sherman Act, since there were already a host of laws in place to regulate the transportation sector. The Court ruled that the legislation contained no such exception and they therefore upheld the application of the Sherman Act. The Trans-Missouri Freight Association decision constitutes the first successful use of the new anti-cartel powers contained in the Sherman Act (for further commentary on this decision, see Chapter 6).

Following on its success in the railroad case, in 1898 the Department of Justice filed an antitrust complaint against the Addyston Pipe and Steel Company (85 F. 271, 6th Cir. 1898). In this litigation, the company, a pipe-making firm, was charged with taking part in a scheme to predetermine bids submitted for public works projects. Except for the designated "winner" of the contract, participating firms would deliberately overbid the job, thereby reducing the bidding process to a charade. The new environment created by the Sherman Act was apparently lost on the defendant's attorneys, who argued that this collusion was a reasonable restraint of trade, and that the Act could not have been intended to forbid all such alliances, a view that would be astonishing today. The Court rejected the company's defense, stating that bid-rigging could be condoned only if a firm's monetary survival were at stake, a ruling that would not hold sway today.

The Addyston case illuminates one of the significant complexities of the US legal system as it applies to antitrust law—the division between state and federal authority. When the Addyston ruling was appealed to the Supreme Court (*Addyston Pipe and Steel Company v. U.S.*, 175 U.S. 211 (1899)), the defense argued that the Sherman Act did not apply since it was confined to matters of interstate commerce. In effect, Addyston's attorneys were arguing that the prosecution was invalid because the company operated wholly within one state. The Court disagreed, stating that the Sherman Act was applicable because Addyston routinely shipped its products between states. This decision provided further reinforcement of the Supreme Court's view that the Sherman Act was enforceable whenever a firm's goods crossed state lines.

The primary antitrust cases brought under the Sherman Act in the 1920s concerned the monopolization of markets (e.g. *U.S. v. American Tobacco Company,* 221 U.S. 106 (1911); and *U.S. v. U.S. Steel*, 251 U.S. 417 (1920)). In June 1932, however, the DOJ took up a watershed antitrust case when it charged the Appalachian Coal Company, a consortium of 137 firms, with conspiring to fix prices among various anthracite producers in Virginia, West Virginia, Kentucky, and Tennessee (Sup. Ct. 288 U.S. 344). The defendants had formed a Central Selling Point (CSP) to market the combined production of the firms (in fact, Appalachian Coals can be regarded as a precursor to the central selling mechanism later utilized by the De Beers Diamond Syndicate). In return for a 10 percent commission on all sales, the CSP of Appalachian Coal was supposed to secure the highest price possible for the coal. The government argued forcefully that this arrangement squelched competition between the coal companies, at the expense of consumers. Appalachian Coals countered that the purpose of the CSP was to increase sales, through intense marketing and research, and to reduce distribution costs by eliminating duplicate staffing. The Court found that the government had provided insufficient evidence of detrimental impacts on the market, particularly since Appalachian Coals was not yet in operation at the time the government filed suit. The Court left open the possibility that the case would have to be revisited after actual experience with the consortium's CSP and its effect on prices. The Appalachian Coals case further illustrates the degree to which antitrust laws have strengthened over time, as this collusive arrangement would be declared illegal today.

Antitrust enforcement in the 1930s was somewhat muted after the passage of the National Industrial Recovery Act (NIRA) in 1933. Cooperative practices that would normally have been judged illegal were now permissible if they ameliorated the effects of the Great Depression. Despite this short-lived suspension of antitrust enforcement, in 1936 the Socony-Vacuum Oil Company was indicted under the Sherman Act for colluding with its competitors to manipulate prices by buying excess oil and removing it from the market (Sup. Ct. 310 US 150). This stockpiling of excess production led to more stable, but also higher, prices. The company used NIRA as a defense, arguing that its business practices were known to the government and that they were in the spirit of the Recovery Act. The government countered that Socony-Vacuum and its partners had not asked for an exemption for collusion as required by NIRA, which placed them in violation of the Sherman Act. The Court found in favor of the DOJ, ruling that Socony-Vacuum and its co-conspirators violated the provisions of the Act by engaging in cooperative, anticompetitive practices.

The two preceding cases illustrate the development of various schemes by businesses to price-fix without the appearance of colluding. It can be argued that Central Selling Points increase efficiency by not requiring firms to market their products by way of redundant sales operations, precisely the argument that was made by the defense in *US v. Appalachian Coals*, 288 U.S. 344 (1933). In the Socony-Vacuum trial, the defendants could argue that they were taking advantage of excess supply by sopping it up at reduced prices. The findings in favor of the government indicated that the Courts were willing to consider cases in which outright price-fixing was not involved. In a word, antitrust law was becoming more nuanced.

In 1969, the Supreme Court pushed the accepted definition of collusion further in *U.S. v. Container Corporation of America* (393 U.S. 333, 1969), a case involving the growing corrugated container industry in the southeast. Entry into this market was relatively easy and capacity had expanded well beyond demand. The result of this excess capacity was a sustained decline in prices, a situation that vexed the larger manufacturers. As purveyors of an intermediate product, with no retail price structure, a firm had only a general idea of the prices its competitors set. The "solution" to this uncertainty was an unusual arrangement under which, upon request, firms would supply their latest pricing data to competitors. The information was understood to accurately represent the firm's bid price on new business. This information-sharing among the businesses in the industry resulted in a smoothing of the downward trend in prices.

Although the firms had forged no formal arrangement to adhere to pricing agreements, the systematic sharing of prices undermined competition. According to court documents, the collusion on prices was judged to be "concerted action sufficient to establish the combination or conspiracy ingredient of the Act" (referring to the Sherman Act). It was also found that the exchange of price information had impaired competition. The Court's concern was that firms had privately conveyed price information that they would not have acquired through regular business practices. It was the direct exchange of information between competitors that made the practice illegal.

By the 1960s, US antitrust case law had coalesced into a cohesive structure that was ever more strident in its application. In the case involving American Radiator and Standard Sanitary Corporation and five of its competitors, it was determined that a conspiracy had been perpetrated through meetings of a trade group, the Plumbing Fixtures Manufacturers Association (PFMA). Under the cover of meetings held between 1962 and 1966, member groups of the PFMA rigged prices for enameled cast iron and china plumbing equipment. Even beyond the customary setting of prices, the conspirators in the PFMA sought to stifle competition by establishing maximum allowable discounts, negotiating future prices, publishing the colluded prices in their trade journals, and collectively eliminating low-cost product lines.

On October 6, 1966, indictments were returned against American Radiator and its five co-conspirators. Three executives of American Radiator and five executives from the other corporations were also indicted—one of the earliest instances in which corporate managers were singled out for prosecution. The defense argued that the pricing patterns of the plumbing fixtures market reflected ordinary economic forces, an argument that the jury did not accept, returning guilty verdicts for all the defendants. The details of the judgment demonstrate the critical role played by the PFMA in managing the conspiracy. The case was subsequently appealed to the 3rd Circuit Court of Appeals (433 F. 2d 174), where the earlier court decisions were upheld.

Further nuances of the Court's interpretation of the Sherman Act were established in cases from the 1970s. In *National Society of Professional Engineers v. U.S.*, 435 U.S. 679, tried in 1978, the Court examined whether professional associations could establish obligatory pricing policies for their members. The defendants argued that competitive bidding would produce engineering services of inferior quality, resulting in the construction of unsafe structures. But by eliminating pricing from the initial bidding process for contracts, the engineering services sector ceased to compete. The Court was asked to rule if both the practice of prohibiting bidding, even in the interest of public safety, and also the diffusion of engineering services, which could be argued did not rise to the level of interstate commerce, were in violation of the Sherman Act. The Court found in favor of the DOJ (435 U.S. 679), and noted that a claim of safeguarding the public does not justify prohibiting competition. In *Goldfarb et ux v. Virginia State Bar et al.* (421 U.S. 773), litigated in 1975, the Supreme Court similarly ruled that professional associations (in this case, the State Bar) cannot establish minimum fees for services. The petitioners, a couple that sought to purchase a home in Virginia, encountered a state-wide fixed fee schedule for performing a title search, a situation that they believed constituted an unreasonable constraint on competition. The Court agreed, and the practice of setting minimum charges for like services was ended. The State Bar argued that the Sherman Act was not applicable because the practice of law is a "learned profession," outside the realm of commerce (this argument had been accepted by a court of appeals in an earlier denial of the government's case). The Court's reversal in this case, coupled with its finding in *National Society of Professional Engineers v. U.S.* (435 U.S. 679 (1978)), sent a clear message to professional societies that antitrust prosecutions would not be confined to brick-and-mortar industries. One of the unusual aspects of the 1975 case was the Court's finding that the practices of the Virginia State Bar impacted interstate commerce. This interpretation of what constitutes cross-state commercial transactions was broader than judgments rendered in previous court decisions.

In May 1980, the Supreme Court extended the meaning of "price collusion" in its decision, *Catalano Inc. v. Target Sales, Inc.* (446 U.S. 643 (1980)). The plaintiffs, Catalano, Inc., alleged that coordinated changes in the credit practices of beer wholesalers—the refusal to accept credit or allow a customary 30- to 42-day delay in making payment—constituted price collusion under the Sherman Act. The 9th Circuit Court of Appeals had earlier ruled that the change in practices was not a form of price-fixing, and might actually be pro-competitive, since it removed a perceived barrier to entry (the ability to grant credit), and made prices more transparent. The Supreme Court reversed the earlier ruling, and firmly equated the harmonization of credit policies with price fixing.

The ruling in *Catalano v. Target Sales* put corporations on notice that back-door collusive pricing arrangements were illegal. In making its ruling, the Supreme Court cited the case of the National Society of Professional Engineers as an example of an illegal pricing agreement that did not require the actual setting of prices. It also cited the Socony-Vacuum ruling, in which competitors bought surplus oil to maintain higher prices, as an example of illegal activity that ultimately set prices despite the lack of a price target. Moving forward, businesses should have assumed that all activities directed at manipulating prices were illegal, even if they differed considerably from the traditional cartel practice of setting actual prices.

A big exception: agricultural cooperatives

In its Section 6, the Clayton Act of 1914 granted the farming sector an exception to the Sherman Act's wholesale prohibition on price-fixing by permitting some vaguely defined mutual activities. The DOJ took a dim view of this exclusion for agriculture and narrowed its interpretation, allowing only for the joint marketing of farm products. Supporters of farm co-ops worked to broaden the DOJ's exemption, and with the passage of the Capper-Volstead Act (CVA) in 1922, agricultural cooperatives were given the right to jointly process, prepare, and market their goods. The CVA specifically mentioned the marketing of products both across state lines and internationally, placing the issue squarely into federal, rather than state, courts.

The intent of the exclusions in both the Clayton Act's Section 6 and in the Capper-Volstead Act is clear: permit small farmers to collectively market their agricultural goods as a means of reducing costs and enabling competition with larger farms. These exceptions to antitrust law developed during a period in which consolidation was threatening the viability of small family farms. The only other exemption for allowing cooperation among firms would occur during the Great Depression (see Chapter 3 below). The farming exclusions created problems for the courts, which were left with the difficult task of interpreting and enforcing the provisions of the Acts.

In the first of a string of cases that helped define the boundaries of the law with regard to cooperatives, the Supreme Court ruled in *US v. Borden* (308 US 188 1939) that even if prices do not rise as result of their actions, co-ops cannot restrain trade or monopolize a market. That ruling was reinforced in 1960, when the courts determined that collective marketing was permissible under the Clayton Act's Section 6 and the CVA so long as the resulting co-op did not possess monopoly power (see *Maryland and Virginia Milk Producers v. U.S.*, 362 US 458 (1960)). Reversing its position in a 1980 decision, the courts ruled that cooperatives have the right of monopolization, an opinion that effectively granted co-ops an exception to the Sherman Act (*Fairdale Farms v. Yankee Milk* (635 F.2d 1037 (1980)).

An unusual exception to the ever-increasing forcefulness of both antitrust law and its enforcement, the Capper-Volstead Act can be regarded as a part of a long history of federal assistance to the US agricultural sector (e.g. agricultural price supports). Support for private farming has always been politically popular and advocating legislation that bolsters the viability of the family farm produces goodwill in the voting box. Whereas only 2 percent of today's labor force is actively employed in the agricultural sector, the CVA was passed at a time when over a quarter of the US population made its living on the farm.

European integration and the problem of parallelism

Although Europe has embraced the concept of regionalism to a degree not seen elsewhere in the world, its march towards economic and political integration has been characterized by the parallel development of both intra- and extra-national institutions. Action against pan-European price-fixing is now primarily the responsibility of the European Commission, yet within the centralized structure of the EU, each state still maintains its own antitrust agencies. This problem of overlapping responsibilities for antitrust enforcement mirrors the larger problems posed by parallel governmental institutions. Although a comprehensive examination of the internal competition policies instituted by each of the EU member states is beyond the scope of this book, a brief review of the French and German antitrust pratices, placed within the over-arching authority of the European Commission, will illustrate how domestic measures can co-exist within a larger union of states.

French and German antitrust policy—parallelism of legal legislation in the European Union

The formation of the Western European states into a regional trading block during the post-war period resulted in antitrust legislation that was both domestically driven and cross-national in reach. As the EU moves toward deeper integration, conflicts over legal jurisdiction become more pronounced. In the case of antitrust law, the trend is for independent domestic policies to adhere more closely to central EU dictates.

French antitrust law

Antitrust policies in France are considered the most rigorous of any country in the EU. Modern French antitrust law dates to Ordinance No. 45-1243 of June 30, 1945. In a major modification of the original legislation, dated to 1977 (Law No. 77-806) and 1986 (No. 86-1243), the French legislature addressed growing concerns over the concentration of industries brought about by mergers. The 1986 law, Liberalization of Prices and Competition, supplanted the original antitrust statute of 1945. Before August 2008, French antitrust investigations were carried out by two separate agencies, the General Directorate of Competition, Consumption and Fraud Repression (DGCCRF), and the Conseil de la Concurrence. After 2008, the name of the latter office was changed to "Autorité de la Concurrence" (i.e. the Competition Authority) and assumed all responsibility for investigating antitrust violations. The Competition Authority promotes itself as an advocate for competition in markets—a broad mandate that permits the agency to evaluate the state of competition in any sector it judges to be overly concentrated. To ensure competition, the office holds the power to force a sale of assets.

The provisions of the Law on Liberalization of Prices and Competition (1986) are consistent with the statutes adopted in other strong antitrust legislation. Article 13 and Article 17 of the law provide the Competition Authority with the right to impose fines. Article 17 further permits the office to utilize prison sentences for key players in fraudulent breaches of French antitrust laws, a penalty that has never been pursued by the European Commission. Although merger notification is voluntary (Article 38), the ordinance allows for the reversal of anticompetitive mergers. Article 7 and Article 8 ban a variety of practices commonly used by cartels, including price-fixing, contingent contracts, market divisions, and output restraints.

Forming part of the Code de Commerce, France's Leniency Program (Leniency Programme in the documents) was created by statute in May 2001 under Article L. 464-2 III. Similar to initiatives in the US and the EU, the Leniency Programme offers partial or full immunity from penalties under the following circumstances:

> Immunity from any fine or a reduction of fine may be granted to an undertaking or body which has, with others, implemented a practice prohibited by Article L.420-1 if it has contributed in establishing the reality of the prohibited practice and to identifying the perpetrators by providing information which the Conseil de la concurrence or the administration did not have previously. Following the steps taken by the undertaking or body, the Conseil de la Concurrence shall adopt for this purpose a leniency opinion, which shall specify the conditions attached to the envisaged immunity, after the Government Official and the undertaking or body concerned have presented their observations.
>
> Leniency Programme, Code de Commerce

In September 2006, the European Competition Network (ECN) proposed that EU members alter their leniency policies to achieve a greater degree of uniformity across nations. The Conseil de la Concurrence published a proposed draft of a new Leniency Policy in January 2007,[1] and adopted the changes in April of that year.

German antitrust law

Before the late nineteenth century, German courts did nothing to prevent the formation of cartels, for they viewed price-fixing agreements as legitimate legal contracts. By the early twentieth century, there were between 550 and 600 cartels operating openly in the German Republic (Feldenkirchen, 1992: 258). Consumer complaints of abusive cartel practices led to the passage in 1923 of the Cartel Law. Although intended to regulate cartelized sectors of the economy, by recognizing and cataloging the myriad cartels in existence, the legislators actually legitimized industries that practiced collusion. Except during the Great Depression, when the German government reduced prices fixed by colluding firms, the country's antitrust policy remained friendly to cartelization (for an extensive list of German industries that utilized price-fixing agreements, see Feldenkirchen, 1992: 260).

After years of pressure from US authorities, in 1958 Germany enacted the Act Against the Restraint of Competition, which prohibited most cartels. The authority to manage competition was granted to the Federal Control Office (FCO or Bundeskartellamt). As noted by the OECD (OECD, 2003b), the law was less stringent than US statutes in addressing the problem of horizontal price-fixing. The FCO banned collusion "subject to exemption." In practice, cartels were banned unless strict conditions were met. Revsions in competition law adopted in 1973 were primarily targeted at merger control.

In May 1998, the German laws against restraint of competition were amended once again, primarily to achieve a greater degree of synchronization with EU competition legislation. Prior to 1998, Germany did not prosecute firms for price-fixing until the agreements left the boardroom and were implemented in the market. Article 1 of the Cartel Law prohibits "decisions by associations of undertakings and concerted practices which have as their object or effect the prevention, restriction or distortion of competition". The amendment of 1998 continues to exempt prohibitions on price-fixing when, for example, agreements between small- and medium-sized corporations are aimed at supporting efficiency. Exemptions for export or import cartels have been removed. Even though Article 16 of the Cartel Law includes a substantial list of prohibited activities, German law remains weak in terms of vertical restraints. For more on German antitrust law, see Heidenhain et al. (1999), and Harris and Goldman (2001).

German antitrust statutes were further amended in 2005 in an effort to bring them more closely in line with EU Policies. Germany's prohibition against restrictive practices is now fully consistent with the Union's Article 81. This revision redefines the process in which parallel prosecutions by both German and EU competition authorities can occur. In addition, the powers of the FCO have been increased to include the imposition of immediate restraints on firms engaged in collusion if economic harm is imminent. In addition, the FCO has been granted the authority to undo block exemptions that were previously granted by the EU.

Leniency policy in Germany

The German Leniency Program was issued by the country's Federal Cartel Office in 2006 (Notice no. 9/2006). A firm seeking relief from penalties for collusion must provide the FCO with sufficient information to secure a search warrant for corporate offices and not have acted as the ringleader of the cartel. Contact with the FCO must occur prior to the office obtaining ample evidence to pursue an investigation on its own. Consistent with EU law, the German statutes permit partial leniency (up to a 50 percent reduction in fines) for firms that do not meet all the criteria necessary for full immunity. Section D of Germany's program stipulates that cooperation must be full and continuous for the leniency provision to apply. The first confessor must provide information on all the cartel's participants, both past and present. Article 13 notes that an application to the FCO may instead be transferred to the EU Commission if the price-fixing agreement is more transnational in scope. The transfer of leniency applications from the FCO to the EU Commission illustrates the complexity of parallel legal frameworks operating in a single jurisdiction.

The German power cable cartel: a case study

The German power cable industry, which produces high-voltage cable for electricity suppliers and public transportation systems, began colluding in 1901. Originally, the market was managed through both price floors and sales quotas. By 1945, the regulatory climate in post-war Germany had changed sufficiently to make the cartel's activities illegal. Operating with an unwieldy 34 firms in 1958, the cartel became somewhat more concentrated over time, and yet in 1990 there still remained 21 members in the organization (according to Normann and Tan (2005), the concentration ratio in the mid-1990s was 84 percent). Although a large number of producers existed during this period, the market was dominated by Siemens, AEG (later, Alcatel), and Felten & Guilleaume. The cartel managed the power cable market by fixing the price that producers paid for raw materials, specifically metals. By manipulating input costs rather than applying the more common practice of setting end prices, the cartel assumed that authorities would not react to its collusion. The final prices, in turn, could be surreptitiously corrupted by requiring that member firms produce only certain grades of cable.

Even with the passage in 1958 of the Act Against the Restraint of ompetition, the cable cartel operated with impunity for over a decade, until in 1972, and again in 1974, fines were imposed. From 1975 to 1985, the cartel operated openly and legally once again under an exemption in German law, the so-called "rationalization of markets" initiative. With the influx of new producers following the reunification of Germany, the cable cartel briefly dissolved in the early 1990s, but later reformed and was active until 1997, when German antitrust policies tightened and the FCO imposed fines against it totaling DM 300 m.

The history of the power cable cartel illustrates the tentative nature of antitrust enforcement against collusion in Germany. The exception for "rationalization" of markets in the 1970s and 1980s constituted a wavering in policy that left firms without a clear message regarding tolerated activities. The cable cartel would not have been tolerated in the most recent period of German antitrust enforcement, especially after the country introduced stricter competition laws in 2005 in order to synchronize its policies with those of the EU.

Antitrust legislation in the European Union—Article 81 and Article 82

Despite their regulatory disparities, the member nations of the European Union have constructed common antitrust codes and enforcement regimes. Adopted by the European Community as part of the Treaty of Rome, Article 81 lays out specific activities that will trigger prosecution by the Commission, including price fixing, market sharing, price discrimination, and contingent contracts that are clearly in restraint of trade (see Appendix 1.3). Provision 3 of the article, however, permits some of these activities if agreement has been reached between parties, and the effect of such agreements is to increase efficiency to the benefit of consumers. The potential ambiguity of this third provision is somewhat lessened by sub-provision (b), which forbids such activities if their effect is the elimination of competition. Thus industry associations are permitted if they do not reduce competition. Cooperation by firms on the development of new means of production or distribution is also allowed if the goal is to raise efficiency and lower prices.

Like the Sherman Antitrust Act, Article 81 is a relatively brief document, particularly given the immensity of the problem it addresses. While Section 3 of the Sherman Act clearly lays out the possibility of criminal penalties being imposed upon individuals, there is no mention of penalties in Article 81. As argued earlier, if corporations come to regard antitrust fines as a cost of doing business, imprisonment of key executives may provide the only deterrence to collusion. Section 3 of Article 81 further distinguishes itself from the strident provisions of the Sherman Act by nullifying prosecution if the ultimate effect of collusion is to rationalize markets.

Article 82 (see Appendix 1.4) is intended to raise the specificity of the prohibitions in Article 81, in much the same way that the Clayton Act clarified some of the generalities present in the Sherman Antitrust Act. Article 82 forbids the imposition of unfair trading prices or practices on contracts enforceable within the EU. If the effect is to place some businesses at a competitive disadvantage, firms are forbidden from "applying dissimilar conditions to equivalent contracts." This again raises the issues of legal price discrimination (i.e. preferential pricing based on different elasticities of demand), and of how the European court system should interpret what is legal behavior. Article 82 also prohibits limiting production or product development if those limitations are to the detriment of consumers. Finally, Article 82 forbids the use of contingent contracts, that is, obligations to participate in "supplementary" activities unrelated to the contract being enforced. As noted above, the Clayton Act contains language very similar to this.

Working together, Article 81 and Article 82 provide substantial firepower for regulators to prosecute businesses that act in restraint of trade. As noted by Nicolaïdis and Vernon (1997), however, EU policy has a distinctly European flavor, as the European Commission is given the power to exempt activities that may contribute to competition if certain conditions are met. Specifically, collusive agreements may be permitted if they spur technological or economic development or benefit consumers. Firms seeking to establish such agreements must secure the blessing of the Commission. Whereas US antitrust policies and enforcement actively seek to squelch all collusive practices, the EU seems willing to tolerate a degree of collaboration if it can be shown to be in the public interest.

In general, however, since the early 1990s the EU Commission has stepped up prosecutions for collusion. The next logical step for both US and European antitrust authorities was to expose more cartels. While this exposure was partly accomplished through more aggressive enforcement, it was apparent that providing relief to firms that were willing to confess held even greater potential for uncovering price-fixing. Neither US nor EU antitrust legislation includes leniency provisions, which leaves it to judicial authorities to develop appropriate policies.

Leniency policy in the United States and Europe

In August 1993, the US DOJ enacted a leniency policy with the intention to create uncertainty and destabilize cartels (see Appendix 1.5). Leniency is afforded to firms that expose collusive agreements, thereby raising suspicion among the cartel members. A firm seeking the designation "first confessor" needs to meet six stringent pre-conditions. First, the business revealing an illegal activity has to demonstrate that it took immediate steps to end the violation. Such decisive measures would not be possible if collusion was endemic to the entire firm. Secondly, the corporation must provide full details of the cartel to the DOJ and cooperate with the ensuing investigation. In addition, the admission of wrongdoing must come from the corporation itself, not from whistleblowers. Fourth, the corporation is expected to make financial restitution to those harmed by the cartel, if such restitution is possible. Finally, the confessor cannot be the lead firm of the collusive agreement. These strict criteria eliminate from the start the opportunity for some firms to take advantage of the leniency provision. The DOJ does not want to hear from initiators of cartels or corporations in which collusion has become an accepted way of doing business. If the DOJ has already begun an investigation of the cartel, a firm may be granted leniency if the following additional criteria can be met: 1) authorities must lack sufficient evidence for a conviction in the absence of the firm's cooperation; and 2) the granting of leniency is not deemed unfair to the other corporations involved.

In Section C of its leniency policy, the DOJ addresses clemency for corporate directors, officers, and employees. If the corporation qualifies for leniency under Section A, all personnel who both admit their role in the conspiracy and cooperate fully with the investigation will be granted immunity from criminal prosecution. If the corporation itself is not immune under Section A, individuals within the firm may still be eligible for leniency if they come forward as part of the corporate "confession."

In comparison to the DOJ's straightforward leniency provisions, the EU Commission's Notice on Immunity from Fines and Reduction of Fines in Cartel Cases is lengthy and complex (for excerpts, see Appendix 1.6). The Notice on Immunity begins with a summary of the economic damage that cartels cause (Items (1) and (2)) as a sort of preamble for justifying the need for leniency. Items (4) and (5) note that corporate cooperation in a Commission investigation may have intrinsic value, and therefore a reduction in fines for firms assisting in the inquiry is justified. In Section II, items (8) through (11) lay out the conditions that must be met before leniency is granted. In some ways, these stipulations mirror the requirements set forth in the DOJ's leniency requirements. In the EU's program, a business seeking immunity must:

- Submit a detailed statement describing the alleged cartel, including product coverage, geographic coverage, dates of meetings, etc.
- Provide a statement of the cartel's goals and plans for achieving these objectives.
- Include a list with the names and addresses of all individuals who participated in the illegal activity.
- Surrender sufficient information to enable the Commission to be reasonably sure of a conviction of the cartel's other participants.

Immunity from fines is granted only if, at the time of application, the Commission could not already sustain a decision affirming cartelization of the industry.

Once a first confessor reveals the existence of a cartel to authorities, other firms involved in the violation can be granted partial immunity—in the form of reduced fines—if their testimony provides details unknown to or not in the possession of the initial confessor (Section III, Item 26, Leniency Notice). The "value-added" (i.e. the incremental deposition) provided by the ancillary firm can take the form of written documents that provide greater detail than the evidence already in hand (see Section III, Item 25). The Notice on Immunity emphasizes the value of testimonial information that corroborates what has already been revealed by the initial confessor.

After the initial exposure of the cartel, the next confessor to provide evidence with significant value can expect a reduction of fines in the range of 30 to 50 percent. The third confessor is eligible for a 20 to 30 percent diminution of fines. The leniency notice further specifies a reduction of up to 20 percent for all additional businesses that assist in the investigation. An examination of the numerous cartel cases outlined in Chapter 5 demonstrates that leniency is generally offered to only one or two firms. It is curious that more firms have not taken advantage of this provision in the Leniency Notice. Perhaps some corporations would rather pay the full fine and leave open the possibility of engaging in a future collusive agreement, a door that may be closed if they turn in their co-conspirators.

History of the US Federal Trade Commission and its predecessor

Following the passage of the Sherman Act, it became clear that antitrust enforcement could not be left to the courts alone. At the very least, an agency was needed to investigate the competitive impact of market changes such as mergers and acquisitions.

In an effort to rein in excessive corporate power in major industrial sectors, Congress created the Department of Commerce and Labor in

1903. By the same legislation, and acting as an independent agency of this new department, the Bureau of Corporations was charged with investigating the competitive structure of critical US industries. During its 11-year lifespan, this bureau focused on investigating competitive conditions in key industries such as petroleum, steel, and lumber. When the Federal Trade Commission (FTC) replaced the Bureau of Corporations in 1915 (by way of a law passed in September 1914), the practice of generating detailed analyses of important economic sectors continued, but the objective was now on providing necessary documentation for legislative initiatives.

The FTC was structured to be as independent from congressional pressure as possible. It was to be managed by a board of five Commissioners, nominated by the President and approved by the Senate. The Commissioners were forbidden from engaging in another business or vocation during their tenure. In the Act creating the FTC, the agency's duties were defined as follows:

> The Commission is hereby empowered and directed to prevent persons, partnerships, or corporations, except banks and common carriers subject to the Acts to regulate commerce, from using unfair methods of competition in commerce.
>
> Whenever the Commission shall have reason to believe that any such person, partnership, or corporation has been or is using any unfair method of competition in commerce, and it shall appear to the Commission that a proceeding by it in respect thereof would be to the interest of the public, it shall issue and serve upon such person, partnership or corporation a complaint stating its charges in that respect, and containing a notice of hearing upon a day at a place herein fixed at least thirty days after the service of said complaint. The person, partnership, or corporation so complained shall have the right to appear at the place and time so fixed and show cause why an order should not be entered by the Commission requiring such person, partnership, or corporation to cease and desist from the violation of the law so charged in said complaint.
>
> (SEC. 5, Act to create a Federal Trade Commission)

Continuing in Section 6:

> The Commission shall also have power
>
> a) To gather and compile information concerning, and to investigate from time to time the organization, business, conduct, practices, and management of any corporation engaged in commerce, excepting banks and common carriers subject to the Act to regulate commerce, and its relation to other corporations and to individuals, associations and partnerships. ...

As in the Sherman and Clayton Acts, the FTC's charge was written in general terms and its impact on the business environment was uncertain at the time of its passage. The statement that the FTC shall act "whenever the Commission shall have reason to believe that any such person, partnership, or corporation has been or is using any unfair method of competition" captures the imprecise language of the offices' mandate of maintaining an even playing field.

In its role as enforcer of the Sherman and Clayton Acts, the FTC has been particularly vexed by Section 7 of the Clayton Act (See Appendix 1.4). Zimmerman (1964) provided an early examination of the Commission's application of this section of the Act, and noted the difficulty facing both the FTC and the courts in properly interpreting what constitutes an action that will "substantially lessen competition or tend to create a monopoly." As Zimmerman noted, pivotal prosecutions have rested on the evaluation of what constitutes a market when substitutability between products is possible (*U.S. v. E.I. DuPont de Nemours and Company*, 351 U.S. 377 (1956)). The courts then wrestled with the issue of illegality as it pertained to market share (*Brown Shoe v. U.S.*, 370 U.S. 294 (1962)). Direct FTC intervention to challenge a merger under Section 7 occurred in the Commission's challenge of Pillsbury Mills' proposed acquisition of Ballard and Duff (*Pillsbury Inc. v. FTC*, 354 F.2d 952 (1966)).

In its Horizontal Merger Guidelines (issued in 1992 and revised in 1997) the FTC laid out the guiding principles of its antitrust policy and elucidated its approach to defining markets, measuring concentration within an industry, and evaluating the potential harm posed by mergers. The Guidelines state that a market can represent a product or group of products. Item (1) under Section 1.1 states that the FTC will consider "evidence that buyers have shifted or have considered shifting purchases between products in response to relative changes in price," and that to warrant intervention, a merger must threaten a significant reduction in competition.

Once an investigation has been completed, the FTC may order firms to cease and desist from a method of doing business that the Commission finds in restraint of trade. If the firm fails to comply with the order, the Act specifies that the findings be presented before the appropriate Circuit Court of the district in which the investigation took place. The Court may then order an additional gathering of facts before either affirming the FTC's conclusions or finding for the corporation. If the firm's behavior is found to be anticompetitive, the business may appeal the ruling to the US Supreme Court.

The FTC was charged with complementing and amplifying, not replacing, earlier landmark antitrust legislation:

> Nothing contained in this Act shall be construed to prevent or interfere with the enforcement of the provisions of the antitrust Acts or the Acts to regulate commerce, nor shall anything contained in the Act be

> construed to alter, modify, or repeal the said antitrust Acts or the Acts to regulate commerce or any parts thereof.[1]

Essentially, the FTC's mission is to manage legal market consolidation, whereas the DOJ's charge is to control illicit collusive behavior. As discussed in Chapter 6, working in concert to enhance competition, the FTC and DOJ can sometimes box a struggling corporation into bankruptcy, an outcome that is inimical to the objective of preserving vibrant markets.

Evaluations of FTC merger policy and enforcement

Several studies have examined the history of FTC enforcement. Langenfeld and Silvia (2004) detailed the Commission's activities against horizontal restraints of trade (including mergers) from 1980 to 2003. In the post-industrial economy of the US, it is not surprising that the vast majority of complaints occur in the service sector (Langenfield and Silvia, 2004: 534). Most of the cases involve illicit pricing arrangements rather than mergers, and the authors note that currently trade associations form the root of most antitrust problems. Coate (2005) considered how the revision of the merger guidelines in 1992 impacted enforcement. He posited that the FTC has shifted its focus to so-called "unilateral effects," circumstances in which a firm, working alone, can increase market prices (Coate, 2005: 281–3). The guidelines established in 1992 tout the value of consumer complaints, historical events, and contemporary (i.e. "hot") documents as effective tools for analyzing competitive outcomes. Reviewing case studies, Coate examined which of these evidentiary forms would most likely trigger FTC action (Coate, 2005: 293).

The Antitrust Modernization Act of 2002 established a commission to evaluate the state of competition policy in the US. It was believed that the Sherman and Clayton Acts, together with more recent legislation, might not be sufficient to secure competition in our information-based economy. The commission completed its work in 2007, the expiration date of its mandate, and reported that the US antitrust framework remains viable, even in the New Economy (see www.amc.gov).

Merger policy in the European Union

The European Union's merger policy has been regulated by Council Regulation EEC 4064/89, which was adopted in December 1989. This document overrode a number of domestic merger policies already in force across Europe and replaced them with a single enforcement regime. In the preface it is noted that "whereas this resolution should therefore be based not only on Article 87 but, principally, on Article 235 of the Treaty, under which the Community may give itself the additional powers of action necessary for the attainment of its objectives ..." As with other merger regulations, this codification of a unified merger policy was a natural step in the integration process, and the need for rationalization of antitrust law superseded sovereign interests.

Article 1 of document 4064/89 specifies the characteristics of industries that are to be monitored by competition authorities. In (1(2)a) it is stated that only sectors with annual worldwide sales of over five billion ecu are subject to monitoring (the European Currency Unit (ecu), predecessor to the euro, was a unit of account used to stabilize currency values across member nations; it never became a true currency). In addition, at least two firms in the industry must have annual turnover of 250 million ecu (see 1(2)(b)). With these conditions met, the EU Commission then looks to other characteristics of the industry in order to determine the best way of preserving and developing "effective competition within the common market." The monetary criteria stated above were to be reviewed after four years to determine if the thresholds were still appropriate (Article 1(3)). The general criterion to be used by the Commission in assessing a merger is stated in Article 1(3): "A concentration which creates or strengthens a dominant position as a result of which effective competition would be significantly impeded in the common market or in a substantial part of it shall be declared incompatible with the common market." Article 4 establishes reporting requirements for the Community; for example, mergers or acquisitions that have a "Community dimension" are to be reported to the Commission within one week of their completion. If the Commission determines that the merger falls under Regulation 4064/89, then the specifics of the proposed union are to be published to permit public commentary.

Article 5 stipulates how industry concentration is to be determined. For most sectors, the appropriate measure consists of annual sales exclusive of value-added and other taxes. In Article 5(4)(b), however, it is specified that businesses that fall directly under the control of another firm—through ownership of assets or voting rights—shall be part of the calculation of that firm's sales. For financial institutions, market concentration is measured not in annual sales but rather as a proportion of assets (5(3)(a)). Article B describes the authority granted to the European Commission to issue a decision declaring a merger "incompatible with the common market: (8(3)). Continuing in 8(4), it is stated: "Where a concentration has already been implemented, the Commission may, in a decision pursuant to paragraph 3 or by a separate decision, require the undertakings or assets brought together to be separated or the cessation of joint Control ..." These broad powers are constrained only by the right of the affected parties to pursue a legal remedy through the European Court of Justice (Article 21(1)). The powers and rights of Regulation 4064/89 are to supersede national antitrust powers whenever a case has implications for the common market (see 21(2)). Article 13 defines the broad powers of investigation granted to the Commission. Commission officials are to have unfettered access to the premises of businesses under review, and are to receive copies of necessary financial documents (13(1)(a-d)). Firms that fail to comply with these requests are subject to significant fines (outlined in Article 14).

The EU council's Regulation 4064/89 is comparable in its intent to the act that created the Federal Trade Commission in the US, and yet it is far longer than its American counterpart, reflecting as it does several additional decades of antitrust case law. Moreover, the EU document needed to reconcile domestic with regional competition policy.

Council Regulation 139 and current European merger policy

Much has changed in the EU since the implementation of Regulation 4064/89, not the least of which was the adoption of a common currency in 1999. Recognizing that the heavily amended Regulation 4064/89 of 1989 needed revising, in January 2004 the European Council passed Regulation 139, "On the Control of Concentration between Undertakings." Judicial setbacks, including court reversals of Commission decisions, had spurred the Council to introduce the new legislation (see Lyons, 2004). To account for economic growth and inflation, Article (1)(1–3) raised the threshold levels of industries subject to merger regulation to an aggregate sales figure of five billion euros. The provisions of Regulation 4064/89, Article 2, were not substantially changed, although the Commission's concerns about vertical integration ((2)(5)) were made more explicit. Article 4 of 139, "Prior Notification of Concentrations and Pre-notification Referral at the Request of the Notifying Parties," emphasizes the Commission's time-line of notification and decision-making. Despite these changes, Regulation 139 is actually quite similar to the document it replaced.

A minimalist approach—antitrust legislation in Japan

Working under the guidance of the US occupying forces in 1947, the Japanese government constructed an antitrust document entitled "Act on the Prohibition of Private Monopolization and Maintenance of Fair Trade," commonly known as the Antimonopoly Law. Like the Sherman Act and the EU's Articles 81 and 82, the Antimonopoly Law set out strong prohibitions on collusive activities (for excerpts, see Appendix 1.7). The Japanese edict prohibits monopolization of markets and both domestic and international restraints of trade (Chapter II, Articles 3–7). The protracted length of the Antimonopoly Law (147 pages versus the laconic 6 of the Sherman Act) owes to the inclusion of details that would have been provided by case precedent in the US and Europe. An example of this specificity is found in Article 8, which discusses prohibitions on the activities of trade associations, including restricting entry of new firms into the market.

In Chapter IV (Stockholdings, Interlocking Directors, Mergers, Demergers, and Acquisition of Businesses), significant detail is presented on corporate governance structures that are deemed anticompetitive. Firms are forbidden from holding stocks of competing businesses if to do so substantially reduces competition. Individuals are forbidden from holding multiple board or directorate positions if this representation thwarts competition (Chapter 5, Article 13). In addition, corporations are not permitted to purchase stock or acquire control of rival firms (Chapter 5, Article 18).

The prescribed penalties for engagement in anticompetitive practices are outlined in Article 89 of the Antimonopoly Law. Managers who have "effected private monopolization or unreasonable restraint of trade" or have "effected substantial restraint of competition in any particular field" are subject to imprisonment with work for not more than three years, together with a fine of not more than five million yen. The sanctions for engaging in cross-national restraint of trade are lower, with the jail sentence limited to two years, and the maximum fine set at 3 million yen (see Articles 89 and 90).

The adoption of antitrust legislation under the tutelage of the US military did not free the Japanese economy from a history of entrenched collusion and other forms of market restraints. Prior to the Great Depression, Japanese law openly promoted cartels (e.g. "the Export Society Law" and the "Major Export Commodities Industrial Association Law," both dating from 1925). Major industries could adopt collusive agreements under the guidance and supervision of the Japanese government. The onset of the Great Depression only intensified interest in industrial co-operation, leading to the adoption in 1931 of the" Law Concerning the Control of Important Industries," which authorized cartels for most industries. As the nation prepared for full-scale war in the late 1930s, even stronger legislation promoting collusion was passed. The "National General Mobilization Law" of 1938 not only permitted cartels, but also provided mechanisms by which the government could enforce these agreements. Ramseyer (1985) noted that litigation runs counter to the Japanese ethos and legal action against price-fixing, particularly by private individuals, is rare. In the period from 1937 to 1984, the Japanese FTC, acting under the authority of the Antimonopoly Act, opened hundreds of investigations but pursued only six prosecutions (Ramseyer, 1985: 616).

The case of Japan runs counter to the assumption that collusion is abhorred by national governments, and that only legislative or judicial failures permit cartelization. Lacking societal imperatives to control cartels, the Japanese government viewed collusive agreements as an efficient mechanism for organizing industrial production during a period of crisis. When the allied occupation forces required the Japanese to reject cartelization, there was no indigenous legal framework to build upon. From the Japanese perspective, with markets in turmoil and producers struggling to provide basic necessities to the population, the post-war seemed an inopportune time to strictly enforce a new set of unfamiliar laws. As noted by Hadley (1970), cracks in antitrust enforcement in Japan appeared almost immediately. Forged in 1953, the Amendments to the Antimonopoly Law (the Anti-depression and Rationalization Clauses) allowed firms to apply for exemption from antitrust dictates. From 1953 to 1965, approximately 20 industries were exempted from compliance with the Antimonopoly Law. More importantly, as the Ministry of International Trade and Industry (MITI) became a major force in Japan's economy, the number of industries seeking to circumvent the Antimonopoly Law ballooned. By 1961, for example, over 600 industrial and commercial societies existed, many with the stated purpose of "managing" production and pricing (Hadley, 1970: 376). The clear delineation between Japan's conception of antitrust law and the regulatory milieu of the US and Europe is demonstrated by the fact that MITI was given authority to enforce collusive agreements. As a result, by 1963 there were an astonishing 1,002 known cartels operating in Japan.

There are statutes besides the Anti-depression and Rationalization Clauses of the Antimonopoly Law that allow Japanese firms to collude within specific industries. For example, the Marine Transportation Law (1989) exempts shipping consortiums, the Road Transportation Law (1951) permits cartelization of the trucking and bus industries, and the Small and Medium-Size Business Organization Law (1963, amended in 1999), allows small firms to cartelize. In addition to these standing exemptions, there is a long list of now-expired legislation that once covered the electronics, machinery, and information technology sectors (see Suzumura, 1997: 448–9).

Even when an enterprise violates Japan's effete antitrust laws, enforcement and prosecution is lax, as the JFTC is reluctant to use criminal penalties and fines. Japanese antitrust measures generally take the form of recommendations rather than penalties (see Haley, 2001). In addition, the JFTC's rulings are case-specific to such an extent that firms charged with collusion will sometimes disband and then reorganize only shortly after a decision is rendered. Since the legal system in Japan discourages civil suits, there is no mechanism outside the federal jurisdiction for imposing penalties and collusion becomes ever more attractive (see Haley, 2001: 146).

Some scholars have argued that the institutional tolerance—even promotion—of collusion in Japan has not necessarily harmed consumers. Dick (1992a, 1992b, 1993) observed that despite the lax antitrust environment, market concentration and monopoly power in the US are similar to that of Japan. Similarly, Ito and Maruyama (1990) found that the markup rate in both US and Japanese distribution industries is essentially the same.

The already largely unenforced provisions of Japan's Antimonopoly Law were revised and weakened by modifications in 1953, which among other things relaxed the application of the *per se* rule (i.e. the tacit understanding that collusion was illegal in all circumstances). The pendulum swung back in a modification of 1977, when the JFTC was authorized to impose administrative fines on firms to skim off excess rates of returns from collusion. The amendment of 1977 also grants the Commission the power to order firms in concentrated markets to justify concurrent price increases. In a further amendment of 2005, the JFTC was charged with the responsibility for conducting compulsory investigations when collusion is suspected.

This final modification of 2005 also established a leniency program to aid the JFTC in its investigations. Japan's leniency provisions are structured like those of the US and EU, with the degree of clemency dependent on the order of confession and the amount of information the confessor provides to the JFTC. Leniency policy became a viable enforcement tool in Japan only after the legal environment had become sufficiently hostile to collusion, a philosophical shift generally dated to the 1990s.

Two critical cases of the Japanese Fair Trade Commission (JFTC)

In a rare demonstration of regulatory backbone, in 1974 the JFTC initiated and won a major case against Japanese oil distributors. This action was taken in response to the deleterious effects of the oil crisis of 1973, when inflation's impact on a large number of consumer goods made collusive agreements unacceptable to the Japanese public. Investigations by the JFTC showed that the 12 firms responsible for nearly all domestic sales of petroleum-derived products in Japan had met five times in 1973. During the course of these meetings, the cartel members had agreed to fine one another for violations of their pact and also to set monthly sales quotas. Confident that they were acting with the blessings of MITI, the firm's management teams pursued collusion with relative transparency. Whereas the Japanese oil industry had ignored numerous cease and desist orders issued by the JFTC in the 1960s, public anger caused by the fall-out from of the oil crisis forced the government to intervene (see Schaede, 2000).

The two primary court cases involving the petroleum cartel were *Japan v. Sekiyu Renmei* (983 Hanrei jiho 22 Tokyo High Ct. (1980)) and *Japan v. Idemitsu Kosan K.K.*, (985 Hanrei Jiho 3 Tokyo High Ct. (1980)). In the Sekiyu Renmei prosecution, the defendants argued that they were acting at the behest of MITI. In the Idemitsu Kosan K.K. case, however, the courts decided in favor of the JFTC, asserting that the companies themselves manipulated the price of oil by adopting guidelines set by MITI that were in violation of the law. On appeal, the Tokyo High Court in 1980 affirmed the illegality of Idemitsu Kosan K.K.'s behavior, and imposed criminal penalties on both the individual firms in the cartel and the top executives who had managed the price-fixing scheme. This case is regarded as the first expression of the JFTC's authority. For additional analysis of the Japanese oil cartel cases, see Upham (1987).

The history of the Japanese steel cartel illustrates different institutional forces in play that thwarted antitrust enforcement. Like other core sectors of Japanese production, the steel industry pursued cartel-like organization with the approval of MITI. The underlying philosophy of the MITI was that in difficult economic times, competition weakens industry, while cartelization offers risk-reduction that allows firms to invest and grow. In 1965, MITI addressed climbing steel inventories by ordering a 10 percent reduction in each firm's output. When one producer (Sumitomo) rebelled, MITI reigned in the firm by threatening to deny it access to foreign exchange. The prevalence and relatively casual nature of collusion in Japan made it unlikely that Sumitomo would complain about MITI's encouragement of price-fixing.

Fry (2001) provided an analysis of the weaknesses that have persisted in Japanese antitrust policy into the twenty-first century. Nevertheless, there is a growing momentum toward stricter enforcement, demonstrated by the announcement in 2009 that the JFTC was imposing significant fines on three steelmakers for their participation in a cartel. Significantly, Nippon Steel, Nisshin Steel, and Yodogawa Steel were found to have violated the Antimonopoly Law and were collectively fined JP¥ 15.5 billion.

Additional cases that have further defined developing anti-cartel law in Japan include *Toshiba Chemical Company v. JFTC* (906 HANREITIMES 136 Tokyo High Court (1995)) and *Mitsubishi Building Maintenance Case* (Mitsubishibiltechnoservice 41 SINKETUSHU 46 (1994)). Inoue (2007) provided some excellent insights into these and other important anti-cartel cases.

Conclusion

For over a century, governments in the industrialized world have pursued antitrust laws and enforcement mechanisms as the means of unfettering trade. Early legislative efforts in the US, first with the Sherman and Clayton Antitrust Acts, and then with such modifying legislation as the Celler–Kefauver Act, provided the DOJ with a basis for later prosecutions. The basic premise of anti-cartel enforcement in Europe is contained in the EU's Article 81 and Article 82. Although objections to EU Commission antitrust rulings and penalties have been rare, these legal challenges have provided a degree of legal fine-tuning. The absence of significant reform or modification to antitrust legislation in the 50 years since the Celler–Kefauver Act indicates the soundness of competition policy in the US. The same observation cannot be made for Japan, however, where antitrust enforcement was significantly delayed and the ponderous language of the Antimonopoly Law is still actively being interpreted.

Given the simplicity and brevity of early US antitrust legislation, it was natural that the courts would render interpretations in order to establish policy. The judicial system first wrestled with what constituted a monopoly, and then turned its attention to the question of whether the Sherman and Clayton Acts were applicable to intra- as well as interstate-trade. In the Addyston case, the court began laying the framework for what constituted "unreasonable' restraint of trade. The Appalachian Coal decision addressed the limits of cooperative activities among producers. After the initial upheaval of the Great Depression, authorities intervened to limit government-sanctioned co-operation among producers. As the industrial economies were transitioning into the global cartel period, the courts ruled on the permissible degree of information-sharing by corporations (e.g. *Container Corporation*). In the Catalano case, the Supreme Court expanded the meaning of price collusion to include common credit practices.

One of the more intriguing aspects of antitrust law—a topic worthy of its own study—is the development of appropriate leniency policy. Like any criminal or civil prosecutorial tool, the tension between securing the cooperation of conspirators and not providing the guilty with a free pass complicates the task of establishing leniency rules. Instituting tiers of cooperation (i.e. first confessor, provider of significant assistance, etc.) is an efficient means of bringing down cartels. Some of the firms that have received total exemptions from fines, however, went on to become repeat offenders. As will be discussed in Chapter 2, this recidivism suggests the dominant strategy for some businesses is to collude and then turn themselves in as the first confessor. It is unclear if reforms to leniency policy would avoid this outcome.

Another major component of the antitrust frameworks is appropriate merger policy. Without the ability to collude, firms may simply merge, and the impact on competition may be far worse than cartelization. Over time, the Federal Trade Commission and the European Commission have established a fairly consistent set of rulings to guide firms. As argued in Chapter 6, when both the opportunity to collude and the ability to merge are removed, firms under significant competitive pressure may choose to exit the market, an undesirable outcome by any measure.

Appendix 1.1: Text of the Sherman Antitrust Act

An act to protect trade and commerce against unlawful restraints and monopolies, July 2, 1890

Be it Enacted by the Senate and House of Representatives of the United States of America in Congress Assembled

Section 1. Every contract, combination in the form of trust or otherwise, or conspiracy, in restraint of trade or commerce among the several states, or with foreign nations, is hereby declared illegal. Every person who shall make any such contract or engage in any such combination or conspiracy, shall be deemed guilty of a misdemeanor, and, on conviction thereof, shall be punished by fine not exceeding five thousand dollars, or by imprisonment not exceeding one year, or by both said punishments, at the discretion of the courts.

Section 2. Every person who shall monopolize, or attempt to monopolize, or combine or conspire with any other person or persons, to monopolize any part of the trade or commerce among the several states, or with foreign nations, shall be deemed guilty of a misdemeanor, and, on conviction thereof, shall be punished by fine not exceeding five thousand dollars, or by imprisonment not exceeding one year, or by both said punishments, in the discretion of the court.

Section 3. Every contract, combination in the form of trust or otherwise, or conspiracy, in the restraint of trade or commerce in any Territory of the United States or of the District of Columbia, or in restraint of trade or commerce between any such territory and another, or between any such Territory and another, or between any such Territory or Territories and any State or States or the District of Columbia, or with foreign nations, or between the District of Columbia and any State or States or foreign nations, is hereby declared illegal. Every person who shall make any such contract or engage in any such combination or conspiracy, shall be deemed guilty of a misdemeanor, and, on conviction thereof, shall be punished by fine not exceeding five thousand dollars, or by imprisonment not exceeding one year, or by both said punishments, in the discretion of the court.

Section 4. The several circuit courts of the United States are hereby invested with jurisdiction to prevent and restrain violations of this act; and it shall be the duty of the several district attorneys of the United States, in their respective districts, under the direction of the Attorney-General, to institute proceedings in equity to prevent and restrain such violations. Such proceedings may be by way of petition setting forth the case and praying that such violation shall be enjoined or otherwise prohibited. When the parties complained of shall have been duly notified of such petition the court shall proceed, as soon as may be, to the hearing and determination of the case; and pending such petition and before that final decree, the court may at any time make such temporary restraining order or prohibition as shall be deemed just in the premises.

Section 5. Whenever it shall appear to the court before which any proceedings under section four of this act may be pending, that the ends of justice require that other parties shall be brought before the court, the court may cause them to be summoned, whether they reside in the district in which the court is held or not; and subpoenas to that end may be served in any district by the marshal thereof.

Section 6. Any property owned under contract or by any combination, or pursuant to any conspiracy (and being the subject thereof) mentioned in section one of this act, and being in the course of transportation from one State to another, or to a foreign country, shall be forfeited to the United States, and may be seized and condemned by like proceedings as those provided by law for the forfeiture, seizure, and condemnation of property imported into the United States contrary to law.

Section 7. Any person who shall be injured in his business or property by any other person or corporation by reason of anything forbidden or declared to be unlawful by this act, may sue thereof in any circuit court of the United States in the district in which the defendant resides or is found, without respect to the amount in controversy, and shall recover three fold the damages by him sustained, and the costs of suit, including a reasonable attorney's fee.

Section 8. That the word "person" or "persons" wherever used this act shall be deemed to include corporations and associations existing under or authorized by the laws of either the United States, the laws of any of the Territories, the laws of any State, or the laws of any foreign country.

Approved, July 2, 1890, Fifty-First Congress of the U.S.

Appendix 1.2: Key provisions of the Clayton Antitrust Act

An act to supplement existing laws against unlawful restraints and monopolies, and for other purposes, October 15, 1914

Section 2. That it shall be unlawful for any person engaged in commerce, in the course of such commerce, either directly or indirectly to discriminate in price between different purchasers of commodities, which commodities are sold for use, consumption, or resale within the United States or any Territory thereof or the District of Columbia or any insular possession or any other place under the jurisdiction of the United States, where the effect of such discrimination may be to substantially lessen competition or tend to create a monopoly in any line of commerce; provided, that nothing herein contained shall prevent discrimination in price between purchasers of commodities on account of differences in the grade, quality or quantity of the commodity sold, or that makes only due allowance for difference in the cost of selling or transportation, or discrimination in price in the same or different communities made in good faith to meet competition: And provided further, that nothing herein contained shall prevent persons from selecting their own customers in bona fide transactions and not in restraint of trade.

Section 3. That it shall be unlawful for any person engaged in commerce, in the course of such commerce, to lease or make a sale or contract for sale of goods, wares, merchandise, machinery, supplies or other commodities, whether patented or unpatented, for use, consumption or resale within the United States or any other Territory thereof or the District of Columbia or any insular possession or other place under the jurisdiction of the United States, or fix a price charged thereof, or discount from, or rebate upon, such price, on the condition, agreement or understanding that the lessee or purchaser thereof shall not use or deal in the goods, wares, merchandise, machinery, supplies or other commodities of a competitor or competitors of the lessor or seller, where the effect of such lease, sale, or contract for sale of such condition, agreement or understanding may be to substantially lessen competition or tend to create a monopoly in any line of commerce.

Section 7. That no corporation engaged in commerce shall acquire, directly or indirectly, the whole or any part of the stock or other share capital of another corporation engaged also in commerce, where the effect of such acquisition may be to substantially lessen competition between the corporation whose stock is so acquired and the corporation making the acquisition, or to restrain such commerce in any section of the community, or tend to create a monopoly of any line of commerce.

Enacted October 15, 1914

Appendix 1.3 Antitrust provisions of the European Union (Article 81)

1. The following shall be prohibited as incompatible with the common market: all agreements between undertakings, decisions by associations of undertakings and concerted practices which may affect trade between Member States and which have as their object or effect the prevention, restriction or distortion of competition within the common market, and in particular those which:

(a) directly or indirectly fix purchase or selling prices or any other trading condition;
(b) limit or control production, markets, technical development, or investment;
(c) share markets or sources of supply;
(d) apply dissimilar conditions to equivalent transactions with other trading parties, thereby placing them at a competitive disadvantage;
(e) make the conclusion of contracts subject to acceptance by the other parties of supplementary obligations which, by their nature of according to commercial usage, have no connection with the subject of such contracts.

2. Any agreements or decisions prohibited pursuant to this article shall be automatically void.

3. The provisions of paragraph 1 may, however, be declared inapplicable in the case of:

- any agreement or category of agreements between undertakings,
- any decision or category of decisions by associations or undertakings,
- any concerted practice or category of concerted practices,

which contribute to improving production or distribution of goods or to promoting technical or economic progress, while allowing consumers a fair share of the resulting benefit, and which does not:

(a) impose on the undertakings concerned restrictions which are not indispensable to the attainment of these objectives;
(b) afford the possibility of eliminating competition in respect of a substantial part of the products in question.

Appendix 1.4: Antitrust provisions of the European Union (Article 82)

Any abuse by one or more undertakings of a dominant position within the common market or in a substantial part of it shall be prohibited as incompatible with the common market in so far as it may affect trade between Member States.

Such abuse may, in particular, consist in:

(a) directly or indirectly imposing unfair purchases or selling prices or other trading conditions;
(b) limiting production, markets or technical development to the prejudice of consumers;
(c) applying dissimilar conditions to equivalent transactions with other trading partiers, thereby placing them at a competitive disadvantage;
(d) making the conclusion of contracts subject to acceptance by the other parties of supplementary obligations which, by their nature or according to commercial usage, have no connection with the subject of such contracts.

Appendix 1.5 Corporate leniency policy, US Department of Justice, issued August 10, 1993

The Division has a policy of according leniency to corporations reporting their illegal antitrust activity at an early stage, if they meet certain conditions. "Leniency" means not charging such a firm criminally for the activity being reported. (The policy also is known as the corporate amnesty or corporate immunity policy.)

A. Leniency before an investigation has begun

Leniency will be granted to a corporation reporting illegal activity before an investigation has begun, if the following six conditions are met:

1 At the time the corporation comes forward to report the illegal activity, the Division has not received information about the illegal activity being reported from any other source;
2 The corporation, upon its discovery of the illegal activity being reported, took prompt and effective action to terminate its part in that activity;

3 The corporation reports the wrongdoing with candor and completeness and provides full, continuing and complete cooperation to the Division throughout the investigation;
4 The confession of wrongdoing is truly a corporate act, as opposed to isolated confessions of individual executives or officials;
5 Where possible, the corporation makes restitution to injured parties; and
6 The corporation did not coerce another party to participate in the illegal activity and clearly was not the leader in, or originator of, the activity.

B. Alternative requirements for leniency

If a corporation comes forward to report illegal antitrust activity and does not meet all six of the conditions set out in Part A, above, the corporation, whether it comes forward before or after an investigation has begun, will be granted leniency if the following seven conditions are met:

1 The corporation is the first one to come forward and qualify for leniency with respect to the illegal activity being reported;
2 The Division, at the time the corporation comes in, does not yet have evidence against the company that is likely to result in a sustainable conviction;
3 The corporation, upon its discovery of the illegal activity being reported, took prompt and effective action to terminate its part in the activity;
4 The corporation reports the wrongdoing with candor and completeness and provides full, continuing and complete cooperation that advances the Division in its investigation;
5 The confession of wrongdoing is truly a corporate act, as opposed to isolated confessions of individual executives or officials;
6 Where possible, the corporation makes restitution to injured parties; and
7 The Division determines that granting leniency would not be unfair to others, considering the nature of the illegal activity, the confessing corporation's role in it, and when the corporation comes forward.

In applying condition 7, the primary consideration will be how early the corporation comes forward and whether the corporation coerced another party to participate in the illegal activity or clearly was the leader in, or originator of, the activity. The burden of satisfying condition 7 will be low if the corporation comes forward before the Division has begun an investigation into the illegal activity. That burden will increase the closer the Division comes to having evidence that is likely to result in a sustainable conviction.

C. Leniency for corporate directors, officers, and employees

If a corporation qualifies for leniency under Part A, all directors, officers, employees of the corporation who admit their involvement in the illegal antitrust activity as part of the corporate confession will receive leniency, in the form of not being charged criminally for the illegal activity, if they admit their wrongdoing with candor and completeness and continue to assist the Division throughout the investigation.

If a corporation does not qualify for leniency under Part A above, the directors, officers, and employees who come forward with the corporation will be considered for immunity from criminal prosecution on the same basis as if they had approached the Division individually.

D. Leniency procedure

If the staff that receives the request for leniency believes the corporation qualifies for and should be accorded leniency, it should forward a favorable recommendation to the Office of Operations, setting forth the reasons why leniency should be granted. Staff should not delay making such a recommendation until a fact memo recommending prosecution of others is prepared. The Director of Operations will review the request and forward it to the Assistant Attorney General for final decision. If the staff recommends against leniency, corporate counsel may wish to seek an appointment with the Director of Operations to make their views known. Counsel are not entitled to such a meeting as a matter of right, but the opportunity will generally be afforded.

Appendix 1.6 Excerpts from the European Union's leniency notice

Commission notice on immunity from fines and reduction of fines in cartel cases (2006/ C 298/11)

I. Introduction

(1) This notice sets out the framework for rewarding cooperation in the Commission investigation by undertakings which are or have been party to secret cartels affecting the Community. Cartels are agreements and/or concerted practices between two or more competitors aimed at coordinating their competitive behavior on the market and/or influencing the relevant parameters of competition through practices such as the fixing of purchase or selling prices or other trading conditions, the allocation of production or sales quotas, the sharing of markets including bid-rigging, restrictions of imports or exports and/or anti-competitive actions against other copetitors. Such practices are among the most serious violations of Article 81 EC.

(2) By artificially limiting the competition that would normally prevail between them, undertakings avoid exactly those pressures that lead them to innovate, both in terms of product development and introduction of more efficient production methods. Such practices also lead to more expensive raw materials and components for the Community companies that purchase from such producers. They ultimately result in artificial prices

and reduced choice for the consumer. In the long term, they lead to a loss of competitiveness and reduced employment opportunities.

(3) By their very nature, secret cartels are often difficult to detect and investigate without the cooperation of undertakings or individuals implicated in them. Therefore, the Commission considers that it is in the Community interest to reward undertakings involved in this type of illegal practices, which are willing to put an end to their participation and co-operate in the Commission's investigation, independently of the rest of the undertakings involved in the cartel. The interest of consumers and citizens in ensuring that secret cartels are detected and punished outweighs the interest in fining those undertakings that enable the Commission to detect and prohibit such practices.

(4) The Commission considers that the collaboration of an undertaking in the detection of the existence of a cartel has an intrinsic value. A decisive contribution to the opening of an investigation or to the finding of an infringement may justify the granting of immunity from any fine to the undertaking in question, on condition that certain additional requirements are fulfilled.

(5) Moreover, co-operation by one or more of the undertakings may justify a reduction of a fine by the Commission. Any reduction of a fine must reflect an undertaking's actual contribution, in terms of quality and timing, to the Commission's establishment of the infringement. Reductions are to be limited to those undertakings that provide the Commission with evidence that adds significant value to that already in the Commission's possession.

(6) In addition to submitting pre-existing documents, undertakings may provide the Commission with voluntary presentations of their knowledge of a cartel and their role therein prepared specially to be submitted under this Leniency Programme. These initiatives have proved to be useful for the effective investigation and termination of cartel infringements and they should not be discouraged by discovery orders issued in civil litigation. Potential leniency applicants might be dissuaded from cooperating with the Commission under this Notice if this could impair their position in civil proceedings, as compared to companies who do not cooperate. Such undesirable effect would significantly harm the public interest in ensuring effective public enforcement of Article 81 EC in cartel cases and thus its subsequent or parallel effective private enforcement.

(7) The supervisory task conferred on the Commission by the Treaty in competition matters does not only include the duty to investigate and punish individual infringements, but also encompasses the duty to pursue a general policy. The protector of corporate statements in the public interest is not a bar to their disclosure to other addresses of the statement of objections in order to safeguard their rights of defence in the procedure before the Commission, to the extent that it is technically possible to combine both interests by rendering corporate statements accessible only at the Commission premises and normally on a single occasion following the formal notification

of the objections. Moreover, the Commission will process personal data in the context of this notice in conformity with its obligations under Regulation (EC) no 45/2001.

II. Immunity from fines

A. REQUIREMENTS TO QUALIFY FOR IMMUNITY FROM FINES

(8) The Commission will grant immunity from any fine which would otherwise have been imposed to an undertaking disclosing its participation in an alleged cartel affecting the Community if that undertaking is the first to submit information and evidence which in the Commission's view will enable it to:

(a) carry out a targeted inspection in connection with the alleged cartel; or
(b) find an infringement of Article 81 EC in connection with the alleged cartel

(9) For the Commission to be able to carry out a targeted inspection within the meaning of point (8)(a), the undertakings must provide the Commission with the information and evidence listed below, to the extent that this, in the Commission's view, would not jeopardize the inspections:

(a) A corporate statement which includes, in so far as it is known to the applicant at the time of the submission:

A detailed description of the alleged cartel arrangement, including for instance its aims, activities and functioning; the product or service concerned, the geographic scope, the duration of and the estimated market volumes affected by the alleged cartel; the specific dates, locations, content of and participants in alleged cartel contracts, and all relevant explanations in connection with the pieces of evidence provided in support of the application.

The name and address of the legal entity submitting the immunity application as well as the names and addresses of all the other undertakings that participate(d) in the alleged cartel. The names, positions, office locations and, where necessary, home addresses of all individuals who, to the applicants knowledge, are or have been involved in the alleged cartel, including those individuals which have been involved on the applicant's behalf;

(10) Immunity pursuant to point (8)(a) will not be granted if, at the time of the submission, the Commission had already sufficient evidence to adopt a decision to carry out an inspection in connection with the alleged cartel or had already carried out such an inspection.

(11) Immunity pursuant to point (8)(b) will only be granted on the cumulative conditions that the commission did not have, at the time of the submission, sufficient evidence to find an infringement of Article 81 EC in

connection with the alleged cartel and that no undertaking had been granted conditional immunity under from fines under point (8)(a) in connection with the alleged cartel. In order to qualify, and undertaking must be the first to provide contemporaneous, incriminating evidence of the alleged cartel as well as a corporate statement containing the kind of information specified in point (9)(a), which would enable the commission to find an infringement of Article 81 EC.

Continues to end of section II, items 12-22.

III. Reduction of fines

A. REQUIREMENTS TO QUALIFY FOR A REDUCTION OF A FINE

(23) Undertakings disclosing their participation in an alleged cartel affecting the Community that do not meet the conditions under section II above may be eligible to benefit from a reduction of any fine that would otherwise have been imposed.

(24) In order to qualify, an undertaking must provide the commission with evidence of the alleged infringement which represents significant added value with respect to the evidence already in the Commission's possession and must meet the cumulative conditions set out in (12)(a) to (12)(c) above.

(25) The concept of "added value" refers to the extent to which the evidence provided strengthens, by its very nature and/or its level of detail, the Commission's ability to prove the alleged cartel. In this assessment, the Commission will generally consider written evidence originating from the period of time to which the facts pertain to have a greater value than evidence subsequently established. Incriminating evidence directly relevant to the facts in question will generally be considered to have a greater value than that with only indirect relevance. Similarly, the degree of corroboration from other sources required for the evidence submitted to be relied upon against other undertakings involved in the case will have an impact on the value of that evidence, so that compelling evidence will be attributed a greater value than evidence such as statements which require corroboration if contested.

(26) The Commission will determine in any final decision adopted at the end of the administrative procedure the level of reduction an undertaking will benefit from, relative to the fine which would otherwise be imposed. For the:

- first undertaking to provide significant added value: a reduction of 30–50%
- second undertaking to provide significant added value: a reduction of 20–30%
- subsequent undertakings that provide significant added value: a reduction of up to 20%

In order to determine the level of reduction within each of these bands, the Commission will take into account the time at which the evidence fulfilling the condition in point (24) was submitted and the extent to which it represents added value. If the applicant for a reduction of a fine is the first to submit compelling evidence in the sense of point (25) which the Commission uses to establish additional facts increasing the gravity or duration of the infringement, the Commission will not take such additional facts into account when setting any fine to be imposed on the undertaking which provided this evidence.

Continues through points 27 to 40 to end

Appendix 1.7 Excerpts from Japan's Antimonopoly Law

Act on the prohibition of private monopolization and maintenance of fair trade: Act No. 54, April 14, 1947.

Translated from the Japanese—application of the Antimonopoly Law to actual cases should utilize the original document published in the Official Gazette.

Chapter I—General provisions

Article 1

The purpose of this Act is, by prohibiting private monopolization, unreasonable restraint of trade and unfair trading practices, by preventing excessive concentration of economic power and by eliminating unreasonable restraint of production, sale, price, technology, etc. and all other unjust restrictions on business activities through combinations, agreements, etc. to promote fair and free competition, to stimulate the creative initiative of entrepreneurs, to encourage business activities, to heighten the level of employment and actual national income, and thereby to promote the democratic and wholesome development of the national economy as well as to ensure the interests of general consumers.

Chapter II—Private monopolization and unreasonable restraint of trade

Article 3

No entrepreneur shall effect monopolization or unreasonable restraint of trade.

Article 6

No entrepreneur shall enter into an agreement or an international contract which contains such matters as fall under unreasonable restraint of trade or unfair trade practices.

Article 7

(1) In case there exists any act in violation of the provisions of Article 3 or the preceding article, the Fair Trade Commission may, pursuant to the procedures as provided for in Section II of Chapter VIII, order the relevant entrepreneur to cease and desist from the said acts, to transfer a part of his business, or take any other measures necessary to eliminate such acts in violation of the said provisions.

(2) The Fair Trade Commission may, when it finds it particularly necessary, even when an act in violation of the provisions of Article 3 or the preceding Article has already ceased to exist, pursuant to the procedures as provided for in Section II of Chapter VIII, order the relevant entrepreneur, to take measures to make public that the said act has been discontinued and any other measures necessary to ensure elimination of the said act; provided, however, that this shall not apply to cases where three years have passed since the date of discontinuation of the said act.

Article 7–2

(1) In case any entrepreneur effects an unreasonable restraint of trade or enters into an international agreement or an international contract containing such matters as fall under unreasonable restraint of trade, and such act falls under any of the following items, the Fair Trade Commission shall order the said entrepreneur to, pursuant to the procedures as provided for in Section II of Chapter VIII, to pay to the national treasury a surcharge of an amount equivalent to and calculated by multiplying the sales amount of the relevant goods or services calculated pursuant to the method provided for in the Cabinet Order—(rest of article not presented).

Chapter III—Trade associations

Article 8

(1) No trade association shall engage in any act which falls under any of the following items:

i. Substantially restraining competition in any particular field of trade;
ii. Entering into an international agreement or an international contract as provided for in Article 6;
iii. Limiting the present or future number of entrepreneurs in any particular field of business:
iv. Unjustly restricting the functions or activities of the constituent entrepreneurs—meaning an entrepreneur who is a member of the trade association; the same apply hereinafter
v. Inducing entrepreneurs to employ such act as falls under unfair trade practices.

Article 8–2

(1) In case there exists an act in violation of the provisions of paragraph 1 of the preceding Article, the Fair Trade Commission may, pursuant to the procedures as provided for in Section ii of Chapter VIII, order the trade association to cease and desist from the said act, to dissolve itself, or to take other measures necessary to eliminate the said act.

Chapter III—II

Article 8–4

(1) When a monopolistic situation exists, the Fair Trade commission may order the relevant entrepreneur, pursuant to the procedures provided for in Section II of Chapter VIII, to transfer a part of its business or to take any other measures necessary to restore competition with respect to the relevant goods or services; provided, however, that this shall not apply to cases where it is found that such measures may, in relation to said entrepreneur, reduce the scale of business to such an extent that the expenses required for the supply of goods or services which the said entrepreneur supplies will rise sharply, undermine its financial position, or make it difficult to maintain its international competitiveness, or where such alternative measures may be taken that is found sufficient to restore competition with respect to the relevant goods and services.

Chapter IV—Stockholdings, interlocking directors, mergers, demergers, and acquisition of businesses

Article 9

(1) Any corporation, which may be to cause excessive concentration of economic power through holding of the stocks—including shares held by a member; the same shall apply hereinafter—of other corporations in Japan, shall not be established.

(2) A corporation—including a foreign corporation; the same shall apply hereinafter—shall not become a corporation which may be to cause excessive concentration of economic power in Japan through acquisition or holding of the stocks of other corporations in Japan.

Article 10

(1) No corporation shall acquire of hold stocks of any other corporations where the effect of such acquisition or holding of stocks may be substantially to restrain competition in any particular fields of trade, or shall acquire or hold stocks of other corporations through unfair trade practices.

Article 13

(1) Neither a director nor an employee—meaning in this article a person other than directors engaged in the business of a corporation on a regular basis—of a corporation shall hold at the same time a position as a director of another corporation where the effect of such an interlocking directorate may be substantially to restrain competition in any particular field of trade.

(2) No corporation shall coerce another corporation in competition with it in Japan through unfair trade practices, to admit its directors concurrently to the position of director or employee of the latter corporation, or to admit its employee concurrently to the position of director of the latter corporation.

Article 14

No person other than corporations shall acquire or hold stocks of a corporation where the effect of such acquisitions or holding of stocks may be substantially to reduce competition in any particular field of trade, or shall acquire or hold stocks of a corporation through unfair trade practices.

Article 18

(1) No corporation shall perform an act falling under any of the following acts, where the effect of such act may be substantially to restrain competition in any particular field of trade, or through unfair trade practices:

i. Acquiring the whole or substantial part of the business or another corporation;
ii. Acquiring the whole or a substantial part of the fixed assets used for the business of another corporation;
iii. Taking on a lease of the whole or a substantial part of the business of another corporation;
iv. Undertaking the management of the whole or a substantial part of the business of another corporation;
v. Entering into a contract which provides for a joint profit and loss account for business with another corporation.

Article 89

(1) Any person who falls under any of the following items shall be punished by imprisonment with work for not more than three years or by a fine of not more than five million yen.

i. Any person who, in violation of the provisions of Article 3, has effected private monopolization or unreasonable restraint of trade; or
ii. Any person who, in violation of the provisions of item 1 of paragraph 1 of Article 8 has effected substantial restraint of competition in any particular field or trade.

Article 90

Any person who falls under any of the following items shall be punished by imprisonment with work for not more than two years or by a fine of not more than three million yen:

i. Any person who, in violation of the provisions of Article 8 or item 2 of paragraph 1 of Article 8 has entered into an international agreement or an international contract which contains such as matters as fall under unreasonable restraint of trade;
ii. Any person who violated the provisions of item 3 or 4 of paragraph 1 of Article 8; or

Any person who fails to comply with a cease and desist order of a decision as provided for in Article 65 or paragraph 1 of Article 67 after it has become final and binding.[2]

2 Oligopoly markets, collusion, and the operation of cartels

The manipulation of market prices through collusive agreements dates back to the beginning of industrialization. During the period from the 1890s to roughly 1950, lax enforcement of antitrust laws essentially permitted cartels to operate, and collusion was common and relatively transparent, particularly in commodity markets. From the mid-1960s to the mid-1980s, the United Nations and its agencies encouraged developing nations to adopt commodity price agreements that circumvented the legal constraints imposed by the industrialized nations. In contrast to the extra-legal model common to the developing world, collusion in the United States and Western Europe since 1950 has been driven underground by the threat of legal sanctions. The means by which cartels fix prices differs considerably from one period to the next. Cartels that operate in the open can utilize many mechanisms to affect prices, whereas cartels that function clandestinely are constrained by antitrust laws and thereby rely on fewer methods to manipulate markets. This chapter will examine the theoretical basis for the pricing structures utilized by cartels within the context of the periods noted above (see Table 2.1 for an illustration of the periods and characteristics of cartels). In markets that are free from antitrust regulations, price manipulations can take the form of buffer stocks, central selling points, export controls, and straightforward pricing agreements (as in bid-rigging). Conversely, in countries that abide by antitrust laws, price-fixing—whether it takes the form of a verbal agreement or a more formal arrangement—is the only option for collusion. The conditions favorable to cartelization will be examined first, as these factors determine the

Table 2.1 Historical patterns of cartelization under different antitrust regimes

No Antitrust Enforcement—Before Passage of Sherman Antitrust Act (pre-1891)	Weak Antitrust Enforcement—Anticompetitive Practices Common (1891–1950)	Stricter Antitrust Enforcement within Industrialized Nations—Int'l Cartel Period for Developing World (1950–1990)	Active Phase of Illicit Globalized Cartels in Industrialized World (1990–present)

structure, function, and longevity of cartels. The conclusions drawn from this analysis will then be applied to the recent wave of illegal collusive agreements in the industrialized world.

The condition for cartelization

The experience of the developing nations in attempting to cartelize commodity markets will be utilized here to illustrate the conditions that must be met for price-fixing to be effective. The visibility of these efforts at collusion make them an instructive means of analyzing the circumstances under which price-fixing can be implemented successfully.

It was with considerable pride and fanfare that the so-called "Group of 77," a block of developing nations from across the globe, pushed the United Nations Commission on Trade and Development (UNCTAD) in 1976 to adopt Resolution 93-IV, known as the *Integrated Programme for Commodities* (IPC). After years of declining or unstable commodity prices, the IPC sought a fundamental alteration of the terms of trade between developing and developed nations. Under the IPC initiative, the prices received for goods exported by the developing nations were to be raised through non-market—some would say, anti-market — mechanisms.[1] This flexing of muscle by the developing nations was a startling rejection of the primacy of free markets in international trade. See Rothstein (1979) and Goodwin and Mayall (1980) for extensive evaluations of UNCTAD's accomplishments under the IPC.

The UNCTAD proclamation foresaw the use of cartels in a multitude of markets, including agricultural commodities markets such as coffee, cocoa, and sugar, as well as in the markets of raw materials, including minerals such as iron ore, copper, and tin. Despite the broad appeal that the initiative had for nations in the developing world, in practice the IPC's goals were doomed to failure from the start. The list of commodities targeted by the IPC for price controls included some goods produced in the industrialized world (for example, copper, sugar, meat, and vegetable oil). The developed nations did not welcome the market intrusion posed by the IPC and, without the participation of significant producers in the industrialized sphere, many of the cartels envisioned under the UNCTAD resolution never materialized. Moreover, although the IPC provided political affirmation for the cartels that already existed in seven world commodity markets (petroleum, coffee, cocoa, sugar, tin, natural rubber, and bauxite), for the most part these markets did not possess the conditions favorable to sustainable cartelization. Indeed, although key producers in these markets put production or export controls in place, for various reasons (detailed in Chapter 3) price increases remained elusive.

The use of cartelization to manipulate market prices requires that five conditions be met. First, in order for effective policing of the agreement the number of producers within the cartel must be limited. As will be discussed later in this chapter, firms engaged in a cartel have a significant incentive to cheat. With too many participants, it becomes impossible for the cartel to monitor the pricing and production of its members and the agreement is likely to collapse. The fact that the International Sugar Agreements or ISAs (detailed in Chapter 3) never managed to significantly influence prices was due, in part, to the inability of the participating nations to secure durable agreements on production and exports. Similarly, the International Coffee Organization (ICO) was unable to permanently secure higher and more stable coffee prices for its nearly two dozen members. Of the seven commodity products mentioned above, only the producers of cocoa and natural rubber fit the criterion of limited membership (just four producers oversee the bulk of world production) and yet they too were unable to manage the market.

The traditional measure of industry concentration is the four-firm concentration ratio—namely, the percentage of industry sales that is attributable to the top four firms. According to this model, if this ratio exceeds 60 percent, the firm is deemed an oligopoly and the likelihood of collusion is considered greater. Currently, industry concentration is most frequently measured using the Herfindahl–Hirschman Index (HHI). The HHI is the sum of the squared market share of each firm in the industry (in percentage terms):

$$\text{HHI} = \sum_{i=1}^{n} S_i^2$$

The HHI is considered a superior way of measuring oligopolistic power, as it places greater weight on cartel members who hold the greatest market share. Thus a market that is comprised of four firms, one of which is very large, will have a much higher HHI than a market in which the bulk of the revenues is controlled by four firms of equal size. As noted by Hovenkamp (2005), approval of a merger may rest upon the pre- and post-value of the HHI, with industries having a value of 1,800 or more considered highly concentrated. As described in Chapter 5, the industries in which collusion was pursued were typically those with a limited number of firms.

Paradoxically, the price increases affected by cartelization are likely to draw additional producers into the market, thereby weakening or eliminating the cartel's ability to manipulate prices. Working collusive agreements require that some form of barrier to entry exist to keep out additional producers, these impediments constituting the second condition for cartelization. Effective barriers to entry can take the form of climatic conditions required to grow a particular crop (cocoa, for example) or the geographic distribution of natural resources (e.g. petroleum, tin, and bauxite). In the international sugar market, however, the barriers to entry are weak owing to the fact that world sugar output can be derived from both the tropically-grown sugar cane as well as the sugar beets of temperate zones. Ultimately, the significant and persistent over-production of both of these crops led to the failure of the International Sugar Agreements. The production of natural materials such as petroleum, of course, is geographically contained and therefore less susceptible to the entry of new producers.

A third requisite condition for the successful formation of a cartel is that the product being promoted be homogeneous. Commodities such as sugar, cocoa, and natural rubber conform well to this criterion. Many of the products mentioned in UNCTAD's proclamation, however, lack homogeneity. So, for example, the existence of two grades of petroleum, low-sulfur (sweet) and high-sulfur (sour), has forced the Organization of Petroleum Exporting Countries (OPEC) to adopt a two-tier pricing structure. Similarly, the division of the coffee market into the higher grade Arabica and more disease-resistant but lower quality robusta beans, and then within these two product grades, additional classifications by geography and roast (e.g. Sumatran, Kenyan AA, etc.), complicated efforts to secure prices through the International Coffee Agreements. In the presence of multiple grades or varieties of a given commodity, the pricing structure can become divisive, forcing the cartel to impose a product hierarchy that de facto rewards some members and penalizes others.

The primary goal of cartelization frequently was to raise rather than smooth commodity prices. Faced with an elevated price for a cartelized product, the consumer may seek a more affordable alternative, and when attractive product substitutes exist, the cartel's control over prices is greatly weakened. The relative likelihood of substitution therefore constitutes another factor that impacts the success of a cartel. In the case of the International Rubber Agreements, for example, the cartel was so successful in manipulating the world market for natural rubber that the industrialized nations stepped up their production of synthetic rubber (a near-perfect substitute, except in the case of automobile tires, which require the use of natural rubber). As for the tropical crop cane sugar, which is largely a product of the developing world, the attempts to rein in world exports and firm prices under the International Sugar Agreements were thwarted by the fact that beet sugar provided an economical substitute.

The final condition needed for successful collusion concerns the physical characteristics of the commodity in question; how the intrinsic physical characteristics of a product affect the supply side of price manipulation. As will be discussed below, cartels have utilized a number of methods to stabilize or increase prices. These approaches involve restricting the quantity of a product available on international markets. Thus if the cartel is to succeed either output must be curtailed or excess production must be removed and stored for later sale. For commodities such as petroleum, tin and bauxite, a reduction in output eliminates the need and expense of storing the product. For agricultural goods, on the other hand, cyclical crop variations (e.g. inches of annual rainfall, relative temperatures) make it difficult to manage supply and so it is left to the cartel members to limit their exports. For the agricultural products discussed in Chapter 3, medium-term storage is possible and therefore the cartel can avoid the unpopular practice of destroying crops as a means of adjusting prices. Yet for many of the other crops that UNCTAD mentions in the 1976 proclamation (e.g. bananas and meat), storage of sufficient duration to allow for market prices to firm is impossible. The issue of long-term storage of commodities was one of the key factors limiting cartels to a relatively small number of markets.

Connor (2007: 443) noted that there are additional market characteristics that affect the feasibility and sustainability of cartels. As a corollary to significant concentration in production, Connor proposed that cartel pricing is more likely to be successful if buyer concentration is low. In addition, Connor (2001: 545) also noted that if competing firms have an established legal relationship, as through trade associations or joint ventures, for example, then the jump to illegal cooperative behavior becomes more likely.

Statistical inference about the number of cartels and cartel characteristics

All suppositions about populations are based on inferences drawn from samples and applied to those populations. Under most circumstances this is appropriate, since concerns about these conclusions can be addressed through application of the model to larger sample sizes. In circumstances where the phenomenon being measured is illegal, however, obtaining a sample that is provably unbiased is impossible. Statistical interferences on the population of those engaged in tax evasion or illegal immigration necessarily involves supposition. The development of theory surrounding collusion, particularly the assumed nature of firms and industries that are engaged in price-fixing, depends almost entirely upon the characteristics of a potentially biased sample, namely the minority of instances where collusion is uncovered. What we "know" about collusion is inferred from a sample of observables that may not reflect the characteristics of the actual population.

Based on these observations, it is commonly assumed that cartelization is confined to industries with a limited number of firms, producing a homogeneous product with no close substitutes, and characterized by significant barriers to entry. More recent analysis has led to the conclusion that price-fixing arrangements are more common in industries producing intermediate products. As a final price is not observable, it is more difficult for such agreements to be uncovered by antitrust authorities. In addition, collusion is more likely to occur in sectors producing "mature" products that are well along their life-cycle. Innovation and product differentiation is more difficult in these sectors, and collusion may appear to be the only route to higher returns. Finally, increased exposure to competition is regarded as a catalyst for price-fixing, suggesting that investigative resources should be targeted towards industries experiencing newfound rivalry. Exceptions to these assumptions are regarded as interesting counterexamples that assist in refining models of collusion.

Unlike most theoretical inference, however, the analysis of collusion and collusive behavior suffers from a significant flaw. Conclusions are drawn from the subset of firms that are both engaged in collusion and ensnared by antitrust authorities (thought to be as little as one-sixth of the firms actually engaged in price-fixing). It is assumed that this sub-sample of businesses prosecuted for price-fixing is a reasonable representation of the actual population of colluding firms. Unlike other situations where increasing the sample size will likely eliminate any potential bias, the illegality of price-fixing results in a population that remains largely an unknown. Equally important, the control population, those firms not colluding, is an unknown. If antitrust authorities are able to uncover only a small minority of actual instances of price-fixing, then a number of corporations in the control group may actually be engaged in some form of collusion. Inferences drawn from these observations are likely to be suspect. Inferences drawn about the Underground Economy in the US (the off-cited statistic that 70 percent of such activities are unreported legal activities) are also based on imperfect sampling.

Unlike other circumstances where empirical testing is done, the illegality of cartels suggests that information obtained about the behavior of colluding firms is likely to be unreliable. A similar situation is likely to exist for firms that engage in other illicit behavior, such as predatory pricing. Although it is assumed that predatory pricing can only occur in industries with barriers to entry and low price elasticity of demand, this is based upon evidence drawn from proven violations of antitrust law. It is impossible to determine if this sample is representative of the population of firms engaged in predation. Equally important, as in the case with collusion, the characteristics of the control group (those not engaged in predatory pricing) are unknown, as there is no means of stating with certainty that a given firm has not engaged in aggressive pricing that crossed the line into illegality. This problem with incomplete (erroneous) sampling is becoming increasing critical, as antitrust authorities move towards some form of early-warning system that is based upon industry characteristics and observed pricing behavior.

Drawing inferences about collusion with incomplete information

The difficulty for regulators (and those analyzing collusive behavior) is that the fundamental assumptions (e.g. limited number of firms) outlined above may or may not hold, particularly when the data set used to support such assumptions is composed largely of unknowns. If we use A to represent the situation that an industry is colluding, and ***B*** to denote that the industry fulfills most or all of the conditions above, then it is generally held that:

(1) ***A/B***	True in a subset of cases
(2) ***B/A***	Assumed true
(3) ***Not A/Not B***	Mostly true
(4) ***Not B/Not A***	Possibly true

Situation number 1 represents the standard treatment of cartel theory under which collusion is assumed to take place primarily in those industries where the requisite conditions for price-fixing prevail. Situation 2 denotes the fact that if collusion is taking place, the industry likely fulfills the necessary conditions for collusion. Numbers (3) and (4) are more problematic. Assumption 3 notes that if firms are not colluding, then the conditions for cartelization are not present. This may be true, but since the actual sample of colluding firms is an unknown, it is impossible to state with any certainty that (3) is valid. A similar situation exists for assumption (4). Firms that are not engaged in price-fixing may not fulfill the necessary conditions for collusion, but this cannot be known with any confidence. Statements about the conditions for collusion are based upon the nature of firms that engage in cartel behavior (and are caught), but must also rely upon the characteristics of the control group. In this instance, with neither the sample of colluding firms nor the control group known, all statistical inference is suspect. Models that are intended to provide antitrust regulators with some form of advanced warning about price-fixing are essentially untestable.

Statistical sampling in the absence of "clean" samples

As noted by Jandl (2004), this inability to construct a representative sample is common when illegal activities are involved. The author notes that sampling to determine the prevalence of drunk-driving, prostitution, illegal immigration and tax evasion are all problematic (Jandl, 2008: 1). Further complications arise if the intent is to determine not just the incidence of an illegal activity, but the characteristics of the population involved in that activity; precisely what is required if the supposedly known traits of colluding firms are to be observationally proven.

Jandl (2008: 5–13) details a number of different techniques that have been used to estimate populations when random sampling is impossible, including the use of multipliers, capture–recapture models, and the outcome of regularization (legalization) policies. All these approaches involve significant assumptions and the estimates are superior only to no information at all. Multipliers can be derived by using interviews of known offenders to determine what proportion of a particular group that is involved in a specific offense. Multiplying this by the number of persons in that population that were captured for the same offense gives an estimate of the total. Similarly, capture–recapture models (see Jandl, 2004 for an application) use recidivism rates to determine the size of a population. Suppose 100 persons from a particular group are arrested and eventually released. If five out of 100 subsequent detentions involve re-arrests of these same individuals, then the original 100 persons arrested made up 5 percent of the total population. Clearly, both of these methods have significant flaws. Multipliers rely upon survey data from offenders that is highly suspect. Capture–recapture models assume that repeat offenders are representative of an entire population. Yet, lacking an alternative, these approaches provide at least some estimate of an essentially unknowable population. Regularization or amnesty programs (whether for tax evasion or illicit immigration) probably provide better estimates, as hidden populations are suddenly out in the open. Such programs are by necessity irregular, however, and an estimate derived from any amnesty program is likely to be usable only in the near term.

The problem with these techniques when applied to price-fixing is that they are used primarily to estimate population size and not population characteristics. Using a capture–recapture procedure provides an estimate of the population of colluding firms but, given the small size of the sample, little opportunity to draw inferences about what those firms might look like. The European Union and US Department of Justice (DOJ) leniency provisions mimic amnesty programs by allowing firms to confess to price-fixing and avoid most, if not all, penalties. Yet, these are rolling programs—continuously available to all corporations. They are unlikely to produce a large response from corporations during any given time period, since they are available during subsequent periods. Confessions under either program trickle in, and do not provide the kind of "clean" sample necessary to make statistical inferences. In addition, unlike tax or immigration amnesty programs, the reward for admitting guilt is a mixed blessing. The firm avoids a potential fine, and its executives potential jail time, but the excess profits extracted through collusion are gone, potentially forever. Post-confession, the corporation is likely to be viewed as an unreliable partner in crime, unlikely to be invited to join future price-fixing schemes. Although capture–recapture methodologies present significant challenges, an application of this technique to a sample of cartelized firms will be presented in Chapter 5.

Price manipulation under collusive agreements

Given the inherent heterogeneity of international commodity markets, cartels have naturally adopted a variety of ways to manipulate prices. The success and durability of these mechanisms has varied greatly. This section first examines each of these methods as they apply to the commodity cartels of the period from 1965 to 1985, when collusive agreements in the developing world were extra-legal. Also to be considered are the cartels operating in the developed world since 1950, which have avoided using methods that would expose them to the sanctions of antitrust authorities. In an ideal world—ideal, at least, for the members of the cartel—all collusive agreements would utilize buffer stocks as a means of achieving price stability. With buffer stocks, the degree of cooperation necessary to make the cartel function is minimal. In this scenario, members agree on a target price and jointly fund a buffer stock. In turn, markets are stabilized through the buying and selling of the commodity. As long as supply and demand are approximately equal over the long term, the buffer stock can maintain the target price without being forced to secure additional resources. The cost to the participants is minor and enforcement costs are negligible. Indeed, because the manager of the buffer stock will buy when prices are low and sell when prices are high, this arrangement generally results in a net profit. As will be discussed in Chapter 3, the International Tin Agreements (ITAs) involved the use of buffer stock that successfully managed prices until the mid-1980s, when supply outpaced demand to such a degree that the buffer stock exhausted its financial resources and collapsed.

In markets in which persistent excess supply exists—as in coffee and sugar commodities—a buffer stock mechanism will not successfully stabilize or increase prices. In this case, the use of a buffer stock would require unlimited resources and the permanent stockpiling of significant quantities of the commodities. To counter the negative effects of excess supply, the International Coffee Association (ICA) and the International Sugar Agreements (ISAs) required members to curtail exports in order to realize higher world prices. When the coffee and sugar markets were roughly in equilibrium in the 1970s, export controls provided a practical approach to improving market conditions for producers. When in the 1980s supplies of coffee and sugar greatly outstripped demand, export controls left members of the cartels with large quantities of unsold output and the agreements collapsed. For the ICA, in particular, the fact that the coffee plant does not produce beans for the first five to seven years after planting meant that the crop production could never be tailored precisely to demand.

In contrast to agricultural goods, mineral production is suited to the use of export controls providing, that is, that the key producers can be persuaded to match production to demand. Despite its notoriety, OPEC, for example, has an uneven record in its drive to manipulate world oil prices. Increasing oil prices frequently occurred prior to actions by OPEC. In 1973, OPEC initiated a generalized commodity price boom that led to a period of global inflation, yet by the end of the decade it was political events—in particular, the Iran Hostage Crisis—rather than market events that were determining oil prices. OPEC's loss of its tenuous hold on the market was further demonstrated by the complete collapse of petroleum prices in 1986, when the cost of a barrel of oil briefly fell to ten dollars (for an analysis of the cartel's behavior under conditions of falling petroleum prices, see Jones, 1990). The wild swings in petroleum prices in 2008 further demonstrate the imperfect control that OPEC exerts upon world prices. In early 2008, with real petroleum prices at historical highs, OPEC lacked sufficient capacity to bring prices back down to desirable levels. One-hundred-forty-seven-dollar per barrel oil encourages conservation and substitution and therefore inflated prices are not in the best interests of the cartel in the long term. Following the economic crisis in the fall of 2008, OPEC was powerless to affect prices, and even its real and threatened reductions of output did little to solidify prices, which fell some 70 percent from their highs for the year.

With the threat of antitrust prosecution always present, firms in the industrialized world avoid transparent forms of price manipulation (in particular, production controls) and rely instead on less detectable methods, especially bid-rigging.[2] The rigging of bids provides both secrecy and a predetermined "winning" price, which exceeds the outcome that would prevail in an unhampered market. In 2006, the US DOJ announced that Elpida Memory of Japan, Infineon Technologies of Germany, and the South Korean firms Hynix Semiconductor and Samsung Semiconductor had conspired to fix prices on DRAM computer chips sold to US manufacturers. In addition to its guilty plea to the price-fixing charge, Elpida also admitted that it had worked with the cartel to bid-rig sales to Sun Microsystems by setting minimum contract bidding prices. In 2004, the EU uncovered bid-rigging among 11 firms selling Gas Insulated Switchgear (GIS). In this case, the cartel members coordinated their bidding by establishing minimum offering prices. In an attempt to secure even higher returns, they also agreed to a geographic partitioning of the GIS market. Further details on these cartels will be presented in Chapter 5.

Perhaps the most successful international cartel to ever function is the De Beers diamond syndicate. For decades, De Beers utilized exclusive production agreements and maintained a tight control of supply in order to artificially inflate the price of diamonds.[3] On the surface, it appears that the cartel simply used export controls to restrict supply and maintain higher prices. Yet the success of the De Beers cartel actually relied on the use of a Central Selling Point (CSP) to raise prices and prevent cheating by participants. As new diamond mines were discovered and additional output entered the world market, De Beers negotiated the control of the new capacity. In particular, excess diamonds were withdrawn from the market to maintain target prices; in 2001, it appeared that over $3 billion dollars in unsold inventory was held by the cartel. Wholesalers who attempted to secure sources for diamonds outside of the CSP were denied future access to the high quality diamonds held by the cartel. Diamond producers who cheated on the cartel were similarly punished. Indeed, when in the early 1980s Zaire attempted to sell their industrial-grade diamonds outside the CSP, De Beers flooded the market with inventory and the price soon collapsed. Although De Beers successfully manipulated market prices for many years, their "model" of collusion is not easily applicable to other commodity markets (for a thorough discussion of cartelization of the diamond market, see Bergenstock, 2006). Unless most of the output of a particular product can be brought under the control of a centralized marketing entity, it is unlikely that prices can be tightly controlled through collusion.

Application of the cartel model in the presence of antitrust enforcement

A consideration of the history of the commodity cartels of the 1970s and 1980s provides important insights into the functioning of collusive agreements. The business environment changed dramatically in the late 1980s, when the commodity cartels sanctioned under UNCTAD dissolved in the face of market and political pressures. OPEC stands as the notable exception to the demise of commodity cartels during this period. The commodity agreements that were supported by UNCTAD and the developing nations were extra-national and impervious to the legal controls that existed in the industrialized world. As the commodity cartels of the developing world waned, the developed world experienced a surge of collusive agreements. As previously noted, secrecy was paramount to those engaging in collusion in the industrialized nations. Unlike the earlier commodity agreements, which operated freely and often lasted for decades, the pressures exerted on the cartels in the developed world tended to limit their duration. There may, of course, be long-standing collusive arrangements functioning in the industrialized world that simply have not yet been routed by antitrust agencies, but in general these cartels have a lifespan of only three to five years. Although penalties for engaging in cartelization have increased significantly, and now include not only monetary penalties but also the potential for criminal sanctions, cartels continue to form. As was the case with commodity markets, for a cartel to function successfully in the industrialized world it, too, must conform to the market conditions of: limited membership, product homogeneity, effective barriers to entry, storability or other means of controlling supply, and lack of attractive substitution.

The worldwide lysine cartel active from 1992 to 1995 provides an illustration of how a successful cartel functions in the developed world (for further discussion of this cartel, see Chapter 5). At the urging of fellow executives, Mark Whitacre, president of the lysine division of Archer Daniels Midland (ADM), met in April 1992 with representatives of the major Japanese producers Kyowa Hakko Kogyo and Ajinomoto. The initial meeting was followed by a "trade association" conference in Mexico City in June 1992, during the course of which the three firms discussed price-fixing. These companies were later joined by two major South Korean producers, Sewon and Cheil Jedung. World lysine prices had fallen significantly, to approximately 60 cents per pound, a figure that guaranteed losses for even the most efficient producer of the group, ADM. The collusive cooperation between the five firms resulted in the firming of prices to nearly $1.30 per pound by 1995. Unbeknownst to the cartel, the FBI had begun investigating ADM as early as November 1992. In time, Whitacre became an FBI mole, and for nearly three years he gathered evidence to support a DOJ charge of collusion. By 1996, ADM, Ajinomoto, and Kyowa had agreed to pay fines to settle the price-fixing allegations (for a detailed discussion of the lysine conspiracy, see Connor, 2001).

The lysine cartel was a stable association that disintegrated as a result of a federal probe rather than owing to any inherent characteristics. The market for lysine was dominated by five producers, which made it simple for the participants to agree on pricing and monitor adherence to the agreement. There are no cost-effective substitutes for lysine, an amino acid used in the pork, chicken, and fish industries. Although the barriers to entry are not insurmountable, additional capacity cannot be put in place in the short- to medium-term, as expansion of production facilities takes approximately three years. Lysine is a homogeneous product, making price-fixing far easier to implement than if there were multiple grades or varieties of the product. Finally, lysine production can be adjusted to achieve a target price, a factor equivalent to the fifth condition discussed above, which requires the existence of some means of removing excess production from the market. The conspirators benefited from another fundamental characteristic of the market, namely, that lysine production is not intended for final consumption and therefore price increases in the market are less discernible.

Like most cartels formed in the industrialized world, the lysine conspiracy relied on firms to manipulate output in order to achieve a target price. The need for secrecy prevented the cartel's use of other mechanisms such as a Central Selling Point. Although production controls like those employed by the lysine cartel are more likely to lead to cheating on the agreement, it appears that the greatest threat to the longevity of collusive agreements is their illegality.

Profit-maximization under the cartel model

Although the cartels of the industrialized world continue to thrive even in the new era of strict antitrust enforcement, their ability to form is constrained by the conditions for cartelization previously discussed. The requirement that the cartelized market be dominated by only a few firms suggests that collusion is primarily a movement away from oligopolistic "competition" (that is, tacit cooperation) toward explicit cooperation that resembles monopoly.

Traditionally, oligopolistic behavior has been modeled utilizing Sweezey's Kinked-Demand Curve (Sweezey, 1939). Modern analysis of oligopolies, on the other hand, has turned to game theory as a means of explaining cooperative pricing under this market structure. In Table 2.2, price competition in a duopolistic (two-firm) industry results in lower profits for both firms. Starting

Table 2.2 Pricing under conditions of duopoly

	Firm 2	
	High price	Low price
High price	Profits high for both firms	Profits high for Firm 2, very low for firm 1
	Firm 1	
Low price	Profits high for Firm 1, very low for Firm 2	Profits low for both firms

in the upper left-hand corner of the diagram, one sees that when Firm 1 reduces its price, the dominant strategy for Firm 2 is to institute a similar price reduction, resulting in an outcome shown in the lower right-hand corner. Both firms are now worse off and it is likely that prices will eventually return to their original (i.e. high) level. This "game" of price competition will be repeated until both firms, realizing that it is not in their best interest to compete on price, turn to tacit cooperation.[4] While the profitability of both firms rises as a result of the cessation of price competition, profits will still be well below where they would stand under conditions of monopoly.

The problem for regulators is that the outcome of this game—with both firms charging an identical price—resembles the collusive result. Lacking evidence that cooperation on pricing has taken place, antitrust authorities must undertake the complex task of unraveling the behavior and costs of the firm before a charge of illicit cooperation can be made. As demonstrated in Chapter 5, the US DOJ and the EU Commission have uncovered most cartels through some form of outside assistance. In most cases, investigations have begun after the dissemination of insider knowledge, the confession of a participant in the cartel, or the reception of consumer complaints.

The Cournot–Nash model of oligopoly behavior

Game theory is a simple and straightforward means of examining the behavior of oligopolies and cartels. This simplicity, however, makes the model somewhat unsuitable for evaluating more complex behavioral issues such as the response of cartel members to clemency provisions. The traditional exposition of oligopoly behavior presented in the Cournot–Nash Model is better suited than game theory for analyzing complicated issues like leniency. Let us suppose a duopoly market with q_1 representing the output of Firm 1, and q_2 representing the output of Firm 2. The price in the market is dependent on the combined output of the two firms:

$$P = P(q_1 + q_2) \tag{1}$$

Firm 1's highest level of profits is determined by maximizing:

$$P(q_1 + q_2)q_1 - C_1(q_1) = \Pi_1, \tag{2}$$

where:

$C_1(q_1)$ = Firm 1's cost function,

Π_1 = profit of Firm 1.

Likewise, Firm 2 profit-maximizes utilizing the function:

$$P(q_1 + q_2)q_2 - C_2(q_2) = \Pi_2 \tag{3}$$

A Cournot–Nash Equilibrium (Nash, 1950) occurs when the quantities determined through these two maximizations are consistent. The first-order condition for Firm 1 is:

$$P(q_1^* + q_2) + q_1^* P`(q_1^* + q_2) - C_1`(q_1^*) = 0, \tag{4}$$

where:

q_1^* = the optimal quantity for Firm 1;

implying:

$$P(q_1^* + q_2) + C_1`(q_1^*) - q_1^* P`(q_1^* + q_2). \tag{5}$$

Likewise, Firm 2's optimal price decision will fulfill:

$$P(q_1 + q_2^*) + q_2^* P`(q_1 + q_2^*) - C_2`(q_2^*) = 0, \tag{6}$$

or:

$$P(q_1 + q_2^*) = C_2`(q_2^*) - q_2^* P`(q_1 + q_2^*). \tag{7}$$

Each firm is making an implicit assumption about the output of the other firm—namely, that the output will remain constant. When the presumed outputs are equal to the actual outputs, the market is in equilibrium. Since equilibrium in the Cournot–Nash Model requires that the price be set by the combined output of the two firms (equations 5 and 7), both firms will therefore charge an identical price for the product, a situation that might be falsely interpreted as a sign of collusion.

The outcome of the Cournot–Nash Model illustrates the problem for antitrust regulators—the profit-maximizing price chosen by each firm is identical, yet no collusion has taken place. In oligopolistic sectors such as the US commercial airline industry, this outcome is inevitable in the long run. Since competition on price is destructive, each firm will eventually settle into a pricing pattern that closely mirrors its competition. This cooperate outcome is neither unanticipated, nor illegal.

The collusive outcome: the basics

When a market is cartelized, a variety of pricing strategies can be adopted to maximize the profits of the industry as a whole. Utilizing the variables from Cournot–Nash (see above), profit-maximization by the cartel would imply:

$$P(q_1 + q_2)\,(q_1 + q_2) - C_1(q_1) - C_2(q_2) = \Pi_{\text{industry}}. \tag{8}$$

Price is set by the combined output of the two firms and the overall outcome is equivalent to a monopolist possessing two centers of production. The two first-order conditions are:

$$P`\,(q_1^* + q_2^*)\,(q_1^* + q_2^*) + P(q_1^* + q_2^*) - C_1`\,(q_1^*) = 0, \tag{9}$$

and:

$$P`\,(q_1^* + q_2^*)\,(q_1^* + q_2^*) + P(q_1^* + q_2^*) - C_2`\,(q_2^*) = 0. \tag{10}$$

Since the first two terms in (9) and (10) are identical, the result implies that the marginal cost for the first producer must equal that of the second producer. If both firms have identical cost functions, the outputs will be equal. Otherwise, the producer with the lowest costs will realize a greater proportion of the combine cartel output.

Although equations (9) and (10) represent the "ideal" outcome under a cartel (understanding that except for the two participants of the duopoly, the non-competitive outcome is far from ideal), collusive agreements in the real world only approximate the result described above. As noted in Chapter 5, many of the pricing and output decisions in cartel arrangements formed since 1990 were reduced to simple agreements that the firms stay off of one another's turf. The international commodity cartels that were prevalent in the developing world under UNCTAD involved complex agreements and compromises on production and exports. It is difficult to imagine either process resulting in a collusive ideal. Thus the theoretical outcome outlined above should be regarded as a tendency of a cartel rather than a true description of cartel behavior.

Antitrust policy and firm behavior

The analysis presented above does not include the potential fines that may arise from antitrust action taken against cartel members. With some low but significant probability, the firm can expect to have the collusive agreement exposed, and fines levied as a result. If the fines are of sufficient magnitude, this may ultimately bring about a change in how firms view the returns to collusion, and a subsequent reduction in the number of cartels. The search for an appropriately severe fine that would bring about such an outcome is detailed in the latter part of this chapter. Perhaps the most significant revision of antitrust policy has been, however, the introduction of so-called leniency policy in the US and EU; policies that permit a firm to expose a price-fixing agreement that it is party to, yet avoid any penalties for its participation. This innovation has altered the expected payoff to corporations considering collusion.

The cartel game in the presence of a "payoff" for snitching

When antitrust agencies realized that a significant number of cartels were escaping detection in the US and Europe, the decision was made to adopt leniency clauses that would encourage firms to confess their own transgressions and also turn in their co-conspirators. A cartel member can receive clemency, in the form of exemption of fines, by being the first member of the collusive agreement to admit to violating antitrust laws. Although an amnesty policy existed in the US as early as 1978, the DOJ did not adopt a formal program until the creation of the Corporate Leniency Program in 1993. The EU's Leniency Notice dates to 1996; in 2006, the EU Commission published a proposed major revision, IP/06/1705. Corporations that are offered leniency agree to provide the authorities with full details of the collusive agreement and to expose all participants. In some instances, "second confessors" (that is, firms that agree to cooperate after a partner firm has already exposed the cartel) are also granted a degree of leniency. The effectiveness of these leniency provisions is made less clear by the preferential treatment of these second confessors.

The probability that a firm would be eligible for a leniency judgment is a factor that, together with the expectation of excess returns and the risk of detection, greatly complicates a firm's ability to determine optimal profit-maximizing behavior. The result of this uncertainty is that leniency programs can result in mixed outcomes. Not surprisingly, Motta (2004) determined that the effectiveness of leniency provisions is measurably enhanced as cartel penalties rise and leniency "discounts" increase. The author also noted that raising the probability of detection made these programs more effective. Conversely, Stephan (2005) argued that in nearly three-quarters of cases, cartel members that came forward to benefit from the Corporate Leniency Program were already under investigation by the DOJ. Motta and Polo (2003) analyzed the impact of leniency programs by incorporating the longer-term interests of participants. By undermining the trust that is essential to cartelization, the amnesty programs of the US and the EU may permanently eliminate the possibility of future collusion. This breakdown of trust is not played out when cartels are uncovered by authorities; in fact, some cartels have returned to collusive cooperation even after being exposed. A cartel member therefore may find the benefits of being the "first confessor" not as attractive as maintaining the trust of co-conspirators.

Zane (2003) argued that when a firm is deciding whether to expose its co-conspirators or keep the cartel intact it has to take into account the possibility that it may incur civil penalties from a confession—penalties that could be far greater than those imposed by the DOJ or the courts. If the firm has international operations, an admission of collusion in the US may lead to criminal and civil penalties abroad. Following the exposure of collusion, the firm's management may face lawsuits from stockholders as well as substantial fines for violating securities laws. Unlike other white-collar crimes, the extent of the prosecutions and penalties can be nearly limitless. As Zane noted (2003: 3), "A defendant that pleads guilty now gives civil plaintiffs the opportunity to use the defendant's guilty plea as evidence against the defendant in their civil cases;" this confession also "alerts enforcers in other jurisdictions that there may be an anticompetitive problem." The author identified this conflict as a classic example of the Prisoner's Dilemma and noted that non-cooperation is in some circumstances the dominant strategy. Clearly, this assessment is not good news for antitrust authorities, who have increasingly turned to higher penalties to realize compliance.

The introduction of leniency measures into antitrust laws substantially alters the payoff matrix facing a firm that colludes. In contrast to the payoff matrix for cartels' behavior described above, the situation with leniency terms now corresponds more closely to the Prisoner's Dilemma version of game theory. Firm 1 faces a situation in which it can raise its profits through collusion yet it risks substantial penalties—including civil fines—if its partner(s) expose the cartel.

Where:

δ_1 = Probability of partner exposing cartel, Firm 1,
δ_2 = Probability of partner exposing cartel, Firm 2,
F_1 = Anticipated fine, Firm 1,
F_2 = Anticipated fine, Firm 2.

Table 2.3 Profitability of oligopoly firms—Cournot–Nash outcome versus cartel

	Cartel price—Firm 2	*Cournot–Nash price—Firm 2*
Cartel price—Firm 1	Highly profitable—δ F_1/ Highly profitable—δ F_2	
Cournot–Nash price—Firm 1		Less profitable/less profitable

Each corporation must now evaluate several strategies:

- cooperate in a collusive agreement in spite of the risk that its partner(s) will expose the cartel;
- abandon the cartel and settle for the normal cooperative oligopoly rate of return;
- engage in the cartel with the intention of being the first to expose its existence to the antitrust authorities and thereby avoid significant fines.

Without question, the third option provides the highest rate of return for the colluding firm. The firm faces the risk, however, that its co-conspirators will evaluate the cartel arrangement in a similar fashion and move to be the first one to confess.

These contradictory incentives pose a significant problem for antitrust regulators. In the absence of the leniency provision, collusion is profitable yet potentially high fines make the expected rate of return lower. With a leniency program in place, a firm can avoid fines by being the first confessor and therefore the risks associated with the collusion are diminished. For a detailed rationale for the leniency provisions and their relative effectiveness, see Blum et al. (2008).

The incentive to cheat

One of the tenets of cartels is that the incentive to cheat renders them unstable. The assumption is that as long as their subterfuge is not uncovered, firms can secure additional profits by violating the terms of the collusive agreement. Specifically, when prices are managed by the cartel rather than the market, firms can increase sales and profits by charging a price that lies between the oligopoly equilibrium implied by the Cournot–Nash Model and the price imposed by the cartel. One of the fundamental problems facing firms that engage in collusion in the industrialized world is that their need to operate under the radar of antitrust authority makes it more difficult for them to police their own illegal association and punish "cheaters." It is assumed that cartels will be short-lived, as cheating by one participant will effectively destroy the cooperation of the group.

The early literature on the stability within cartels supported the view that collusive agreements are inherent unsustainable. In his seminal piece on cartel behavior, Stigler (1964) argued that cheating is the natural outcome of the price manipulation carried out by cartels. With cartelized prices in place, as in equations (9) and (10), a firm can obtain incremental profits by remaining in the cartel and secretly offering its product at reduced prices and securing additional sales. The temptation to cheat creates somewhat of a double-bind for participants of collusive arrangements: deceit can boost the individual incremental profits of the rogue member, but should this deception be uncovered the cartel would inevitably break down and the cheater would have to accept the lower returns of open market competition. Porter (1983) and Green and Porter (1984) went as far as to assert that the fear of renewed competition is the source of the stability in cartels. For their overview of the literature on the duration of cartels, Levenstein and Suslow (2006) drew upon nine comprehensive studies on the impacts of collusion. Although the data presented by these various researchers are somewhat inconsistent, there is evidence to suggest that the longevity of cartels has been increasing over the course of time (Levenstein and Suslow, 2006: 51). Similarly, these authors presented figures on the causes of the demise of individual cartels. In all but one of these studies, the primary trigger to the dissolution of collusive agreements was cheating (with the entry of new firms and product substitution following in importance). A study by Marquez (1994) found that increased market concentration prolongs the life of cartels, while rapid growth in demand tends to shorten this duration. Griffin and Xiong (1997) examined the incentive to cheat specifically from the viewpoint of OPEC members and concluded that the allocation system used by the organization—a system that favors small producers—invites deception by participants who consider their share of the market to be too modest.

The tendency toward instability in cartels is most apparent in the pricing and production agreements utilized in international commodity agreements. Many members of OPEC, for example, violated their production limits in the early 1980s, which lead to a price collapse in 1986. Similarly, sugar producers, who were never able to fully implement the output controls established under the International Sugar Agreements, suffered decades of weak prices. The cartels that function in the developing world are likely to experience cheating for the simple reason that production and sales figures for the non-industrialized world are often unreliable, and therefore excess production can be concealed more easily.

Given the penchant for cheating in collusive accords, a number of cartels have turned to methods that are much less likely to result in agreement violations. Firms may simply agree not to sell on one another's turf or they may agree to specific quotas when doing so. If market segmentation is combined with price floors, an effective collusive agreement can be achieved without the need for negotiations about market share. In certain cases, cartel members publicized their pricing structures through trade journals or other venues, and this "signaling" became an effective enforcement tool. This was the case with the lysine cartel. The cartels recently uncovered in the US and Europe represent only about one-sixth of the total number of working collusive agreements, and of this number, most were brought to light through antitrust investigations. The findings suggest that most firms that operate collusively would rather sustain their accords and preserve higher rates of return over the long term, than resort to cheating and the promise of higher short-term profits.

Establishing penalties to deter cartel behavior—the interaction of traditional factors and leniency policy

Connor (2006 and 2007) noted the difficulty of determining fines that are sufficiently high to deter collusive agreements yet are not at variance with the penalties in other antitrust cases. Given that the EU Commission has now dealt with more than one instance of repeat offenders in the world of cartels, the most important next step in antitrust enforcement may be determining a fine that most effectively dissuades firms from colluding. Very high monetary penalties in themselves may deter collusion, yet fines that are too high pose the risk of causing business failure—hardly a good outcome in the quest for increased competition. The deterrent effect of US and European punitive policies toward cartels involves other factors as well, including whether executives are subject to criminal penalties (fines, jail time or both), as well as the availability of leniency provisions. Executives that are considering entering into a collusive relationship consider the probability of all of these factors.

A number of authors have examined optimal sanctions for collusion or other anti-competitive activities. Landes (1983) was the first to consider the theoretical underpinnings of an optimal fine; he then applied the concept to various antitrust violations. In 2002, the Organization for Economic Cooperation and Development (OECD) filed the report "Fighting Hard-Core Cartels: Harm, Effective Sanctions and Leniency Programs" (OECD, 202), which detailed the experience of the EU in imposing fines and sanctions to deter cartels. Connor and Landes (2007) compared the actual economic damage brought by cartels to the magnitude of fines currently imposed through the US DOJ. They found that cartels tend to raise prices by an average of 31–49 percent (this range reflecting the two different data sets employed by the authors). The figures, however, purport that DOJ sentencing guidelines assume a price increase of only 10 percent. The authors concluded that higher fines are not only justifiable, but also far more likely to effectively provide deterrence. As noted by Combe et al. (2008), the success of antitrust penalties also depends on the probability of getting caught. Cyrenne (1999) examined whether pricing information can be used to detect cartels and argued that fines must be of sufficient size to deter collusion. As noted in Chapter 5, price data alone are usually not a fruitful route for antitrust investigators, since most illegal agreements affect prices of intermediate goods for which data is largely invisible.

The firm's incentive function

In consideration of these various influences, the incentive to conspire for the [i^{th}] firm can be expressed as:

$$\underset{(+)}{\mathrm{F}\,(\mathrm{Ret}_i},\ \underset{(-)}{\delta_{1,I} * F_i},\ \underset{(+)}{\delta_{2,i}},\ \underset{(-)}{\delta_{3,i} * \mathrm{Crim}_i},\ \underset{(-)}{\delta_{4,i} * \mathrm{Civil}_i)}$$

Where:

Ret_i	=	Firm 1's estimate of the excess returns available by colluding,
$\delta_{1,I}{}^{*}F_i$	=	Firm 1's subjective estimate of the probability of getting caught, multiplied by the estimated fine,
$\delta_{2,I}$	=	Firm 1's subjective of the probability of being able to use a leniency provision,
$\delta_{3,i}{}^{*}$ $Crim_i$	=	Firm 1's estimate of the likelihood of charges being sustained against executives times the magnitude of the of the resulting penalties—this component is complicated by the possibility that criminal punishment might consist of a prison term as opposed to fines.
$\delta_{4,i}{}^{*}Civil_i$	=	Firm 1's estimate of the likelihood of civil penalties being levied, multiplied by the projected fine.

Equation (1) demonstrates the difficult task facing antitrust authorities. Increasing either the magnitude of criminal and civil penalties or raising the probability of getting caught can increase the terms $\delta_{1,I}{}^{*}$ F_i, $\delta_{3,i}{}^{*}$ $Crim_i$ and $\delta_{4,I}{}^{*}$ $Civil_i$. The exact mechanism of raising $\delta_{1,i}$ $\delta_{4,i}$ is the subject of intense debate, particularly as it relates to the effectiveness of leniency provisions. Regulatory bodies can do little to influence either the firm's estimate of the available excess returns or the probability that any individual firm can use the leniency program. The level of uncertainty associated with this latter impact rises with the size of the cartel and contributes further to the conclusion that collusive agreements are largely confined to industries that are highly concentrated.

The term $\delta_{3,i}$ raises significant issues, for the US DOJ and the EU Commission have demonstrated an increasing willingness to expand criminal prosecutions to include not only corporations but their top executives as well. Fines paid under antitrust prosecutions may be regarded by some firms as simply a cost of doing business, particularly with the relatively low probability of getting caught. In several cases, however, the imposition of corporate fines typical of traditional antitrust enforcement has been combined with fines and jail time for company executives. An example of this dual enforcement can be found in the international vitamin cartel. As reported by the US DOJ in April 2000, four managers from the member firms pled guilty to "conspiracy to suppress and eliminate competition (US DOJ, #179: 04-06-00), and agreed to serve jail time and pay substantial fines. The criminal sentences in this case, although only five months in duration, nonetheless demonstrated that the "halcyon days" of corporations simply paying a fine and resuming business as usual were over. Executive culpability adds a new dimension to the analysis of the behavior of firms, for managers must now consider their own welfare when determining whether to engage in collusion on behalf of their employers.

Trade associations, information sharing, and collusion

One of the most difficult problems facing regulators is the level of awareness among corporations as to what constitutes illegal activity. Representatives of firms that meet regularly as members of a trade association may, for example, be unaware of the legal limits of information sharing. Similarly, illegal institutional arrangements such as interlocking boards may develop without criminal intent. Who better to help a firm with pricing guidance than another firm working in the same industry? There are cases in which perfectly legal activities gradually slipped into the realm of unacceptable. Indeed, when participants begin using aliases during their meetings it should become clear to authorities that corporate cooperation has stepped over the line of propriety.

Petersen (2001) examined the extent to which small businesses are aware of the legal ramifications of their competitive practices. Of the 254 executives of small companies in his sample, many were unaware that practices such as interlocking boards, agreements to divide markets or predator pricing were illegal (see also Petersen, 1998). Cason (1994) concentrated his study on the role that trade associations play in the dissemination of market information. His work utilized reaction functions to compare how corporations behave when in the possession of partial as compared to perfect information obtained through illegal cooperation. Kirby (1988) also appraised the significance of trade associations as conduits of information. Earlier studies of information sharing under conditions of oligopoly include Gal-Or (1985) and Shapiro (1986). Miller et al. (1993) considered the controversial practice of "price signaling," whereby firms announce price increases in advance, ostensibly to give customers time to adapt to the impending changes, but with the actual intention of colluding. They cite cases in which the DOJ has initiated action against collusive "price signaling" in the manufacturing sectors of anti-knock additives and hardwood materials. As noted in Chapter 5, the sorbate cartel—one of the longest-lived collusive arrangements in modern history—functioned by posting price changes in the trade publication the *Chemical Market Reporter*.

The establishment of price agreements, either through activities in trade associations or by undertaking "price signaling," presents special challenges to antitrust agencies. In these cases the ostensible corporate activity—the forging of corporate ties through industry associations and the posting of future prices—is perfectly legal even though its outcome may not be. When cooperation takes either of these forms, particular vigilance is necessary in order to expose the collusive association.

Conclusion

There is a natural tendency toward collusion in oligopolistic markets. Faced with price interdependency, firms either follow the path of tacit cooperation or they find a means by which to collude. Before the introduction of antitrust legislation in the late nineteenth century, firms in oligopolistic industries turned to collusion if they could overcome the incentive to cheat on such agreements. During the international cartel period from the 1950s to roughly 1990, producers in the developing world functioned outside the constraints of antitrust authority, and collusion for them required only that they form an alliance and then incentivize one another to abide by joint price and product agreements. The period from 1990 to the present has been characterized by strong antitrust enforcement in the industrial world. Despite the efforts to quash anticompetitive accords, however, numerous cartels have still sprung up in US and Europe. If the product fulfills the universal conditions for cartelization (as detailed above), then the inducement to form a collusive agreement is greater.

The recent adoption of leniency provisions in the US and the EU further complicates the decision making of the firm. Profit maximizing strategy is to collude first and then confess before one's co-conspirators can act. Even in the presence of aggressive antitrust action, a firm's decision to engage in cartelization involves weighing the risks and rewards of collusion.

Regulators face the arduous task of determining whether common pricing is the natural result of oligopolistic "competition" or the outcome of illicit collusion. That recent cartels have been concentrated in industries selling intermediate products with opaque pricing makes the antitrust investigations even more difficult. Authorities have relied on two measures—the increased probability of conviction through incentive programs and greater penalties—as the means for curbing the rise of cartels. Specifically, the implementation of leniency provisions for first-confessors is considered the best tool for creating uncertainty and therefore instability within a cartel. The EU Commission has encouraged parties harmed by cartels to pursue civil suits beyond the prosecutions of antitrust agencies, and these settlements can expose the colluders to huge additional fines.

The inherent characteristics of a particular good may also be the predominant reason that firms turn to cartelization. Businesses that produce intermediate goods (e.g. food additives) or those that sell their products through competitive bidding arrangements (e.g. electrical transformers) are more likely to turn to collusion to reduce price uncertainty. The absence of a market price in these sectors places firms in the difficult position of formulating bids without the benefit of knowing what their competitors are charging. In these circumstances, price-fixing not only eliminates the potential for lost profits through under-pricing, but it also leads to coordinated price increases. Not surprisingly, the phenomenon of cartelization is increasingly concentrated in the markets of intermediate products (this trend is discussed in greater detail in Chapter 5).

Ever more prevalent since 1990, trade associations have become conduits of information sharing and signaling, yet their activities are difficult to monitor and susceptible to collusion. It would be undemocratic to outlaw professional organizations, yet it is very possible that when key producers of an industry gather in a conference hall some illicit information will be shared.

The history of cartelization from the mid-nineteenth century to 1990 is treated in Chapter 3. Cartels first emerged in the mid-1800s during the Industrial Revolution when businesses seeking increased rates of return could engage in an open process of market segmentation without penalty. The excesses of this free-wheeling period resulted in the passage of the Sherman Antitrust Act of 1891, but from that point up to the end of World War II, antitrust enforcement was largely ineffective and firms easily evaded the restrictions on collusion. The Sherman Antitrust Act, and the later Clayton Act (1914) were not strictly enforced until approximately the mid-twentieth century. Many scholars point to the landmark case *U.S. v. Alcoa*, 91 F. Supp. 333 SDNY (1950)—in which Alcoa was forced to divest itself of Alcan—as the pivotal moment that ushered in a new era of antitrust policing. Globalization is an accelerating phenomenon in the period after 1950, and its impact on competition has led to the recent developments in international collusion. The so-called international cartel period, developed under UNCTAD, will also be discussed in more detail, particularly with regard to how cartels operate in the absence of any threat of prosecution. Chapter 5 provides an examination of the numerous collusive agreements that have been uncovered since approximately 1990. A comparison of the means and outcomes of cartelization during the international cartel period and the current era of enforcement are discussed in Chapter 4. Finally, proposals for controlling anticompetitive market practices are treated in Chapter 6.

3 The historical background

Beginning in the 1920s, corporations increasingly banded together to manipulate supplies including those of aluminum, tin, natural rubber, and sugar. Various mechanisms, including production cuts and price floors were used to elevate returns. Although regulatory authorities placed pressure on firms to abandon such practices, collusion remained a vexing but accepted part of doing business. All of that changed in 1950, when the landmark decision in the case of *US v. Alcoa* was rendered. In this renowned ruling, which had implications for markets around the world, the Department of Justice forced Alcoa to divest itself of its Canadian subsidiary, Alcan Aluminum, which had been charged with manipulating the international price of aluminum. The DOJ's action ended an era of relative tolerance of collusion in the United States.

Collusive activity in the twentieth century can be segmented into four major phases. The initial period, from roughly 1870 to the 1920s, coincides with the industrialization of the production and transportation sectors in US and Europe. The second period, dated from the 1920s to 1950, is marked by lax antitrust enforcement. During the third period, from 1950 to the mid-1980s, developing nations sought to restructure the terms of trade in international markets by increasing the price of commodities and raw materials. Little could be done to address these new global cartels, as they lay outside the jurisdiction of authorities. Although market forces eventually dismantled most of these arrangements, the Organization of Petroleum Exporting Countries (OPEC) has survived for nearly 50 years. The fourth and partially overlapping phase of cartelization involves price-fixing within the developed world, which has continued despite strict antitrust enforcement. This most recent phase of cartelization will be examined in Chapter 5.

The initial cartel phase—1870 to the inter-war period

The formation of collusive arrangements dates to the advent of industrialization. Until the passage of the Sherman Act in 1891, for example, railroads in the US openly colluded. When it became clear that the courts were going to enforce the Sherman Act, collusion simply went underground and was not pursued by competition authorities.

Cartelization within transportation and manufacturing sectors

Cartelization of the US rail transportation industry was evident as early as the mid-nineteenth century. As noted by Hilton (1966) and Binder (1988), this early foray into the manipulation of markets was legal at the time. The cartel found it difficult to monitor and enforce its agreements, however, and in the 1870s, the railroads adopted more sophisticated controls for dividing the available rail miles and revenues among members (so-called "pooling"). Although the agreements were sometimes short-lived, by incorporating a system of fines for violating the accord, the cartel enjoyed a degree of success (see Binder, 1988: 444). In 1887, the Interstate Commerce Act made pooling illegal and the railroads resorted to rate-fixing to maintain their collusive agreement. Prior to passage of the Sherman Antitrust Act, the railroads essentially divided the US market for freight transportation and thereby secured both higher freight rates and increased profit margins.

One of the first tests of the Sherman Act was the complaint filed against the Trans-Missouri Freight Association in 1892. The lower federal courts had ruled in favor of the railroads, accepting the argument that the Interstate Commerce Act rather than the Sherman Act held authority over the railroads. Upon appeal, in 1897 the Supreme Court issued a ruling against the freight companies. An analogous case brought against the Joint Traffic Association (which represented 33 railroads) resulted in a similar ruling, also in the government's favor. While there is an extensive debate in the literature about the impact these rulings had on competition, it was clear that the days of open collusion were over. The railroads then transitioned to a system of price-fixing that was so successful it became a standard means of market-sharing. Specifically, members of the railroad trade associations secretly negotiated tariffs and then published these rates to ensure compliance. Although this tangible form of cooperation exposed the firms to the possibility of legal action, prosecutions were unusual in the early years immediately following the passage of the Sherman Act, and railroad executives were willing to take the risk.

International commodity cartels—Alcoa and the international aluminum market

When Alcoa and AIG of Switzerland agreed in 1896 not to export to each other's markets, they initiated a decades-long manipulation of prices in the international aluminum market. In 1901, the agreement was expanded to include Froges and Pechney (both of France) and British Aluminium. In addition to export controls, this multi-firm arrangement established a world price and apportioned demand across the five producers. Initially, prices firmed, but the inevitable entry of new firms attracted to these higher returns led to a weakening of the cartel's power. In addition, Alcoa was under pressure from the US DOJ to abandon its participation in the collusive agreement. By the second decade of the twentieth century, the industry was once again competing on price.

In 1923, the European firms again sought relief from downward pressure on prices by informally agreeing not to export to the US market. Alcoa, in turn, made a similar pledge regarding exports to Europe, and prices began to stabilize, so that by 1924, aluminum prices in the US were up over 42 percent. Price increases in Europe were smaller (Holloway, 1988: 25). Subsequent agreements between Alcoa and its European counterparts were even more stringent, with quotas, uniform prices, and even penalties for over-production put into place. Facing ever-increasing pressure from the DOJ, Alcoa began acting only through its Canadian subsidiary, Alcan. A degree of market manipulation continued until 1950 when, as noted above, Alcoa was forced to sell Alcan and "fully" comply with US anti-trust regulations. Adams (1951) asserted that even this severe judgment against Alcoa entailed very few meaningful market divestment requirements, an indication that rigorous antitrust enforcement was still to come. A degree of competition returned to the aluminum industry until the formation in 1974 of the International Bauxite Association, a consortium of developing nations that acted as a supply cartel for the ore used in aluminum production.

Although pressure had been successfully applied to Alcoa to end its cooperation with competitors, the regulatory environment remained lax during the first half of the twentieth century. In today's antitrust regime, the DOJ would impose fines rather than attempt to cajole a firm into compliance. As discussed in Chapter 5, in the current enforcement period (dated from the 1980s to the present), parties engaged in collusion routinely go to great lengths to hide their illicit pricing practices and personal identities, even resorting to the use of pseudonyms when registering at hotels.

The aluminum cartel illustrates the importance of the five conditions for cartelization outlined in Chapter 2. Aluminum is a homogeneous product, offered by a limited number of firms. There is no practical substitute for aluminum in most instances, as other metals lack its combination of strength and malleability. Aluminum smelting and distribution is characterized by significant economies of scale, which act as a strong barrier to entry. A workable aluminum cartel was feasible, something that cannot be said for collusive efforts in other commodity markets.

International sugar controls

Between 1920 and 1925, under mounting pressure from over-production, the world price of sugar fell from eleven to three cents per pound. World producers, particularly Cuba, sought the US government's help in reducing the excess supply. In October of 1927, Congress passed legislation allowing the President to impose quotas on Cuban production. From a level of 5.8 million tons of output in 1925, by 1928 Cuban production has fallen to 4.6 million tons and world sugar prices stabilized. With the world heading into the Great Depression, sugar prices fell again and the quotas were abandoned.

In 1931, representatives of seven interested nations initiated the Chadbourne Plan, which imposed a five-year limitation on sugar exports for its members. The US and Britain's decision not to join the cartel prevented any meaningful reduction in world sugar supply. Despite production and export cuts by both Cuba and Java prices did not firm, and the Chadbourne Plan was not renewed. When an intergovernmental arrangement comprising 21 countries and representing nearly 90 per cent of world sugar output was signed in 1937, prices firmed from 1.03 to 1.34 cents per pound—significant in percentage terms, but hardly a cause for celebration among producers who had been receiving nearly eight times this amount in 1920. Generally regarded as a failure, the agreement of 1937 was soon abandoned. For further details on the early sugar controls, see Stocking and Watkins (1991) and Wilk (1939). The second phase of cartelization in this market began in 1953, when a group of sugar exporters in the developing world, with Cuba taking the lead, formed the International Sugar Association (ISA).

The failure of this initial effort to stabilize sugar prices is not surprising. The barriers to entry in the sugar market are weak, particularly since sugar can also be made from beets, a temperate crop. Production from sugar cane is diffuse, and with so many exporters in the market, negotiating and monitoring controls becomes exceedingly difficult. This non-conformity to two of the key conditions for cartelization made successful price-fixing of sugar problematic.

Natural rubber agreements

With production of natural rubber highly concentrated—just five nations produce approximately 90 percent of world output—exporting nations should be able to exercise a significant degree of price control. But since the development in the 1920s of a near perfect substitute, synthetic rubber, prices of natural rubber have remained depressed.[1] The first attempt to manipulate the price of natural rubber dates to 1920, when the British firms that dominated the Rubber Growers' Association agreed to cut production by 25 per cent. Production further declined when the Dutch also agreed to quotas. American producers, on the other hand, were overstocked and refused to join the British and Dutch in reducing supply. By 1921, rubber prices had bottomed out at 17 cents per pound. In 1922, the British instituted new export controls under the Stevenson Plan. The dramatic rise in the price of natural rubber after the implementation of the plan may be more of a reflection of rapid growth in the industrialized world in the 1920s than an outcome of market manipulation.

With the onset of the Great Depression, the natural rubber market essentially collapsed, with prices falling from a high of 75 cents per pound in 1925 to less than four cents per pound by 1933. In response, the major exporting nations—France, India, the Netherlands, Siam (Thailand) and the United Kingdom—negotiated the first International Rubber Agreement (IRA), which was signed in 1934. Unlike previous accords, the IRA had teeth. Members were assigned export quotas, and nations violating those quotas were subject to fines by the organization. The existence of large stockpiles of natural rubber (nearly a nine months' supply in 1934) made the cartel's quota system difficult to enforce, so members cut their production limits by 30 per cent, and prices finally began to firm. By 1937, the price of natural rubber had risen to 19 cents per pound. The IRA was renewed twice, in 1938 and 1943, but permanently expired in 1944. Price manipulation was not pursued again until 1980, when under the auspices of the New International Economic Order, the Natural Rubber Agreement (NRA) was created. In spite of the downward price pressure that resulted from competition with synthetic rubber, both the IRA and the NRA enjoyed modest success. Overall, the natural rubber market conformed to most of the conditions for successful cartelization, which permitted the market controls to function.

International tin and tea cartels

As with other commodities, the international tin market experienced significant price weakness in the early 1930s. In response, five major producers—Bolivia, China, Malaysia (at that time a British Protectorate), the United Kingdom and The Netherlands—adopted a series of supply restrictions and price targets. Although Siam later joined the arrangement, other major producers, particularly the Congo, refused to enter the agreement and downward pressure on prices remained strong (for a discussion of the tin cartel's attempts to achieve price stability, see Hillman (1988) and (1997)). The Great Depression squelched the initiatives of the tin cartel. Later, with World War II looming on the horizon and the high demand for tin—an important strategic mineral—price collusion became unnecessary. The relatively unsuccessful attempt at cartelization of the market is somewhat ironic in that a subsequent buffer stock arrangement for tin was quite successful.

The malleability and non-toxicity of tin are unique qualities that distinguish it from other metals. The utilization of tin in products that contact food and water (e.g. the canning and plumbing industries) make it an irreplaceable input. Tin is considered a strategic mineral and the US government has over the years maintained stockpiles of the commodity. The failure of pre-war cartels to significantly raise tin prices owes more to economic exigency than any lack of compatibility with the conditions for cartelization.

The tea cartel was formed when the onset of the Great Depression led to weakness in demand and a decline of nearly 50 per cent from peak prices in 1924. The significant increase in cultivated acreage in India, Ceylon, Java and Sumatra during a rapid run-up in prices in the mid-1920s had left the industry with a marked oversupply. In 1930, representatives from India, Ceylon, and the Dutch East Indies signed the first International Tea Agreement to substantially cut production. An examination of the output figures indicates that these cutbacks never occurred and prices continued to fall. With the addition of Java and Sumatra, a second International Tea Agreement was signed in 1933 with the goal of cutting exports by 15 percent over the five-year period that the agreement was to be in force. This time, the accord took hold and the price of tea rose approximately 50 percent by 1935, and prices remained stable until the onset of World War II. The tea cartel is regarded as a collusive agreement that worked. For an analysis of the conditions in the tea market that first prevented, and then permitted, the establishment of a functioning cartel see Gupta (2001).

The interwar period

Even with the civil and criminal penalties prescribed by the Sherman Act, a significant number of cartels formed in Europe and the US during the interwar period. The antitrust legislation was primarily targeted at corporate trusts, particularly that of the petroleum industry, and was applied only haphazardly to other noncompetitive practices such as collusion. The increase in cartelization during the 1920s and 1930s can also be viewed as a response to more open international markets and increased competition. Firms responded to this intrusion into their domestic territories by seeking agreements to divide markets and protect profitability.

Light bulbs

In the 1920s, General Electric experienced competitive pressures from new producers of light bulbs in Europe, who were increasingly breaking free of their reliance on GE's technology and patents. To buoy prices, GE convinced its rivals to adhere to price guidelines. Known as the Phoebus Cartel, this agreement allowed GE to use its superior capital standing to purchase stakes in five European counterparts, who were still recovering from the impacts of World War I. These interlocking boards gave GE the power to coordinate pricing and maintain high rates of return. Unimpeded by regulators, this collusive arrangement worked well for a number of years, until the entry of low-cost Japanese light bulb producers eroded GE's ability to control pricing (Wells, 2002, pp, 19–22, provides a thorough discussion of the Phoebus Cartel).

As with the commodity sectors discussed above, the light bulb industry was well suited to cartelization. The product is relatively homogeneous, marketed by a limited number of producers, and only poor substitutes for electric lamps (candles?) existed. Still, the barriers to entry in the light bulb market were weak, and although the cartel maintained a strong hold on the sector through the 1930s, it fell apart after Japanese manufacturers entered the field.

The steel cartel

Following the cessation of World War I, steel producers experienced a significant drop in demand and a concomitant fall in prices. In 1926, firms from France, Germany, Belgium, the Saar (a German protectorate), and Luxembourg negotiated an accord that restricted output, thereby creating the first international steel cartel. Like the nineteenth-century railroad pricing agreements, this early attempt at collusion lacked the coverage and enforcement powers necessary to ensure true cooperation. Under the increasing financial pressure of the Great Depression, the pact fell into disarray. In the midst of this economic maelstrom, the industry's trade associations had been unable to exercise their mandate of monitoring production and enforcing quotas. As a result, producers openly violated production limits and the cartel suspended its operations in 1931.

Although the early steel cartel did little to stabilize prices during its five-year tenure, its members learned the fundamentals of collusion. When the organization reformed in 1933, the quotas put in place were backed by the threat of fines for exceeding a country's export limits. In turn, each corporate member was given proprietary rights to its domestic market (for an analysis of the second steel cartel, see Barbezat, 1991). The new cartel effected higher prices and soon steel-makers in other nations wanted to participate. Major producers in Great Britain, Poland, Czechoslovakia, and Austria joined in the mid-1930s. With their market directed to domestic use and the threat of antitrust enforcement hanging in the air, US firms at first showed little interest in the cartel (see Wells, 2002: 17). As the domestic market shrank, however, US steel corporations recognized that their diminished economies of scale would encourage a flood of less expensive imports. Now desiring to join the cartel, American steel producers sought to circumvent antitrust prosecution by invoking the Webb-Pomerene Act, a law devised in 1918 to grant US firms immunity from competition laws if their cooperation on exports supported the war effort. Using this legislation as a shield, the US producers joined the cartel in 1938. As a result, export quotas were negotiated and the American steel industry avoided a wave of imports. Ironically, the worldwide cooperation that the steel cartel finally achieved lasted only a year or so, as the onset of World War II effectively dissolved the cartel. Additional details on the formation, structure, and management of the cartel can be found in Barbezat (1989).

The experience of the steel cartel provides an interesting contrast to what transpired in the rail sector. Cartelization of steel production began abroad, beyond the reach of US antitrust authorities, and only came to America after a fully formed cartel was already in place. Rather than operate secretly, US steel firms invoked an exception to the Sherman Act in order to collude.

The interwar period illustrates how cartels function under nominally enforced antitrust laws. Open collusion, as practiced in the steel cartel, was reasonable only when a legislative loophole could be found. Otherwise, one had to find a creative means of manipulating prices while avoiding detection. So it was when GE simply acquired controlling stakes in its European rivals in order to control the market for light bulbs. The discussion of the international cartel period outlined later in this chapter illustrates how cartelization changes when the threat of sanctions is eliminated.

The electrical equipment conspiracy

Although the Alcoa decision is widely regarded as the start of serious antitrust enforcement in the US, the electrical equipment cartel managed to operate for nearly a decade. This was not due, however, to lax antitrust enforcement, but rather the overwhelming size and complexity of the conspiracy. When it was finally put out of business, in a very public airing of the sins of the cartel, the expansiveness of the scheme shocked both legislators and the public.

The collusive accord that manipulated prices in the US electrical equipment market was widespread and enduring. Best estimates suggest that up to 40 firms were involved in the conspiracy, which affected over $2 billion in sales. The impetus behind the conspiracy was excess capacity coupled with flat demand, leading to aggressive competition and falling prices. The conspiracy lasted for much of the 1950s, and as price cooperation persisted over time and between so many firms, collusion simply became the norm in the industry. For those interested in the fine details, Lean et al. (1985), provide an intimate view of the cartel, including a timeline of the conspiracy and details on the participants.

The electrical equipment conspiracy was actually three cartels within a cartel. The market was segmented into three primary products, switchgear, steam turbine generators and transformers, all of which were typically sold through competitive bidding. The major producers hammered out separate agreements for each product line with complex systems put in place to determine the low bidder (see Baker and Faulkner (1993) for an entertaining description of how bidding on switchgear was determined by the phases of the moon). The membership of the cartel was unraveled during a string of indictments brought by the US DOJ. The two dominant firms in the conspiracy were General Electric and Westinghouse. Allis-Chalmers, threatened with indictment and trial, was the first of the smaller firms to plead out (in spring of 1960). Five additional firms agreed to plea deals in exchange for *nolo contendere* acceptance of guilt: Schwager-Wood and Joslyn Manufacturing, which both produced power-switching gear, Federal Pacific and ITE Circuit Breakers in the circuit breaker indictment, and Carrier Corporation, a producer of condensers.

The electrical equipment conspiracy was a classic bid-rigging scheme. In the switchgear industry, key executives established a generalized framework under which contracts would be divided up between participants, and so-called "working groups" of lower-level managers would work out the practical details (see Baker and Faulkner, 1993: 839). Corporations were rotated into the position of "designated winner," and all other firms deliberately over-bid. A similar system was used in the electrical transformer industry. This fairly straightforward system worked quite well, since switchgear and transformers were regarded as homogeneous products, regardless of manufacturer. Conversely, the steam turbine sector was poorly suited to cartelization. Turbines were individually ordered to precise specifications. As no two turbines were exactly the same, it was impossible to set a meaningful price. This part of the conspiracy worked at best imperfectly, and firms tried to skirt their obligations if a sizable order was at stake. In addition, the negotiations that were necessary to produce a workable cartel bidding structure were exceedingly complex, and risked exposing the agreement. Authors (see Hay and Kelley, 1974: 16, for instance) have referred to uneven and unpredictable orders of this kind as "lumpy," and noted that this makes cartelization difficult.

The cartel was finally exposed when officials of the Tennessee Valley Authority (TVA) complained to the DOJ about the pricing structure of bids it received on large infrastructure projects. The subsequent "trial" (most of the charges were pleaded out) involved not only rulings against the corporations involved, but also against 45 individual defendants, two-thirds of whom received jail sentences. The penalties that were handed out appear inexplicably light given the breadth of the conspiracy; approximately $1.7 million in total fines, and brief, frequently suspended, jail time for executives directly involved in the cartel. On the positive side, the conspiracy received a degree of exposure uncommon in antitrust cases. Long, very public Congressional hearings were held by the Kefauver Committee to determine the exact details of how the cartel operated and who was in charge. If prestige was as important as wealth to these key executives, this public humiliation represented a significant loss to those involved.

The electrical equipment conspiracy was a comprehensive, long-lived cartel that defied some of the assumptions upon which collusion is normally based. The complexities of the market, with participants seeking to manipulate prices on a range of products, would normally have made price-fixing extremely difficult. When this is coupled with the large number of firms that joined in the conspiracy, it is surprising that cartelization was possible. Its success was partly due to the fact that the electrical equipment cartel was one of the last wholly domestic price-fixing agreements, and international negotiations and market controls were not necessary. It has also been argued that over-capacity in the industry made unrestrained competition unprofitable, and raised the incentive to cooperate. Perhaps the cartel is most famous for the time-consuming and historic prosecution carried out by the DOJ. No cartel case prior to this had involved an investigation of so many firms involved in so many disparate products.

In addition to the now infamous electrical equipment cartel, there were a vast number of smaller collusive accords that were uncovered in the 1960s and 1970s. The economic impact of many of these was muted by the fact that many were local or regional in nature. Hay and Kelley (1974: 29–38) provide a comprehensive list of the numerous cartels that operated during this period. Of the approximately 70 cartels, 15 were national in scope, affecting industries such as fabricated steel, hydraulic hose and bed springs. None of these had the longevity and economic impact of the electrical equipment conspiracy.

The international cartel era—1953 to 1990

As the regulatory environment in the industrialized world strengthened and authorities began to strictly enforce antitrust laws, blatant collusion became a phenomenon confined largely to emerging economies. Nations outside the industrialized world have always been more resistant to the restrictions of competition policy. In the developing world, the post-colonial period saw the production of many critical commodities fall under the control of newly established governments whose leaders understood the importance of stable commodity prices, particularly when their economies were dependent on only one or two raw materials. A commitment to free markets was seldom a priority because international commodity prices were highly volatile and trending downward. As noted by Goodwin and Mayall (1980) and Rothestein (1979), the pressure to adopt some means of steadying markets had been building within the developing world long before the United Nations passed the UNCTAD proclamation in 1976 condoning cartels. The first International Sugar Agreement of the early 1950s will be used as a useful inaugural date for the cartel era in the developing world.

International sugar agreements

The sugar market is poorly suited to cartelization. In particular, sugar production is widely dispersed, making the negotiation and enforcement of any agreement difficult. Although the concern about international prices has always centered on surplus cane production, output of a rival source of sugar, beets, posed a greater challenge to market stabilization (Mahler (1984) explored the characteristics of this market). Sugar beets are a temperate crop, widely grown in the US and Europe, and any attempt to raise prices incentivizes further production.

The first International Sugar Agreement was signed in 1953. With a significant portion of world cane production under its control, and output managed by a central government, Cuba was well positioned to lead the sugar cartel (for an evaluation of Cuba's role in the management of sugar prices under the ISAs, see Spar (1994)). The ISA succeeded in maintaining its target price through 1955. Poor sugar beet harvests in Europe in 1956 led to a rise in international prices independent of the actions of the cartel. The second ISA, in force from 1959 to 1963, stabilized prices for the first few years of the agreement. In 1963, however, the US-imposed trade embargo on Cuba diverted the country's sugar production onto international markets, which depressed prices. After the mid-1960s, Cuba became a less significant producer, supplanted by nations like Brazil, Thailand, and India. Cuba had forever lost its role as arbiter of the international sugar market.

In 1968, the accords became institutionalized under the auspices of the London-based International Sugar Organization (ISO), comprised of some fifty exporting nations from both the developed and developing worlds, and major importing nations (e.g. the US, Finland, Japan, Korea, Norway, Russia, Sweden, and Switzerland). Mahler (1984) provided an overview of the political and economic considerations that led to the agreement. Setting prices and quotas and therefore acting as a cartel, the ISO was sanctioned by the US government and exempt from antitrust enforcement because it was classified as an intergovernmental body rather than an insular organization serving only corporate interests. The ISO's successor agreement of 1977 could not stem the deterioration of the market caused by over-production, and prices weakened further through the late 1970s (see Table 3.1). Falling output of Cuban sugar cane and also beet production from the Soviet Union in the early 1980s resulted in higher prices and the incentive to expand planted acreage. But soon production once again exceeded world demand, with the per-ton price falling to a low of $185.4 in 1985. Disillusioned with the efficacy of manipulating prices at an international level, the US withdrew from the ISO in 1992. In recognition of its impotency, the ISO drafted a resolution in 1993 that simply listed planted acreage and projected output as mere guidelines for the producers in each participating state. This collapse of the sugar cartel was inevitable given the diffuse nature of production.

International coffee agreements

The coffee market has many of the characteristics necessary for cartelization. The confinement of coffee plantations to the tropics provides an effective barrier to entry. Coffee is storable in the near to medium term, which enables producers to tailor export levels to market conditions. The

Table 3.1 World sugar prices, 1959–1990, dollars per metric ton, Brazil

Year	Price ($)	Year	Price ($)
1959	79.9	1975	642.0
1960	69.3	1976	253.4
1961	75.0	1977	181.3
1962	88.4	1978	169.4
1963	137.9	1979	193.4
1964	130.5	1980	479.4
1965	74.6	1981	372.2
1966	80.1	1982	207.2
1967	80.1	1983	208.1
1968	98.8	1984	201.7
1969	104.5	1985	146.5
1970	112.2	1986	154.7
1971	121.0	1987	149.6
1972	158.8	1988	185.2
1973	197.1	1989	267.1
1974	558.4	1990	350.7

Source: International Monetary Fund.

rejection of roasted chicory as a replacement product during a period of coffee price hikes in the 1970s demonstrates that there is no plausible substitute for coffee. However, factors working against price-fixing in the coffee market include the relatively high number of producers, which makes it more difficult for the cartel to verify compliance. In addition, coffee is not a homogeneous product, with beans identified as being either Arabica (i.e. high-quality beans grown at high altitudes) or Robusta (i.e. mass-marketed and cultivated on the plains). The fact that roasters, acting as wholesalers, will substitute cheaper Robusta beans if prices for Arabicas are elevated means that there is sustained downward pressure on the market as a whole. Another indication of the heterogeneity of coffee, and therefore the difficulty of establishing uniform price structures, is the dizzying array of consumer choices, from Kenyan AA to Jamaican Blue Mountain.

The International Coffee Organization (ICO) was founded in 1962 to stabilize both supply and prices in the international market. Like the International Sugar Organization, the international coffee agreements negotiated by the ICO eventually included both coffee producers and the nations that received the exports. Although the US and other coffee-consuming nations usually opposed this manipulation of markets, coffee prices had been exceedingly volatile and price stability held the promise of benefitting all parties to the agreement. As the greatest producers and exporters of coffee at the time, Brazil and Colombia acted as the leaders of the cartel's exporters, but the target price they set was too high, and Brazil was forced to curtail exports in order to stabilize the market. The ICA was renewed in

1968, but chronic oversupply in the market continued to depress prices. Market equilibrium was finally restored by nature rather than institutions—the severe frost that hit the Brazilian coffee plantations in 1975 eliminated the persistent excess supply.

Even with coffee prices higher and less variable, the ICO pushed for a provisional accord in 1976 to expand participation to 50 exporting nations and two dozen importing countries, but renewed excess production made implementing the accord possible only in 1980. Subsequent coffee price agreements in 1986 and 1989 were never fully implemented and also failed to curtail production. The major importing countries left the coffee cartel after 1989, and the period of cooperation with exporters came to an end. (For an examination of the ICA's impact on Kenyan producers, see McMahon, 1987).

The effect of the International Coffee Agreements on prices appears to have been minimal, with the climatic event of the Brazilian frost exercising a greater influence on the market. Prices were highly variable during the cartel period (see Table 3.2). The 1976 accord, put in force in 1980, was followed by a decade of weak coffee prices (the exception to this occurring in 1986). Still, the collapse of prices following the abandonment of the cartel in 1989 suggests that cooperation firmed prices to some degree. This impact is noted by Tilley and Khaerunisa (1996), who examined the prices received by Indonesia for high-grade beans and concluded that termination of the ICA reduced export prices.

Table 3.2 World coffee prices, 1960–1993, dollars per 60 kilogram bag

Year	*Price ($)*	*Year*	*Price ($)*
1960	59.3	1977	318.9
1961	57.6	1978	244.5
1962	53.8	1979	242.1
1963	52.2	1980	254.0
1964	64.4	1981	169.1
1965	64.0	1982	184.4
1966	62.6	1983	173.8
1967	55.4	1984	190.4
1968	56.2	1985	192.1
1969	59.3	1986	256.8
1970	74.8	1987	148.2
1971	64.7	1988	178.3
1972	73.5	1989	141.2
1973	95.9	1990	117.7
1974	102.8	1991	112.2
1975	107.7	1992	84.0
1976	206.8	1993	95.0

Source: International Monetary Fund.

Clearly, the ICAs are a model of persistence, if not success. Over a period of nearly thirty years, the ICO negotiated four agreements between the producing and consuming nations. The coffee market was simply not well suited to cartelization, however, and the ultimate failure of the ICAs to regulate the market is understandable.

International bauxite agreements

Bauxite is the most concentrated source of aluminum ore. Although bauxite is a ubiquitous mineral, deposits of sufficient aluminum content are concentrated in only a few countries. The International Bauxite Association (IBA) was formed in 1974 through the cooperative efforts of the prime ministers of Jamaica (Michael Manley) and Guyana (Forbes Burnham). Five other major bauxite producing countries—Australia, Guinea, Sierra Leone, Suriname and Yugoslavia—participated in the cartel. The bauxite market is somewhat unusual in that the cartel that developed could not easily influence the price of aluminum (the end product of bauxite processing), since several large multinational companies already controlled that market. Instead, the IBA sought to impose on aluminum processors an increase in the per-ton levies on bauxite (variable according to the concentration of alumina in the ore). This extraction fee ultimately raised the price of finished aluminum on world markets. The largest producer, Jamaica, was the first to raise the levies, and the other members of IBA soon followed suit. With most of the world's production of bauxite confined to these seven nations, consensus in the cartel was easy to achieve and levies were raised again in 1981.

The bauxite cartel is unique in the disconnection between the developing nations producing the input—to the casual observer, a heap of slag in the landscape—and the companies producing the finished product of aluminum ingot. To offset the higher levies charged by the IBA, the diversified aluminum producers raised their prices. The significant increase in bauxite levies in the early 1980s (from $5–15 per ton in 1979, to $6–16 per ton in 1980, and $8–20 per ton in 1981) coincided with falling demand for aluminum (see Table 3.3). Prices did not return to their level of 1980, $1,771 per metric ton, until 1988. In a sense, members of the IBA were able to transfer the market risk of weak prices onto the aluminum multinationals. Consequently, the bauxite cartel worked well, particularly after some producers outside the IBA, notably the US, exited the market. Pyndick (1977) provided a thorough analysis of the pricing structure of the IBA, and concluded that the agreement worked at least as well as OPEC, and should therefore be considered another exception to the rule that cartels are inherently unstable.

International cocoa agreements

As early as 1962, the major producers and exporters of cocoa had attempted to form a collusive agreement. This initial attempt failed, and it was only with

Table 3.3 World bauxite and aluminum prices, 1974–1996, range of levies per metric ton, and market price per metric ton

Year	*Levy ($)*	*Price of aluminum ($)*	*Year*	*Levy ($)*	*Price of aluminum ($)*
1974	5–15	763.2	1986	13–17	1,147.3
1975	5–15	866.6	1987	13–17	1,561.8
1976	5–15	888.1	1988	13–17	2,541.2
1977	5–15	1,141.4	1989	15–20	1,946.6
1978	5–15	1,322.2	1990	15–20	1,636.1
1979	5–15	1,599.4	1991	15–18	1,301.3
1980	6–16	1,771.2	1992	15–18	1,253.6
1981	8–20	1,260.2	1993	15–24	1,137.6
1982	8–20	989.6	1994	15–18	1,472.6
1983	13–20	1,435.5	1995	—	1,801.4
1984	13–20	1,248.9	1996	—	1,503.7
1985	13–20	1,038.6			

Source: International Monetary Fund.

UNCTAD's oversight of negotiations that the first International Cocoa Agreement (ICCA) was created in 1972. This accord, signed by 18 exporting nations and 22 importing countries (with the notable exception of the US), supported the use of both export controls and an international buffer stock to stabilize prices. The participation of countries that produce only negligible cocoa output (e.g. Haiti and Jamaica) only complicated the ICCA's discussions. In the end, the agreement of 1972 was never implemented, as the commodity inflation of the 1970s propelled cocoa prices beyond the ICCA's target.

Even a renegotiated price objective in 1976 was soon exceeded, and by 1977, the price of cocoa had risen to an average of $4,038 per metric ton—far beyond the $1,500 or so per ton that the market had supported in the early 1970s. Subsequently, demand for cocoa dropped off and when prices fell by over 50 percent by 1981, the membership returned to the negotiating table to sign the third ICCA. Even with a new target price of between $2,200 and $3,300 per metric ton, as well as restriction of total exports to 250,000 metric tons, prices continued to slide, in part because the largest producer, Côte D'Ivoire, did not participate in the accord. In desperation, the cartel purchased nearly 100,000 tons of cocoa on the open market in 1982 (with further purchases in 1986), but prices continued to fall, hitting a bottom of $978 per metric ton in 1993. There is no evidence that the ICCA had any significant influence on the world cocoa market. Using a simulation model, Herrmann et al. (1993) determined that the 1982 and 1986 accords impacted prices by less than 4 percent.

The ICCAs were a failure. This outcome is surprising considering that the cocoa market conforms to most of the conditions for cartelization. There are a limited number of producers and the barriers to entry (especially climatic requirements) are significant. There is no true substitute for

Table 3.4 Cocoa prices, 1960–1993, dollars per metric ton, Brazil

Year	*Price ($)*	*Year*	*Price ($)*
1960	550.2	1977	4,037.7
1961	440.0	1978	3,377.7
1962	436.9	1979	3,096.1
1963	508.9	1980	2,355.3
1964	465.1	1981	1,925.0
1965	300.5	1982	1,502.4
1966	449.9	1983	1,828.2
1967	516.3	1984	2,317.0
1968	606.8	1985	2,089.3
1969	880.4	1986	2,024.9
1970	647.2	1987	1,847.1
1971	517.0	1988	1,599.0
1972	577.3	1989	1,250.7
1973	1,067.2	1990	1,079.5
1974	1,613.7	1991	1,045.9
1975	1,245.0	1992	989.8
1976	1,694.4	1993	978.3

Source: International Monetary Fund.

cocoa. Although there are varieties of cocoa beans, the signatories of the various ICCA's were willing to ignore this and treat cocoa as a homogeneous crop. Finally, cocoa can be stored for the medium-term, enabling the cartel to stockpile its product. Van Groenendaal and Vingerhoets (1995) saw in the cocoa agreement of 1986 practical mechanisms (e.g. automatic intervention price adjustments) that should have guaranteed success for the cartel. But the ICCAs never achieved the price stability they sought. The relative ineffectiveness of the cocoa cartel demonstrates the difficulty of pushing back against market forces that are trending in the opposite direction.

The Organization of Petroleum Exporting Countries

While most of the cartel arrangements of the 1960s and 1970s have vanished into obscurity, the Organization of Petroleum Exporting Countries (OPEC) remains highly visible. In fact, despite having a somewhat dubious record as a stabilizer of international petroleum prices, OPEC is nearly synonymous with the word "cartel." Formed in 1960 in response to a decade of declining world petroleum prices, OPEC's 15 members meet at least once annually to set production and export quotas. Although little was accomplished in the cartel's early years, under the leadership of Libya's Muammar Qaddafi, who had just taken power in a coup in 1969, the cartel began negotiating more effective pricing arrangements with the multinational oil firms. The resulting increase in the price-per-barrel of 30 cents—quaint compared to the more recent mushrooming of prices—

represented a significant change in the relationship between the integrated petroleum companies and their partners in the developing world.

OPEC's first significant meddling in the international marketplace occurred in 1973, when it imposed an embargo on the US for its support of Israel during the Yom Kippur War. Petroleum prices soon quadrupled, from just over $3 per barrel to approximately $11 per barrel. The unprecedented rise in oil prices (to an average of $29.22 per barrel in 1979, peaking at $36.68 per barrel in 1980) owes more to the political uncertainty that followed the seizure of the US embassy in Iran than it does to any action taken by OPEC. After 1980, discord in the cartel was high, with most OPEC members exceeding their production quotas by substantial amounts. Ultimately, Saudi Arabia, long regarded as the "policeman" of OPEC, punished its partners by massively overproducing to bring about a collapse of petroleum prices, with a bottom of $14.23 per barrel reached in 1986. Not surprisingly, the others members of the cartel then agreed to production cuts to reestablish some control over prices. It was not until 1999, however, when the cartel added two "associate" members, Mexico and Norway, that OPEC succeeded once again in pushing petroleum prices higher. The significant price increases that have occurred from 2005 onward are the result of OPEC losing control of prices on the upside. With world demand outstripping the available supply, and insufficient capacity to stabilize prices, OPEC has been sidelined.

Table 3.5 Petroleum prices, 1965–2006, dollars per barrel

Year	*Price ($)*	*Year*	*Price ($)*
1965	1.33	1986	14.23
1966	1.33	1987	18.15
1967	1.33	1988	14.72
1968	1.30	1989	17.84
1969	1.28	1990	22.97
1970	2.11	1991	19.33
1971	2.57	1992	19.03
1972	2.80	1993	16.82
1973	3.14	1994	15.90
1974	11.22	1995	17.16
1975	10.60	1996	20.42
1976	11.83	1997	19.3
1977	12.84	1998	13.1
1978	12.95	1999	18.0
1979	29.22	2000	28.2
1980	36.68	2001	24.3
1981	35.27	2002	25.0
1982	32.45	2003	28.9
1983	29.66	2004	37.8
1984	28.56	2005	53.4
1985	27.31	2006	64.3

Source: International Monetary Fund.

The difficulties that OPEC has experienced in manipulating world oil prices are a consequence of the size of the organization, for cartel theory suggests that collusive agreements are difficult to police when the concentration of production lies below a certain threshold. With 15 members, each facing its own significant internal political pressures to maximize oil revenue, OPEC production quotas have been difficult to maintain. In addition, major producers such as the US, Russia, Norway, the United Kingdom, and Mexico remain outside the cartel. In possession of approximately 70 percent of the world's proven reserves, OPEC's power is likely to grow in significance as world oil deposits are depleted later this century.

Natural rubber agreements

The cartel that formed in the natural rubber market between 1920 and 1944 set production and export limits. Following a long hiatus, the natural rubber cartel reformed in 1980, with five developing nations and 20 importing countries in its ranks. Under the Natural Rubber Agreement (NRA), buffer stocks would now be used to eliminate price fluctuations. The NRA provided buy—sell criteria to the buffer stock manager, who was authorized to purchase up to 550,000 tons of natural rubber in total holdings. This stockpiling of rubber eliminated the need for production cuts but required each cartel member to provide financing for the joint purchase. Between 1980 and 1985, weakness in the international rubber market required substantial purchases of the commodity to firm prices. The demand for natural rubber is highly dependent on automobile production levels. In the wake of the recession of 1982, prices fell hard, bottoming out in 1985 at $919.6 per metric ton (they had been $1,431 per ton in 1980). Demand then firmed, with prices rising to an average of $1,279 per metric ton in 1988. As noted by LeClair (2000: 77), the substantial drop in the standard deviation of prices during the period when the NRA was active suggests that both suppliers and consumers of natural rubber may have benefitted from the management of prices (see also Burger and Smit (1990), who provided a detailed analysis of the various factors that impact the price of rubber).

Tensions soon developed between the exporting and importing nations of the natural rubber cartel. In the course of negotiating a renewal of the Natural Rubber Agreement in 1995, the exporters tried but failed to have a premium incorporated into the target price. Struggling in the aftermath of the Asian Currency Crisis in 1997, the rubber-producing nations asked for a 5 percent mark-up. This request was rejected by the importing countries, which instead offered to change the currency used to calculate target prices to the Singapore Dollar, a move that would have effectively propped up prices. The rubber exporters refused this offer. In September 1999, Malaysia, Thailand, and Sri Lanka withdrew from the NRA. The cartel was terminated in December of that year, at which time the buffer stock of 140,000 metric tons of natural rubber was liquidated.

Table 3.6 Natural rubber prices, 1978–2000, dollars per metric ton, New York

Year	*Price ($)*	*Year*	*Price ($)*
1978	972.0	1990	1,005.4
1979	1,250.0	1991	1,018.9
1980	1,430.9	1992	900.5
1981	1,109.9	1993	922.5
1982	881.8	1994	953.3
1983	1,093.8	1995	1,103.7
1984	965.6	1996	1,068.3
1985	803.0	1997	1,043.7
1986	802.3	1998	1,025.4
1987	858.9	1999	996.8
1988	950.8	2000	1,041.9
1989	948.9		

Source: IMF, International Financial Statistics.

The natural rubber market was generally well suited to cartelization. At the time the cartel was formed in 1980, the four-country concentration ratio was 83.3 percent. Entry into the market is difficult because of the climatic requirements of rubber production. In addition, natural rubber is a homogeneous product. Perhaps the greatest obstacle to price stabilization is the parallel market in synthetic rubber. Although the cartel members could count on demand from radial tire production, for all other uses, synthetic rubber offered a competitive substitute.

The international tin agreement

With antitrust enforcement taking hold in the industrialized world in the mid-twentieth century, the long-standing agreements to manage the international tin market transitioned into a "modern" commodity arrangement primarily focused on the welfare of exporting nations. In the first International Tin Accord (ITA) of 1956, signatories from 27 nations, including major importing nations such as the US, joined together to smooth volatile prices. In its early years, the cartel saw the value of tin fall below its price floor only once. But extreme market volatility returned in the mid-1970s, with the price of tin going from $6,682 per metric ton in 1975 to $16,743 per metric ton in 1980.

The United States played a major role in the dissolution of the international tin cartel. A critical wartime metal, tin had been stockpiled by the US government since World War II. The decision to begin divesting a significant portion of the US government's strategic reserves of tin began in 1980 (by 1994, 55,000 metric tons of tin would be dropped) exerted downward pressure on prices. On behalf of the country's industrial sector, the US withdrew from the fifth International Tin Agreement in 1981, delivering another blow to the tin-producing members of the cartel. Deeply in debt and lacking cash

Table 3.7 World tin prices, 1959–1988, dollars per metric ton

Year	*Price ($)*	*Year*	*Price ($)*
1959	2,159.5	1974	8,167.1
1960	2,190.3	1975	6,862.2
1961	2,444.9	1976	7,569.8
1962	2.466.2	1977	10,781.8
1963	2.502.5	1978	12,848.2
1964	3,405.6	1979	15,415.0
1965	3,882.6	1980	16,742.7
1966	3,566.0	1981	14,139.4
1967	3,301.1	1982	12,802.9
1968	3,120.3	1983	12,960.4
1969	3,420.3	1984	12,204.7
1970	3,665.9	1985	11,514.8
1971	3,504.6	1986	6,148.6
1972	3,732.1	1987	6,685.7
1973	4.792.3	1988	7,036.9

Source: International Monetary Fund.

reserves to support its buffer stock, the International Tin Agreement collapsed in 1985. By 1986, the price of tin fell to just $6,149 per metric ton.

Despite the problems that that developed for tin producers after 1980, over the long run price management of the commodity had been moderately successful. This was due to the inherent characteristics of tin, a raw material that is easily stockpiled and exported by very few countries. Working against cartelization is the substitutability of tin in all applications except those that demand non-toxicity. The ultimate failure of the tin cartel in 1985 was due to eroding worldwide demand.

International commodity cartels: a post-mortem

There are some generalizations that can be drawn about the relative effectiveness of the commodity agreements devised after 1953 (for an early assessment of the cartel movement, see Gilbert, 1987). Most of the cartels, particularly the arrangements negotiated for the coffee and sugar markets, were simply too large to be sustainable. The divergent interests of individual nations almost always overrode any shared incentive for price stabilization. Moreover, the inherent characteristics of the cartelized markets (e.g. the lack of homogeneity in the coffee market or the substitution problem of the sugar market) frequently worked against their success. When the so-called Group of 77 developing nations called for a New International Economic Order as part of UNCTAD's Integrated Programme for Commodities in 1976, many world markets were still tightly controlled by tariffs (see Gilbert, 1996). With the advent of globalization, such sweeping initiatives became anachronistic, out of step with the trend towards free markets.

Table 3.8 The major commodity cartels of the 1970s and 1980s

Cartel	*Date*	*Membership*
International Bauxite Association	1974	Jamaica, Guyana, Australia, Guinea, Sierra Leone, Yugoslavia
International Sugar Organization	1953	Over 70 nations
Organization of Petroleum Exporting Countries	1960	Algeria, Ecuador, Indonesia, Iran, Iraq, Kuwait, Libya, Nigeria, Qatar, Saudi Arabia, United Arab Emirates, Venezuela
International Tin Agreement	1956	27 exporting and importing nations
International Cocoa Organization	1973	Exporters: Brazil, Cameroon, Côte d'Ivoire, Ecuador, Gabon, Ghana, Grenada, Guatemala, Haiti, Jamaica, Mexico, Nigeria, Papua New Guinea, Sierra Leone, Togo, Trinidad & Tobago, Venezuela, Western Samoa; Importers: Belgium, Bulgaria, Czech Republic, Denmark, the EU, Finland, France, Germany, Greece, Hungary, Ireland, Italy, Japan, Luxembourg, the Netherlands, Norway, Portugal, Russia, Slovakia, Spain, Sweden, Switzerland, the United Kingdom
International Coffee Agreement	1962	50 exporting nations, as well as a number of importing countries
International Natural Rubber Organization	1980	Exporters: Indonesia, Malaysia, Nigeria, Sri Lanka, Thailand; Importers: Belgium, China, Denmark, the EU, Finland, France, Germany, Greece, Ireland, Italy, Japan, Luxembourg, Morocco, the Netherlands, Norway, Russia, Spain, Sweden, Switzerland, the United Kingdom, the US

However unsuccessful in their outcomes, the commodity cartels provide insight into the ways collusion is undertaken when competition policy is absent. Without the need for secrecy, the cartel members openly manipulated prices through a variety of mechanisms, including export controls, fee management, and buffer stocks. Export controls worked poorly, as producing nations balked at cutting production and the excess supply could not be absorbed domestically. The management of levies by the International Bauxite Association worked quite well and can be regarded as similar to the pricing practices used by cartels active in the industrialized world since 1980. The IBA's pricing structure, however, was public, and therefore far more easily controlled than pricing agreements among private firms, where cheating is so often rampant. Buffer stock arrangements are the superior method of cartel management—they are simple to operate, they transcend national and corporate interests, and they usually turn a profit. For those pursuing this means of managing prices, however, stockpiling would be highly visible to antitrust authorities.

The case of De Beers

Despite the checkered history of commodity cartels, global price-fixing arrangements in raw material markets are still feasible under certain conditions. The De Beers Diamond Corporation is regarded as the best example of a successful, long-standing cartel. In 1880, Cecil Rhodes entered the diamond business through a partial acquisition of the De Beers Mine in South Africa, the country with the world's greatest concentration of diamond deposits. He would eventually buy out the other partners and take full control. His purchase eight years later of the richest single source of South African diamonds, the Kimberley Mine, gave Rhodes control of the majority of the world's output and the ability to manipulate international prices. In particular, Rhodes created a centralized point-of-sale through which member merchants, the so-called Diamond Syndicate, a precursor to the cartel's later London-based Central Selling Organization (CSO), purchased diamonds from his corporation. Until the end of the twentieth century, De Beers successfully maintained target prices for diamonds by acquiring any new mines that threatened to weaken his monopoly of the diamond market.

Although South African diamonds represented less than 10 percent of world production in the late 1990s, De Beers still managed more than 80 percent of world supply through a system of interlocking boards. Jewelry wholesalers that attempted to work around the CSO found few suppliers and faced punishment at the hands of the cartel when they tried to return to the syndicate for new stock. Diamond-producing nations that tried to terminate their cooperation with De Beers were also punished. In 1981, Zaire, an exporter of industrial-grade diamonds, turned away from the CSO. Shortly thereafter, large stockpiles of stones were released into the market and the price for diamonds of this low quality dropped nearly 50 percent (for the circumstances of the Zairian dispute, see Spar, 1994: 62–3). Over the years, the De Beers Corporation used intensive advertising to try to convince consumers that the high prices for diamonds reflects the scarcity of quality gems. The primary concern of the CSO has always been the better stones, as this was the segment of the market with the highest rates of return. Still, the management of De Beers fully recognized the linkage between prices at the upper and lower ends of the market. In effect, prices of even flawed stones were managed to prevent weakness in any portion of the market.

The world diamond market changed significantly in the late 1990s, when the stockpiles of excess diamonds that De Beers held to artificially inflate prices reached an unmanageable level, and carrying costs were eating into the company's profits. The company was also facing a public-relations problem due to intense media coverage of the role diamond sales played in financing civil wars and atrocities in Africa.

In 2000, De Beers announced that it was abandoning its traditional role as the guardian of the diamond market. The firm would no longer explicitly manage the quantity and quality of diamonds available on the market. Instead, De Beers began a campaign to "polish" the image of the diamond market, ensuring customers that their gems were not purchased from sources that funded violence or supported insurrection. It is unclear whether a long-term publicity campaign can undo years of bad press. The final blow to the syndicate may come in the form of synthetic diamonds, which have been used in the industrial sector for decades, but since a technological breakthrough in 2006 are now available in gem-quality virtually indistinguishable from the natural stones (in fact, in January 2007, the Gemological Society of America began grading synthetic diamonds in the same fashion that it had always graded natural diamonds). It is uncertain if De Beers and other diamond distributors will be able to overcome the challenges posed by this fundamental alteration of the market.

Although the strategy of centralized selling utilized by De Beers was unique, it resurfaced in the 1990s with the formation of a cartel in the marine hose industry (i.e. high-strength hose used for unloading petroleum from tankers). Suppliers of the hose were able to establish a Central Selling Point and command a significantly higher price for the product. The hose cartel successfully managed the market until both US and European antitrust authorities moved in and prosecuted the executives who had devised the scheme.

Conclusion

The history of cartelization presented in this chapter demonstrates how collusion has adapted to both changing market conditions and evolving antitrust legislation. Following the passage of the Sherman Act, collusion in the industrialized world went underground. Still, anti-collusion enforcement was inconsistent. After 1950, cartels operated once again in the sunlight, either sanctioned by governments or beyond the reach of antitrust authorities. The international commodity agreements generally failed to secure stable prices, as market forces usually overwhelmed the actions of the cartel. The most visible remnant of the UNCTAD initiatives of the 1960s and 1970s, OPEC continues to set target prices, and yet the cost of oil has been more strongly influenced by the vagaries of supply and demand than the policies of the cartel. Excluding oil, the long-term decline in raw material prices has been inexorable, and the dominant strategy of developing nations should be to pursue trade diversification.

With the unraveling of most of the international commodity agreements in the mid- to late-1980s, concern over the negative impact of collusion shifted back to the industrialized world. Unlike the collusive agreements examined in this chapter, the cartels detailed in Chapter 5 are explicitly illegal, and participation entails substantial risk, both for the firm and its executives. The credible threat of punitive action has transformed the way in which cartels function. Collusive practices such as complex pricing agreements, the use of buffer stocks, and the establishment of Central Selling Points are now impossible within the industrialized world. The segmentation of markets and the utilization of minimum prices are now the most common forms of collusion. The earlier history of industrial and commodity cartels provides guidance to those who pursue collusion in contemporary markets.

4 Globalization and corporate collusion

With the exception of the oil cartel, commodity markets have lacked the intrinsic characteristics necessary for sustained price-fixing—the so-called conditions for cartelization that were discussed in Chapter 2. By the last decade of the twentieth century, collusion had moved from being an objective pursued at a national level to become the prerogative of corporate boardrooms. The wave of worldwide tariff reductions during the last two decades has so eliminated barriers to trade that corporations must view competition through an international lens.

Facing the crunch of increased competition, some firms dismiss the threat of antitrust prosecution and seek cooperation with their rivals. Yet the process by which firms establish collusive agreements has become more complicated as markets are globalized. Collusion within national borders is relatively simple, with the number of competitors limited and agreements possible without the burden of such factors as foreign travel or international monitoring of price accords. Keeping a cartel hidden from antitrust authorities when collusion involves international gatherings is a complicated undertaking.

For executives seeking to establish international market controls, trade associations have often provided a means of operating in plain view. The ever-present threat that a cartel member will expose the conspiracy, however, must seem more ominous when numerous firms—including those headquartered in distant markets—are involved. Globalization also creates an environment in which the unexpected entry of a new overseas competitor can destabilize a cartel.

The internationalization of markets has fundamentally changed both how cartels operate and how regulators enforce antitrust laws. As cartelization became globalized, authorities struggled to keep up. Prosecution of cartel members is complicated in two ways. First, competition officials are responsible for investigating both domestic and foreign firms. In building a strong case on the domestic level, authorities must navigate the policies for public disclosure of each foreign nation whose corporations are represented in the case. Second, in a number of instances, authorities in the US and Europe have engaged in parallel investigations and were barred from releasing certain documentation to one another. It is inefficient and counterproductive to have two independent prosecutions of the same cartel. In addition, differences in the penalties imposed in the US and the EU further complicates any joint action against offenders.

This chapter will examine how cartelization in the industrialized world has changed in response to globalization. The implications for both colluders and regulators in this new environment will be considered. Proposals for strengthening competition law in the age of international free trade will be presented at the end of the chapter.

Trends in trade barriers in twentieth century: the US and Europe

From the later nineteenth century onward, the US and its European trading partners had made substantial cuts in tariffs until by the 1920s, international markets were substantially more open to competition (see Table 4.1). By the early 1920s, the average tariff rate for the US fell to less than 15 percent, a drop of approximately 65 percent from its high in the 1860s. International trade ballooned and it was no longer possible for businesses to restrict their competition strategies to domestic rivals. As discussed below, the 1920s saw the beginning of international "cooperation" between manufacturing firms. When tariffs were raised significantly in 1930 under the Smoot-Hawley Act, US markets were once again shielded from the competition of external trade. This protectionist stance did not change substantially until 1947, with the signing of the original General Agreement on Tariffs and Trade (GATT). By this accord, the industrialized nations committed themselves to multilateralism, whereby negotiated tariff cuts for one nation applied to all countries. Only after additional large tariff cuts were made during the Kennedy Round of GATT (1964 to 1967) were firms exposed to international competition at a level commensurate with that of the 1920s.

Regional integration and the rise of inter-European trade

The second concurrent development of trade liberalization centers on the opening of markets through regional integration (i.e. bilateralism). Beginning with the Treaty of Rome in 1957, Western Europe began an unprecedented push towards open markets. By 1968, the six original members of the European Economic Community (EEC)—Belgium, Germany, France, Italy, Luxembourg, and the Netherlands—were trading without tariff barriers. Denmark, Ireland, and the United Kingdom joined the Community in 1973. The final phase of expansion under the original EEC mandate resulted in membership for Greece in 1981, with Spain and Portugal joining in 1986. Twelve nations strong, the EEC pushed for deeper integration, particularly the pursuit of a common currency and the development of common political institutions (e.g. the European Parliament). The EEC was gradually transformed first into the European Community (EC) and then into the European Union. Countries continued to be admitted, with Austria, Finland, and Sweden joining the EU in 1995. The end of Soviet hegemony over Central and Eastern Europe ed to an unprecedented number of new membership applications, with Cyprus, the Czech Republic, Estonia, Hungary, Latvia, Lithuania, Malta, Poland, Slovakia, and Slovenia admitted in 2004. The final enlargement took place in 2007, with the addition of Bulgaria and Romania. The gross domestic product of the 27 member states of the European Union ($16.6 trillion in 2008) now exceeds that of the US ($14.4 trillion for the same year).

The expansion of the EU has met with some setbacks. Fearing the inevitable loss of autonomy that membership entailed, some nations have refused to join. Norway has twice rejected membership into the EU, once in 1967 and again in 1992. Switzerland's application was "frozen" due to unfavorable public opinion at home. Turkey has repeatedly pushed for but been denied membership. A more difficult challenge to the European model of deep integration occurred in France in May 2005, when voters rejected the proposed European Constitution. As the French have led the movement toward a consolidated Europe, their refusal to cede sovereignty on this scale was startling. Supporters of a comprehensive economic and political union in Europe had to accept that changes were coming too quickly for some, and that further integration would have to wait until public opinion caught up with the institutional consensus.

Until 1995, the progress of the EU could be described as "integration among equals." With the possible exceptions of Portugal and Spain, the first fifteen members of the Union shared similar standards of living and industrial structures. The elimination of tariffs and other trade barriers exposed businesses to direct, unfettered competition, and inevitably led to much greater cross-national price competition. This newfound corporate rivalry resulted in widespread industrial consolidation and illicit cooperation in Western Europe. In the "integration among unequals" that characterizes more recent EU expansion, fundamental differences in the industrial bases of members from Eastern and Central Europe make collusion less likely. Cartelization is still primarily a phenomenon of the higher-income nations of Europe, a truism that is explored more fully in Chapter 5.

In comparison to the EU, regional integration between the US and its neighbors did not present the same challenges for antitrust authorities. The North American Free Trade Agreement (NAFTA), and the US–Canada Free Trade Agreement that preceded it, have not produced a wave of cartels similar to that observed in the EU. For one thing, the manufacturing sectors of the US and Canada were already heavily integrated prior to the passage of NAFTA in 1994. Moreover, the Mexican economy was newly industrialized with a dissimilar manufacturing base from its partners to the north (a case of "integration among unequals").

Combining multilateralism and bilateralism—tariff barriers after 1970

The tariff reductions made through the GATT and its successor, the World Trade Organization, together with those carried out through regional trading agreements, have brought tariff rates down to the single-digits (see Table 4.1). The average tariff rate on imports into the US has fallen from an already historic low of 6.5 percent in 1970 to just over half that value in 1989. The near-zero tariff rates of Germany, France, and Italy illustrate a positive impact of early regional integration. On the other hand, nominal tariff rates such as these are an indicator of a less desirable outcome of regional integration, namely, a reorientation of trade toward other European nations (so-called "trade diversion"). Spain had high tariff rates until its late entry into the EU in 1986, but by 1989 the country's import levies could be compared to those of the US. Japan has resisted efforts at regional integration, and yet its trade barriers have still declined as a result of its obligations under the GATT and WTO (see Table 4.1).

Tariff rates in the low single digits are no longer a meaningful barrier to trade, as transportation and distribution costs normally exceed the impact of tariffs. Overall tariff rates in the US and Europe often conceal high levies

Table 4.1 Trade-weighted average tariff barriers, 1970–1989, US, selected European nations and Japan

Year	*US*	*France*	*Germany*	*Italy*	*UK*	*Spain*	*Japan*
1970	6.50	—	—	—	3.07	13.05	—
1971	6.08	—	1.88	—	3.04	14.92	—
1972	5.65	—	1.32	—	3.47	—	—
1973	5.24	—	0.70	—	1.96	—	—
1974	3.77	—	0.31	—	1.54	—	—
1975	3.92	0.09	0.04	0.34	1.54	13.05	—
1976	3.86	0.07	0.05	1.14	0.64	14.92	—
1977	3.73	0.09	0.04	0.22	0.29	18.05	3.15
1978	4.14	0.09	0.03	0.17	0.07	16.85	3.60
1979	3.50	0.07	0.03	0.12	0.00	17.12	3.21
1980	3.09	0.11	0.02	0.08	0.11	6.00	2.29
1981	3.43	0.08	0.02	0.04	0.24	5.47	2.38
1982	3.59	0.07	0.03	0.06	0.37	6.21	2.31
1983	3.67	0.07	0.02	0.06	0.13	6.01	2.36
1984	3.73	0.07	0.02	0.05	0.03	5.82	2.35
1985	3.80	0.07	0.01	0.05	0.00	7.22	2.34
1986	3.61	0.08	0.01	0.07	0.06	5.24	2.90
1987	3.46	0.06	0.01	0.06	0.00	4.69	3.38
1988	3.44	0.04	0.00	0.09	0.17	4.33	3.40
1989	3.44	0.02	0.00	0.03	0.11	3.54	2.74

Sources: US tariff rates taken from U.S. Bureau of the Census, *Historical Statistics of the United States*. Other figures from World Bank, *World Development Index*.

(some in the double digits) that exist in specific sectors, notably textiles, apparel, and agricultural products. Elevated tariffs on textiles and clothing hold no consequence for the developed nation that imposes such levies, since collusion among manufacturers of dissimilar products is rare. In the case of agricultural commodities, nations that promote their farming sectors through subsidization (generally, price supports) must then apply higher trade barriers to discourage imports. The anti-competitive cycle of using government subsidies to bolster farm prices but then protecting the producers from the downward price pressure of competition through tariff policy has been the focus of the WTO's Doha Round of trade negotiations. Little progress has been made on securing lower international tariffs on these products. The impact of the remaining agricultural barriers to trade is muted, however, since cartelization has been confined primarily to intermediate inputs (e.g. food additives).

The magnitude of international trade

The volume of international trade conducted between the industrialized nations was slow to recover after World War II. Until the Kennedy Round of the GATT, tariff rates remained well above where they had been in the 1920s. Despite these high duties, the economic growth of the 1950s brought a double-digit rise in the level of exports. As shown in Table 4.2, growth in the export of manufactured goods continued to accelerate into the early 1970s, until it was choked off by slow economic growth in the latter half of the decade. Trade again expanded by double digits in the latter half of the 1980s, as the tariffs reductions negotiated in the GATT's Tokyo Round (1977) took hold. Overall growth has slowed since 1990, as the world trading system reached the point of diminishing returns on further tariff reductions. In the years that saw an expansion of the world economy (e.g. from 2003 to 2004), however, the volume of exports expanded even more rapidly than world output.

The impact of over sixty years of tariff reductions under the GATT and its successor organization, the World Trade Organization (WTO), can be discerned in the figures, i.e. imports plus exports have risen significantly, in many cases doubling between 1960 and 2000. Only in nations already fully engaged in international commerce (e.g. Norway) does one observe negligible increases in trade. The glaring exception to this generalization is Japan, whose reluctance to enforce its own Antimonopoly Law has delayed the development of competitive markets that would support more open trade. Consequently, Japan tends to run significant trade surpluses on low trade volume. Despite its massive trade deficits, the US is, by international standards, not particularly dependent on trade as a percentage of GDP—only 26.2 percent of GDP in 2000, a figure that represents the sum of both imports and exports.

Table 4.2 Growth in international trade, manufactures, 1950–2005, percentage change

Year	*Percentage change*	*Year*	*Percentage change*	*Year*	*Percentage change*
1950–1963	10.1	1978	21.6	1993	0.0
1964	15.0	1979	21.3	1994	15.6
1965	10.9	1980	15.9	1995	20.0
1966	10.8	1981	-0.7	1996	3.5
1967	7.7	1982	-3.6	1997	4.6
1968	14.9	1983	0.5	1998	2.3
1969	16.5	1984	8.1	1999	3.3
1970	15.4	1985	3.8	2000	10.1
1971	13.7	1986	20.3	2001	-3.8
1972	19.4	1987	19.7	2002	5.4
1973	34.1	1988	16.1	2003	15.8
1974	31.3	1989	6.9	2004	20.5
1975	8.8	1990	14.7	2005	9.9
1976	12.8	1991	3.3	—	—
1977	14.7	1992	8.0	—	—

Source: World Trade Organization.

Table 4.3 Total external trade (exports plus imports) as a percentage of GDP, OECD countries

Country	*1960*	*2000*
Australia	29.4	45.6
Belgium	79.7	169.3
Canada	35.6	86.8
Switzerland	55.7	87.9
Denmark	64.0	80.1
Spain	15.5	62.2
Finland	43.5	76.0
France	26.4	55.9
UK	41.3	57.9
Germany	n/a	67.1
Greece	24.0	57.9
Italy	25.9	55.6
Japan	20.7	20.1
Netherlands	93.3	129.6
Norway	71.2	77.1
Sweden	45.6	89.0
United States	9.5	26.2

Source: World Trade Organization.

Table 4.4 Summary characteristics of major cartels, 1891*–2008

Product	*Geographic coverage*	*Approximate date*	*Method of cartelization*	*Nationality of cartel members*
Railway Transportation	US	1897	System of common fees	US
Light Bulbs	Europe, US	1924–	System of interlocking boards under tutelage of General Electric	US, Europe
Steel	Europe, US	1933	Quotas, territorial limits (cartel operated with official "permission")	US, Europe
Electrical	US	1950s	Bid-rigging equipment	US
Lysine	Global	1992–1995	Pricing agreements	US, S. Korea, Japan
Bulk Vitamins	Global	1989–1997	Pricing agreements	France, Japan, Germany, Canada, Switzerland
Sorbates	Global	1979–1996	Pricing agreements	Germany, Japan
Zinc Phosphate	Europe	1994–	Pricing agreements	UK, Germany, France, Norway
Beer	Netherlands	1996–1999	Segmentation of markets	Netherlands
Carbonless Paper	Europe	1992	Pricing agreements, sales quotas	UK, Germany, France, Spain, South Africa
Plasterboard	UK, Germany, France, Benelux	1992–1998	Pricing agreements	UK, Germany, France, Belgium
Choline Chloride				
Graphite Electrodes	Europe, US	1992–1998	Pricing agreements	Germany, US Japan
Industrial/ Medical Gases	Netherlands	1989–1997	Pricing agreements	Netherlands
Copper Plumbing Tubes	Europe	1988–2001	Pricing agreements	Sweden, UK Greece, Italy, US, Germany, Finland, Netherlands

(Continued)

Table 4.4 (*Continued*)

Product	*Geographic coverage*	*Approximate date*	*Method of cartelization*	*Nationality of cartel members*
Soda Ash	Europe	1980s	Price rebates	UK, Belgium
Citric Acid	Global	1991–1997	Price floors, quotas	Switzerland, Netherlands, US
Bleaching Agents	Europe	1997–2002	Pricing agreements	Belgium, Italy, Spain, France, Finland, Germany, Netherlands
Elevators/ Escalators	Belgium, Germany, Luxemburg, Netherlands,		Market share agreements	US, Finland, Germany, Switzerland
Flat Glass	Europe	2004–2005	Market segmentation	US, Japan, UK
Switchgear	Europe	1988–2004	Market segmentation, quotas	Japan, France, Germany, Switzerland, Austria
Synthetic Rubber	Europe	1993–2002	Pricing agreements	Germany, US, Japan
DRAM Chips	US		Pricing agreements	Japan, S. Korea, Germany
Marine Hose	US		Bid-rigging, market segmentation	Individuals, not firms
Nucleotides	Global	1988–1998	Pricing agreements, market segmentation	Japan, S. Korea
Fasteners	Europe	1977	Pricing agreements, market segmentation	UK, S. Korea, US, Germany, Japan
Art Auction Services	Europe, US	1993–1999	Common fees, pricing practices	US, UK
Paraffin	Europe	1992–2005	Pricing agreements	UK, Germany, Spain, Italy, Netherlands, Hungary, S. Africa
Consumer Credit Cards	US		Exclusionary rule	US

Note: *Date of the Sherman Act.

This unprecedented increase in international trade between the industrialized economies in the last four decades illustrates the enormous competitive pressures that corporations faced. The GATT accords fundamentally altered the environment in which firms operated. In a sense, it is not entirely surprising that businesses would view collusion as a way of mitigating the impact of relentless competition.

Cartels transformed—collusion in a globalized world

Table 4.4 summarizes the characteristics of the major cartels that were uncovered between 1900 and 2008.[1] Over the century or so under review, reductions in tariff rates have moved collusion from domestic or regional markets onto the global stage. In the Western Hemisphere, this trend played out in the initial collusive accords of the railroad sector, which were followed by cartels in the light bulb and steel industries that involved both the US and Europe. Not surprisingly, the light bulb cartel was formed during a period of historically low tariff rates, with General Electric seeking protection in European markets through control of the boards of competing companies. US steel manufacturers used existing Depression-era laws to cooperate openly with their European counterparts. The brazenness of early cross-national price-fixing agreements is striking when compared to the underhandedness of cartels that have been exposed in the US and Europe in recent years. General Electric was able to end competition on light bulbs by consolidating the management of the industry. With the nod of antitrust authorities, the global steel industry simply assigned markets to domestic producers. In that era of cartelization, big results on pricing and production could be achieved without extensive negotiations.

The higher tariffs put in place in the early 1930s and only slowly removed in the post-war world allowed cartels to once again manipulate domestic markets without the threat of being undercut by rising imports. As detailed by Hay and Kelley (1974), of the numerous price-fixing agreements uncovered in the post-war period, nearly all were categorized as local or regional rather than national in scope. It was not until tariffs were lowered in the Kennedy Round of the GATT that globalized cartels re-emerged as powerful tools for avoiding competition.

Table 4.4 also lists the major cartels active after 1977 and the methods of collusion they used on an international scale during this more strident antitrust regime. In Europe's fasteners industry, a cartel composed of five firms from five countries worked together from 1977 to manipulate prices by segmenting the market. In contrast, the sorbates cartel was the first global concern to rely solely on pricing agreements (the first dated to 1979) to manage competition. Of the five major cartels formed in the 1980s, two relied on price-fixing (vitamins and copper tubes), two on market segmentation (nucleotides and switchgear) and one on volume rebates (soda ash).

Most collusive agreements devised after 1990 rely on pricing agreements, whereby participating firms can enter any market so long as they abide by preset minimums. With price-fixing agreements, market manipulation can be easily hidden. Conversely, market segmentation, the second most common form of collusion in this late period, is a risky strategy in a globalized world. In this scheme, end-users of an input may sense that rivals are not competing, as bids are received from only one supplier, a situation that can lead to exposure of the cartel. Nearly all of the collusive agreements reached after 1990 are either pan-European or global (see Table 4.4).[2] With the elimination of trade barriers, this most recent phase of cartelization has seen an uptick in collusion among firms from the US, the industrialized nations of Europe, and Japan. Connor (2002) examined the collusive agreements that have been exposed in the food and agricultural industries and noted that competition officials are aware that cartelization is a potential downside of globalization. Evenett et al. (2001) argued that the generally accepted principle that cartels crumble as a result of the incentive to cheat was not evident in the 1990s, when many international price-fixing agreements where maintained for years. Bond (2004) pushed these arguments a step further by noting that globalization is itself the impetus for many new cartel arrangements.

The inability of current antitrust regimes to address cartelization on a global basis was addressed by Buxbaum (2004). The author noted that the landmark *F. Hoffman–LaRoche v. Empagran, S.A.* (542 U.S. 155 (2004)) represents the challenge of using national laws to address international antitrust cases. Empagran, an Ecuadorian purchaser of bulk vitamin products, alleged that it had suffered significant economic harm in the US market as a result of Hoffman–La Roche's participation in the global vitamin cartel. The Supreme Court evaluated whether actions by multinational corporations impacted commerce in the US to a sufficient degree to warrant the imposition of penalties under US antitrust laws. In reversing a lower ruling by the 3rd Circuit Court, the Supreme Court found in favor of Hoffman–La Roche, arguing that Empagran's home country was the appropriate venue for pursuing legal action. As noted by Bauxbaum, the Supreme Court's ruling rested on the assumption that Empagran's injuries in its home market were separate from the damages caused by the vitamin cartel in the US market. The decision provided some guidance on the limits of US antitrust law in cases in which damages from a cartel are international in scope. As Buxbaum noted, the Hoffman–La Roche decision did not undermine the Supreme Court's earlier ruling in *Hartford Fire Insurance v. California* (509 SC 764 (1993)), where it had been asserted that foreign companies acting in foreign countries could be held liable for violating the Sherman Act if they conspired to restrict trade within the United States. Klevorick and Sykes (2007) examined the jurisdictional issues of the Hoffman–La Roche judgment and provided a list of the pros and cons of extending US competition policy to international markets.

Industrial cartels with a global reach

The most far-reaching cartels of the last three decades are found in the food additives industry (Table 4.4). The markets for lysine, bulk vitamins, sorbates, citric acid, and nucleotides each posses the characteristics favorable for cartelization. That food additives are intermediate goods whose price structure is based on bids quoted to individual firms further incentivizes producers to collude. With the exception of citric acid, which is manufactured mainly in the US, Switzerland, and the Netherlands, the other food additives under consideration have at least one Asian manufacturer. The global production of these commodities is matched by global utilization.

Case study—lysine

The narrative of how cartels develop and function in input markets is especially apparent in the lysine industry. A naturally occurring amino acid, lysine was first commercially produced by Japan's Ajinomoto Company in the early 1960s. Another Japanese firm, Kyowa Hakko, soon joined the market. In 1976, Ajinomoto teamed up with a French firm, Orsan, to form Eurolysine. Kyowa Hakko, in turn, established new plants in the US, Mexico, and France. Given the lax antitrust environment in Japan during the period, it is not surprising that Ajinomoto and Kyowa began colluding in the late 1970s. The Japanese firms functioned as an unchallenged duopoly until 1980, when South Korea's Sewon Corporation entered the lysine market and refused to join the collusive agreement (Connor, 2007). Additional competitive pressure was exerted when Archer Daniels Midland (ADM) entered the market in 1991. Their plant in Decatur, Illinois soon exceeding in production those of Ajinomoto, Kyowa, and Sewon.

Just as the rivalry between producers was at its fiercest and prices were bending downward, the four corporations—Ajinomoto, Kyowa, Sewon, and ADM—initiated the infamous Lysine Conspiracy of 1992 through 1995. This cartel has been the focus of numerous studies, mainly because in the prosecution of the case, the US Department of Justice made pricing data available in court documents. The release of such documentation is exceptional, as pricing by many collusive accords is based on bid prices for individual orders and therefore does not represent true market prices.

Table 4.5 contains the price of lysine from before the formation of the cartel until after its dissolution. The price of lysine plummeted from $1.12 per pound in October 1991 to only 64 cents per pound in July 1992. This level was far below the average of $1.65 per pound that had prevailed in the late 1980s. When Archer Daniels Midland decided in 1989 to transition from making dextrose, a key input of lysine production, to making the end product itself, potential world production nearly doubled. The collapse in world prices occurred after ADM's new plant went into operation in 1991. As the world's most efficient producer, the company was able to

Table 4.5 Lysine prices October 1991–December 1994, dollars per pound, monthly average

Month	*Price ($)*	*Month*	*Price ($)*	*Month*	*Price ($)*
1991		*1993*		*1994*	
October	1.12	January	0.98	January	1.12
November	1.07	February	0.94	February	1.11
December	0.97	March	0.89	March	1.11
1992		April	0.78	April	1.11
		May	0.66	May	1.11
January	0.92	June	0.62	June	1.11
February	0.84	July	0.76	July	1.09
March	0.82	August	0.88	August	1.11
April	0.80	September	0.98	September	1.16
May	0.78	October	1.08	October	1.20
June	0.69	November	1.10	November	1.22
July	0.64	December	1.13	December	1.22
August	0.70				
September	0.82				
October	0.92				
November	0.98				
December	0.98				

Source: Amino Acid Antitrust Case, Exhibit C, April 1996.

endure falling prices better than its competitors. By April 1992, however, even ADM was looking for some relief from the deteriorating market.

The preliminary price-fixing meetings between ADM and the other major producers of lysine took place in Mexico City in June 1992. By the end of the year, lysine prices had stabilized. As shown in Table 4.5, between October 1992 and February 1993, lysine sold in the range of 92 to 98 cents per pound. Under these conditions, the lysine market was reasonably profitable for ADM, whose break-even price was estimated at 70 cents per pound. The competing firms, however, struggled under the burden of older capacity. A squabble soon developed when Ajinomoto accused ADM of stealing their patented microbes. As noted by Connor (2001: 12), the two firms also argued about the total potential sales of lysine, with Ajinomoto asserting that the cartel members should be able to increase their production levels. The lysine agreement faltered and prices collapsed once again, falling to a new low of 62 cents per pound in June 1993.

Soon after that low point, lysine producers moved to manage global supply, agreeing at a meeting in October 1993 to strictly limit production. Ajinomoto was granted the highest market share (about one-third of the total lysine market). ADM agreed to a slightly smaller allocation. Prices buoyed, reaching a profitable $1.10 per pound within four months of the meeting, and remaining near this level for nearly a year before spiking once again. This highly profitable period for the lysine industry ended only when a federal grand jury in Chicago issued the first in a series of subpoenas. Connor (2001) asserted that the fines imposed on the firms did not adequately reflect the damage done to end-users of lysine. Conversely, White (2001) questioned the purported duration of the cartel presented in Connor's study, and argued that the "but for" price was actually higher than reported.

In contrast to earlier cartels, the Lysine Conspiracy was, in all respects, truly global in its reach. The cartel encompassed essentially all lysine production, with its membership drawn from firms in the US, Asia, and Europe. Whereas market segmentation was the primary means of collusion in the 1990s, the lysine producers established a common worldwide price target, and manipulated production levels to achieve that target.

The antitrust response to globalized collusion

As the legal and legislative integration of the EU has advanced, anti-cartel enforcement has moved from domestic to intra-Union courts. This transfer of sovereignty has required the imposition of uniform laws. The first institution to implement supra-national policies in Western Europe was the so-called High Authority of the European Coal and Steel Community (ECSC), a consortium of six member states—France, Germany, Italy, the Netherlands, Belgium, and Luxembourg—realized in 1951 to rationalize regional markets. With the signing of the Treaty of Rome in 1957 (affected in 1958), these same nations were unified under a central authority, the European Commission, which took as its model the High Authority of the ECSC. In its role as the executive branch of the European Economic Community, the European Commission was charged with overseeing competition policy in all sectors of its member states. The Treaty of Rome also created Euratom, the agency responsible for establishing policy on atomic energy. The High Authority continued to function as a regulator of the coal and steel sectors until 1968 when, together with Euratom, it was subsumed under the aegis of the European Commission (as defined by the Merger Treaty of 1965). The European Commission was retained as the executive body of the European Union, where it still dictates competition policy.

Since the late 1990s, the industrialized nations have sought to establish "best practices" for anti-cartel enforcement, and secure some degree of cooperation in prosecutions involving international price-fixing agreements. These efforts have largely taken place under the auspices of the Organization for Economic Cooperation and Development (OECD). In addition, the US Department of Justice holds recurring workshops on competition policy (especially price-fixing schemes and antitrust strategies) for governmental and law enforcement personnel, including authorities from abroad. The efforts to achieve a coordinated international response to collusive accords in the US, Europe, and Japan have been thwarted by privacy laws that safeguard business information. At the present time, this impasse appears to be intractable. The work of the OECD and the US DOJ has, however, helped illuminate the most effective enforcement practices for industrialized markets.

The OECD's pronouncement of 1998

As noted in Chapter 1, although antitrust policies in the US and the EU have developed independently they share certain attributes. In 1998, the Organization for Economic Cooperation and Development issued the first in a series of studies on regulation and anticompetitive practices.[3] The OECD Anti-Cartel Recommendation and Program outlined the organization's suggestions for responding to collusion. The document called on member nations to examine how effectively their judicial systems rout out collusion. The pronouncement also persuaded OECD nations to cooperate in investigating and prosecuting cartels. Finally, the document encouraged non-OECD nations, especially those undergoing industrialization, to adopt and enforce anti-cartel policies of their own.

The pronouncement of 1998 assessed the strengths and weaknesses of various antitrust regimes, and included an overview of new initiatives adopted in Canada, South Korea, and a number of European nations. The most significant developments in antitrust law are in the area of criminal prosecutions. For example, the OECD documents France's first "criminal referrals," which represented a ratcheting up of the penalties for cartelization in that country. The document also noted that record fines had been imposed in cartel prosecutions in the US, Canada, Ireland, and Norway.

Section II of the OECD's recommendation examined the continuing damage that cartelization inflicts on the marketplace. According to the OECD's estimates, cartels affected approximately $10 billion worth of commerce in the US annually, with a net cost to consumers and corporations of many hundreds of millions of dollars per year. The report acknowledged that the figures for the US were too low, given the "much larger number of undiscovered and unproven international domestic cartels" (OECD, 1998: 5). This rather dark assessment of the economic costs of cartelization was followed by a list of recommended reforms, especially the need for OECD nations to release confidential business information to the investigating bodies of foreign antitrust agencies. The document asserted that confidentiality laws could be relaxed for international prosecution hearings without making proprietary business information available to the general public.

Section II of the report called for other actions to be undertaken in the three years subsequent to the document's release, including:

- obtaining better estimates of the overcharges arising from collusive agreements, together with an assessment of the resulting economic harm;

- estimating the real impact of national laws that forbid certain forms of cross-country cooperation in cartel cases;
- implementing the best investigative tools available for antitrust investigations, and promoting, wherever possible, international cooperation in cartel prosecutions;
- determining optimal sanctions for collusions.

The document sought the convergence of antitrust practices across all OECD countries, and invited non-OECD countries to join the discussion on establishing common policies.

Despite its proposals for coordinating antitrust enforcement, the OECD's report did not contain any sweeping suggestions for reform. As the document acknowledged, the large number of collusive agreements that persist even in the face of antitrust actions will only be reduced when more draconian laws and enforcement practices are put into place. In its report of 1998, the OECD pledged to issue periodic updates to determine if its antitrust goals were being realized.

The OECD's Third Report, dated 2005, on the implementation of the recommendations of 1998

The OECD followed through on its promise to release further reports on the state of anti-cartel enforcement. In a report of 2002, the OECD measured the damage done by cartels and reviewed the efficacy of investigative tools. As in the previous report, emphasis was placed on the need for international cooperation. One of the more interesting outcomes of the report released in 2002 was the conclusion that the fines being imposed on violators were often "substantially" below the optimal level needed for effective deterrence.

In its progress report, "Hard Core Cartels: Third Report on the Implementation of the 1998 Recommendation" (OECD, 2005), the OECD pointed to the high fines imposed by its member nations as evidence of aggressive enforcement. As an example of a stringent penalty, it was noted that fines imposed in cartel cases in Hungary rose by a factor of ten between 2003 and 2004. Similarly, Germany imposed record fines of 717 million euro in 2003. The OECD's assessment also surveyed the imposition of criminal penalties, and pointed to the 10,501 days of jail time that US authorities had imposed for price-fixing in 2004 (OECD, 2005: 9).

The biggest changes noted by the OECD in its report of 2005 were legislative in nature, with the most significant prosecutorial initiatives undertaken outside the US and Europe (e.g. Israel, Korea, Mexico, and Turkey). Yet, in Europe, France introduced legislation to create a leniency program. In the UK, criminal sanctions—with a maximum jail sentence of five years—were added to the list of possible penalties. Similarly, Portugal expanded its enforcement authority to include indictments against not only firms, but also individual executives. The German legislature proposed allowing cross-border cooperation on enforcement, a reform that would have fulfilled one of the main objectives of the OECD's pronouncement of 1998. The OECD looked favorably upon the EU's new European Competition Network (Regulation 1/2003), which seeks to harmonize competition policy between member states. In a demonstration of legislative zeal, in 2004 the US Congress passed the Antitrust Criminal Penalty Enhancement and Reform Act, which raised corporate fines for collusion from a maximum of $10 million to $100 million, increased individual fines from $1 million to $10 million, and elevated maximum jail time from three to ten years (Public Law No. 108-237).

One of the more innovative approaches to antitrust enforcement was undertaken in Canada, where authorities turned to the public for help in uncovering cartels. To this end, the Canadian Competition Bureau created a comprehensive media campaign designed to elucidate the negative effects of cartelization and to showcase the agency's actions against collusion. Media efforts of this kind put the public on guard and thereby increase the likelihood that inexplicable price increases will be reported to authorities. In particular, the Canadian public relations program has publicized the mechanism of bid-rigging to a wide audience. The bureau's campaign educates businesses (particularly small business owners) on what constitutes a violation of antitrust law. Some of the illegal agreements in individual nations owe to a lack of awareness of what constitutes collusion (e.g. interlocking boards) rather than a willful disregard for the law. Canada's Competition Bureau has harnessed public outrage at corporate impropriety to encourage whistle-blowing.

The OECD document of 2005 promoted the value of public awareness of price-fixing by citing a bid-rigging case in Sweden's asphalt industry. Unlike previous cartel cases in that country, the public was kept fully informed of the progress of the antitrust investigation. In particular, media reports made public the monetary cost of the cartel to individual citizens. By publicizing the 20 percent drop in asphalt prices that were affected subsequent to the cartel's exposure, consumers were alerted that price-fixing directly impacts their wallets. As a result of the investigation, local governments in Sweden adopted new procedures to uncover bid-rigging in procurement contracts (OECD, 2005: 22). Duplication of the Canadian and Swedish public education initiatives by other members of the OECD could only help in the fight against cartelization.

Estimates of the economic damage caused by cartels

The OECD's 2005 report provided estimates of the monetary harm done by cartels in the hope that governmental agencies would impose fines of commensurate levels. For example, estimates suggest that recently uncovered cartels in Japan raised prices there by 16.5 percent (OECD, 2005: 25).

The asphalt cartels in Sweden and Finland reportedly raised average prices by between 20 and 25 percent. From a law enforcement perspective, the most salient fact on pricing addressed in the report is that international cartels produce higher overcharges than domestic cartels, presumably because the fear of competition from abroad no longer places constraints on price increases. The document also noted that fines tend to run significantly below the estimated economic impact caused by collusive agreements. In 2005, the OECD reiterated its earlier recommendation (published in the report of 2003) that if deterrence is to be achieved, fines should be set at two to three times the excess profits gained by collusion.

As discussed earlier in this chapter, fines of this magnitude raise compliance with competition law but run the risk of bankrupting one or more of the firms engaged in the cartel. As stated by Parker, any elimination of market players reduces industry competition:

> Whether or not it is legally possible to impose an optimal organizational fine and practically possible to calculate it in a given case, actually imposing it might present problems. The optimal fine could simply be too large for the entity to bear, causing bankruptcy and possible exit from the market, which itself could diminish competition.
>
> (OECD, 2005: 26)

Recognizing that the imposition of onerous fines for collusion can actually reduce competition in the marketplace, the OECD has recommended criminal prosecutions of individuals rather than corporate fines as a superior means of deterring price-fixing.

Changing the enforcement environment—sanctioning individuals

As noted in Chapter 2, rogue corporations may view penalties for collusion as simply a cost of doing business. An executive contemplating whether to engage in price-fixing—with its immediate and tangible benefits to the bottom line—knows that the likelihood of the firm getting caught is slim (only 10 to 30 percent of cartels are ever exposed). But when the managers themselves face the threat of financial penalties and even jail time, collusion appears less attractive. While it has become common for the US DOJ to seek sanctions against individuals within collusive arrangements, the practice is not universal among member nations of the OECD.

The OECD report (OECD, 2005: 26) stated, "individual sanctions can strengthen the incentive of directors and employees to resist corporate pressure to engage in unlawful activity, and thus enhance the level of deterrence." On occasion, cartel meetings have been moved to locations outside the US, in the mistaken belief that the change in venue to another jurisdiction will eliminate the threat of criminal prosecution against the individuals involved. The power of personal sanctions to alter corporate behavior can be observed in numerous cartel prosecutions in the US, in which defendants "repeatedly offered to pay high financial fines if they could avoid jail time" (OECD, 2005: 27). At the time the OECD issued its report in 2005, most member countries still did not have antitrust policies that included prosecution of individuals. The United Kingdom, however, had adopted new antitrust rules that included actions against executives involved in collusion. Australia was considering similar legislation. In order to guarantee that leniency policies continued to be effective, the report recommended that corporations and also individuals be eligible for relief.

A significant proportion of the report of 2005 examined the benefits of international cooperation in cartel enforcement. It had been noted in the OECD's report of 2002 that antitrust authorities were increasingly aware of the global nature of cartels and that jurisdictional coordination between nations was increasing, this despite the fact that national laws normally prohibit agencies in one country from sharing sensitive corporate data with authorities in another. As noted later, when the EU Commission uncovered collusion in the insulated switchgear industry, its prosecutors could not disclose business information that it had collected with Turkish investigators who were undertaking a simultaneous inquiry. Even with these legal barriers in place, cross-national cooperation has increased substantially, with one legal official calling it a "sea change", and asserting that joint prosecutorial activity has "never been more effective" (OECD, 2005).

Championed in the report of 2005 as an example of true cross-national cooperation on antitrust enforcement is a case from 2003 in which the US DOJ worked together with Canadian authorities to prosecute colluders in the Canada-based sulfuric acid sector. As part of its investigation of suspected price-fixing by the mining company, Falconbridge, and Noranda, a copper refiner that produced sulfuric acid as a by-product, the DOJ used the provisions of the Mutual Legal Assistance Treaties (MLAT), signed by the US and Canada in 1990, to request proprietary data on the Canadian firms. Canadian authorities raided the offices of Falconbridge and Noranda and seized incriminating documents, which they then shared with the DOJ. In 2004, the companies challenged the validity of the application of the MLAT, arguing that collusion in their industry was not technically illegal. The Canadian courts ruled that cross-border cooperation between law enforcement agencies in the sulfuric acid case fulfilled one of the primary objectives of the MLATs. It is hoped that this MLAT and other legal assistance treaties in force between the US and its trading partners will support cooperative efforts to curb cartelization.

The OECD's report of 2005 also pointed to the simultaneous prosecutions of 14 producers of heat stabilizers and impact modifiers from nine countries by competition authorities in the US, Canada, the EU, and Japan—a cross-national criminal investigation that included evidentiary office raids. The report complimented antitrust authorities for sharing enforcement tactics even when national laws forbid the conveyance of specific information. The OECD stated, however, that the inability to share confidential corporate information remains the most significant roadblock to battling cartels at the international level. As an example of this institutional entrenchment, the OECD pointed to the insulated switchgear conspiracy, which was uncovered by the EU Commission and simultaneously investigated by authorities in Turkey, a non-member state. The Commission was unable to assist the Turkish investigation due to laws governing the disclosure of confidential data. Clearly, it is not efficient to have parallel investigations being undertaken without the benefit of information sharing.

The OECD strongly supported reforming domestic privacy laws so that antitrust authorities are permitted to share investigatory evidence. The organization argued for "international treaties or domestic laws authorizing a competition authority to exchange confidential information in certain circumstances" (OECD, 2005: 34), and laid out best practices for exchanging information. In addition, the report encouraged proper handling of information that might jeopardize the progress of an investigation, particularly those in which a business has an opportunity to seek relief under a leniency provision.

The OECD reports are not the only forum for debating the merits of harmonizing international competition policy. A nation must balance the interests of its oligopolistic firms with the concerns of an increasingly globalized world. Kerber and Budzinski (2004) noted that some countries may deliberately tolerate anti-competitive behavior if it increases the power of domestic producers. Guzman (2004) outlined the positive changes that joint international prosecutions can foster, including the elimination of costly parallel investigations. In addition, with synchronized competition laws, corporations need not bear the added cost of complying with multiple jurisdictions. Guzman noted that international cooperation can be shallow (e.g. information-sharing) or deep (e.g. coordination of antitrust law through an international body such as the WTO). Still, the competition policies pursued by individual nations reflect domestic goals that make genuine legal uniformity on a global level an unlikely prospect (see Stephen, 2004). Wood (2004) pondered if a global antitrust regime is possible, given that conformity to a worldwide competition framework would necessarily require a loss of sovereignty to a super-national body such as the WTO.

Evaluating current policies—the US Department of Justice's 11th annual competition law & policy workshop

Whereas the OECD documents on "hard core" cartels focus on cooperative means of reforming antitrust law, the US Department of Justice advocates more aggressive steps toward eliminating cartels. In his presentation to the EU Institute in Florence, Italy in June 2006, Thomas Barnett, Assistant

Attorney General of the DOJ's Antitrust Division, laid out a framework for effective cartel deterrence (Barnett, 2006). Barnett argued that since 1994, the DOJ has primarily focused its resources on prosecuting the most egregious violators of antitrust law, particularly executives who "cannot reasonably argue that they failed to grasp the illegality of their actions" (US DOJ, 2006: 3). He also noted that anti-cartel enforcement has been given higher priority than other antitrust activities.

The DOJ is a strong advocate of criminal penalties for individuals who violate US competition statutes, including foreign nationals. At the time of Barnett's presentation, 27 foreign executives had accepted plea agreements that included jail time in the US prisons. In *U.S. v. Ian P. Norris*, Criminal No.: 03-632 (2003), for example, a British citizen was extradited to the US to face criminal charges stemming from his tenure at Morgan Crucible, a ceramic and carbon products manufacturer.

Barnett's conference presentation also addressed the appropriate use of amnesty, in particular, a provision known as "amnesty plus" (US DOJ, 2006: 8). As discussed in chapter five, leniency is commonly granted in cartel prosecutions, even when confessions occur after the investigation is underway. The US DOJ recognizes that one antitrust prosecution can help reveal other cartels. During the DOJ workshop, Deputy Assistant Attorney General Scott Hammond commented on this tendency toward cascading prosecutions:

> Here is a remarkable statistic: Roughly half of the Division's current international cartel investigations were initiated by evidence obtained as a result of an investigation of a completely separate market. Most of the corporate defendants in international cartel cases are multinational companies selling hundreds of different products. It will come as no surprise then to learn that the Division's experience is that if a company is fixing prices in one market, the chances are good that it is doing so in other markets as well.
>
> (US DOJ, 2006: 8)

Amnesty Plus allows executives to confess to all former and current collusive agreements in exchange for comprehensive leniency. As a punitive measure, Amnesty Plus increases penalties if it can be determined that a manager was aware of further antitrust violations within the firm but failed to report those transgressions to the DOJ.

The remainder of the DOJ's presentation in 2006 was devoted to the topic of vigorous criminal sanctions for conspirators within a culpable firm. In particular, the DOJ advocates the use of obstruction of justice charges for executives who fail to fully cooperate in cartel investigations, and publicizes its enforcement efforts so that participants in collusive agreements are aware of the risks of remaining silent. The general thrust of the DOJ's philosophy is that higher penalties, coupled with the threat of exposure, will compel business managers to spurn collusive accords.

Conclusion

This chapter has analyzed the transformation of collusion during the twentieth century, from a largely domestic issue to a global concern. Worldwide cartelization gained a foothold prior to the Great Depression, when international markets were still relatively open to trade. Nations responded to the severe economic contraction of the 1930s by reinstituting significant barriers to trade; international rivalry was restrained and collusion became again a localized phenomenon. After the Kennedy Round of the GATT was completed in 1967, however, tariff and other trade barriers had been reduced to levels that exposed corporations to significant global competition. By the late 1970s, the first global cartels (i.e. those affecting the markets for fasteners and sorbates) were established. By the 1990s, a plethora of price-fixing agreements—most of them international in nature—was exposed. Despite the long list of successful antitrust exposures and prosecutions, it is widely believed that the US DOJ and the EU Commission uncover only about one-sixth of cartels in operation at any given time—a sign of the immense challenge posed to competition authorities.

The globalized reach of collusion has changed the way in which cartel participants manage markets. The complex agreements common to colluding firms before the 1960s—price floors, market segmentation, and quotas—gradually gave way to simplistic targets. The five collusive agreements dating to after c. 1980 that were truly international in nature utilized price targets (see Table 4.4). Unlike market segmentation or quotas, which require firms to refuse sales to certain customers, price targets are less visible to antitrust agencies.

5 Collusion in the industrialized world—the structure of the recent US and European experience

As the decade of the 1980s came to an end the commodity cartels of the previous decades fizzled. As noted in Chapter 4, deep reductions in tariffs under the GATT system beginning in the 1970s had increased global trade. Increasingly, firms found themselves in direct competition with rivals that had previously been constrained by trade barriers—a situation that is likely to make collusion attractive. After a period of relative quiescence, the number of large cartels uncovered in Europe and the US exploded. It is difficult to determine whether this uptick in prosecutions was the product of more aggressive antitrust enforcement. Certainly, policies just coming into force in both the US and Europe provided an impetus for partners within certain cartels to hurry to the magistrate's office in order to be the first to confess to collusion. The competitive pressures of globalization created an environment in which some firms opted to fix prices rather than see their bottom lines threatened.

Collusion in a globalized world—the US and the European Union, 1980–2008

This chapter is devoted to analyzing approximately two dozen collusive arrangements that have been uncovered in the US and the EU. As noted by Connor (2006), over 250 antitrust investigations have been initiated in the US and the European Union between 1990 and 2005. This chapter considers both the prosecutions whose impact has been most widespread, as well as cases—however narrow in breadth—that reveal the workings of cartels or elucidate evolving antitrust responses to collusion. Several of the cases under review involve cartels that were investigated by both the US Department of Justice and the EU Commission, often independent of one another.

The cartels presented here are classified in the following manner:

- Globalized cartels that operate in multiple nations and involve multinational firms.
- Price-fixing arrangements that operate in the US or Europe but involve firms from countries outside the region.
- Regional cartels that involve only corporations from that particular area.

- Localized cartels operating intra-nationally despite exposure to competition from other nations.

Both price-fixing and the antitrust response to collusion are impacted by specific geographical factors.

The truly global cartels

The global lysine cartel: 1992–5

Lysine, a feed additive that promotes muscle growth, is mainly used in the production of poultry, fish and pork. Prior to 1991, the market was dominated by Asian producers. When the American firm Archer Daniels Midland (ADM) entered the US market in 1991, its production levels led almost immediately to a global glut of lysine. Although worldwide sales of this amino acid were growing at a rate of 10 percent per year (reaching $600 million in 1995), excess production quickly drove prices down from $1.20 per pound in 1991 to $0.60 per pound in 1992, gutting the profit margins of ADM and the Asian producers of lysine.

The lysine market was well suited for some form of collusive agreement. Before the entry of ADM, the market was dominated by the Japanese firms, Ajinomoto and Kyowa Hakko Kogyo, and two South Korean corporations, Sewon and Cheil Jedang Corp. The four-firm concentration ratio was over 90 percent in 1994. Lysine is a homogeneous product, and entry into the market is a multi-year process requiring significant capital investment. Lysine output can be tailored to meet demand, so that a cartel arrangement need not manage excess supply. Finally, although soybean meal can act as an imperfect substitute, its lysine concentration is low, and most farmers prefer the feed additive lysine, even if it costs a bit more.

White (2001) provided a thorough examination of the lysine conspiracy and its importance to our understanding of how cartels operate. Connor (1997: 415) noted a few additional characteristics (beyond those listed above) that make the lysine market suitable for price-fixing. First, as an intermediate product, lysine is purchased through private contracts. This lack of visibility makes price manipulation less obvious. Secondly, the collusive agreement is relatively easy to monitor since lysine is typically dispatched in large shipments on a sporadic basis (what Connor referred to as "lumpy sales"). Finally, Connor noted that this market lacked an historical pricing experience that would have permitted tacit cooperation to substitute for collusion. An analysis of the lysine conspiracy by Clarke and Evenett (2003) reached the expected conclusion that cartels will conduct their activities in nations that have a weak antitrust environment.

The lysine cartel began in the spring of 1992, when the head of the lysine division of ADM, Terrance Wilson, instructed his second in command, Mark Whitacre, to meet with Japanese producers to discuss forming a trade association. Connor (2007: 193–203) noted that the cartel's pricing strategy was influenced by the availability of "natural" lysine (i.e. the material contained in soybean meal), which prevented the cartel from significantly raising prices of the dextrose-derived commodity. In June 1992 the firms met in Mexico City to discuss methods for increasing prices, including the imposition of regional sales quotas. At this point, the lysine "trade association" was in violation of US antitrust laws, and was officially recognized as a cartel. The two Korean producers joined the collusive agreement in a later meeting. By early 1993, cooperation between the five firms began to take effect and the price of lysine rose from its low of $0.60 in 1992 to just under $1.00 per pound. Prices collapsed in mid-1993, but firmed again within a year, when they reached $1.30 per pound. In the months preceding the disintegration of the cartel in June 1995, prices fell again to roughly $1.00 per pound.

In late June 1995, FBI agents raided the offices of ADM's lysine plant in Decatur, Illinois. The documents seized provided the identities of other participants in the cartel. In the months that followed, ADM faced not only the pressure of the Justice Department's inquiry, but also experienced an onslaught of dozens of lawsuits by end-users of lysine. Under an agreement reached in April 1996, ADM and its Japanese partners agreed to pay $45 million in compensatory damages to those harmed by the cartel. Given the breadth of the conspiracy and the prosecutorial provision that released ADM from admitting its guilt, the resolution was relatively benign. In August, however, pressure from the Department of Justice's criminal investigation led three of ADM's executives to plead guilty and agree to cooperate fully with the criminal probe. Now the firm was forced to pay $75 million in fines and admit criminality as the instigator of the collusive accord. Unlike most prosecutions for price-fixing, individual executives at ADM were also forced to admit guilt and pay individual fines.

The lysine cartel represents one of the largest industrial conspiracies of all time. It provides insights into the market circumstances that support cartels, including: a high degree of market concentration, the relative invisibility of prices, and the lack of experience of a particular industrial sector with tacit cooperation. Connor (2001) analyzed the fines imposed by the DOJ, and noted that despite the magnitude of the conspiracy, the penalties imposed were not commensurate to the economic damage inflicted by the cartel. The fines were, nevertheless, some of the largest ever imposed in an antitrust case, an indication of the DOJ's determination to dissuade potential conspirators. Even with this highly publicized prosecution, however, just four years later a cartel of even greater scope would be uncovered in the bulk vitamin business.

The global cartel for bulk vitamins

On May 20, 1999, the US Department of Justice announced that the Swiss pharmaceutical firm, Hoffmann–La Roche, had agreed to plead guilty to price-fixing and conspiracy in the world bulk vitamin market. The German pharmaceutical firm, BASF, entered a guilty plea as a co-conspirator, and the French corporation, Rhone Poulenc, cooperated with the Justice Department in exchange for leniency. As the ringleader of the conspiracy, Hoffmann–La Roche agreed to pay a record $500 million fine, while BASF consented to a penalty of $225 million. The Director of Worldwide Marketing for Hoffmann–La Roche was prosecuted for both his participation in the cartel and for lying to investigators, and agreed to a sentence that included jail time (see Department of Justice, 1999).

Collusion in the worldwide vitamin market began in 1989, when Hoffmann–La Roche and BASF forged a price-fixing arrangement to cover bulk sales of vitamins A, B_2, B_5, C, E, and Beta-Carotene, which were used to enrich both animal and human foods. Hoffmann–La Roche and BASF agreed to carve up the global vitamin market, including the US, where little production occurred. In subsequent meetings, the companies plotted how to stabilize prices in a diffuse, oligopolistic market. In 1991, the Japanese producers, Takeda, Eisai, and Daiichi Pharmaceutical, became part of the cartel, and were joined in 1992 by Canada's Chinook and Lonza A.G., from Switzerland. At this point, the cartel controlled the lion's share of world vitamin production.

Market conditions for producers of bulk vitamins had been declining in the 1980s, when excess supply drove prices downward. After the cartel was established, however, prices began to gradually increase, rising from $11.59 per pound in February 1990 to $19.84 per pound in late 1998. So as to avoid detection, the price increases were implemented in a slow and methodical manner. It took nearly a decade for the cartel to crack—longer than the lifespan of most collusive accords and only under the pressure of intense government investigations. As noted by Marshall et al. (2008), the announcement of price increases by the industry looked suspiciously like signaling. During the period in which the cartel functioned, prices increases for various vitamin supplements ranged in the middle to high double-digits, and given the longevity of the collusive accord, it is clear that end-users, particularly US farmers, suffered significant economic damage on these impacts (see Connor, 2007: 274–5). Connor noted the complexity of this conspiracy, with Hoffmann–La Roche the instigator of the collusion, and the Swiss firm, Lonza A.F., taking the lead in the niacin and choline chloride markets. One can only imagine the difficulty antitrust authorities had in determining who was responsible for which part of the scheme.

The most enduring and successful of the recent industrial cartels, the bulk vitamin conspiracy received the highest sanctions of any antitrust case to that date. For the most part, bulk vitamins are well suited to cartelization, as they are homogeneous products without any close substitutes. The dual requirements of significant technical know-how and major capital expenditures act as barriers to entry for new firms. As in the lysine market, the inputs (i.e. bulk vitamins) are not sold directly to consumers and, therefore, prices are easy to conceal. Finally, production can be tailored to fit demand and manipulate prices. An unusual aspect of the vitamin cartel that could have derailed the collusive agreement was the dispersed nature of production. Most successful cartels involve industries with few producers, enabling cooperation, effective policing, and concealment. Although the vitamin cartel began with the world's two largest producers, it grew to include over a dozen manufacturers. Essentially, the continued market dominance of the two major players, Hoffmann–La Roche and BASF, enabled the cartel to function despite its numerous producers.

The sorbate cartel

The sorbate cartel was one of the most long-lived collusive agreements ever uncovered. In operation from 1979 to 1996, the cartel's impact on consumers was muted by the relatively small size of the market. Thus fines announced in 2003 against Hoescht (Germany); and Daicel Chemical, Nippon Synthetic Chemical, Ueno Fine Chemicals, and Chisso (all of Japan), were small in comparison to those meted out in other cartel cases. Sorbates are chemical preservatives used to extend the shelf life of food products. Similar to the situation in the lysine and bulk vitamin markets, sorbates are not sold directly to consumers and price-fixing is, therefore, relatively easy to conceal. In 1998, Japan's Chisso approached the EU Commission under the EU's leniency policy and offered to provide information on the cartel, which had disbanded in 1996. Executives at Chisso may have feared that their co-conspirators would step forward and reap the benefits of being "first confessor."

In a brazen fashion, representatives of the five firms met twice yearly, rotating their meetings between Europe and Japan, and setting both prices and quantities for the affected markets.[1] The Japanese firms usually held a pre-meeting in Tokyo, so that they could approach Hoescht with a uniform proposal for prices and volume. In 2003, when fines were finally leveled against the participants, Hoescht was ordered to pay 99 million euro, while the fines against the three Japanese firms (excluding the "first confessor," Chisso) were far smaller (European Commission, IP/03/1330).

Across the Atlantic, the US DOJ charged four companies with operating a parallel cartel in the sorbate market in the US. The indicted firms included Hoescht, Daicel Chemical, and Nippon Synthetic Chemical—all implicated in the European conspiracy—as well as the US corporation, the Eastman Chemical Company. The collusive arrangement in the US had endured for 17 years and involved over $1 billion in sales (Hess, 2000). In a twist on the usual functioning of a cartel, the participants used the journal *Chemical Market Reporter* to announce price increases through a complex formula meant to hide prices from regulators. In its charges against the cartel, the DOJ accused the companies with price-fixing but also indicted specific executives of Daicel, including the Managing Director, Kunio Kanai. The DOJ's decision in the sorbates case to name both firms and executives in its charges—and include even the threat of significant jail time—provided a new benchmark in antitrust enforcement.

The sorbates industry is well suited to cartelization. The market is dominated by five firms in the European Union and four firms in the US. Similar to lysine and bulk vitamins, sorbates are homogeneous and not marketed directly to the public. Although other food preservatives are available, most are imperfect substitutes to sorbates. In addition, the ability of the cartel participants to communicate price changes through a trade publication enabled the cartel members to "meet without meeting" and avoid tipping off authorities.

The graphite electrode cartel

Graphite electrodes, columns of graphite that have been molded in ceramic, serve as essential components for steel manufactured through the electric-arc process. Production is widely distributed, with major firms in the US, Germany, and Japan. The American firm UCAR International Inc., and SGL Carbon AG of Germany initiated the collusive agreement in 1992. Eventually, the cartel grew to include eight members, including a major producer in Japan (see Table 5.1) In order to conceal their arrangement, the colluders used code names for executives and paid in cash for travel expenses to cartel meetings. Manipulation of graphite electrode prices in the European market continued from that time until 1998, even after antitrust investigations had been launched in the US, Europe, and Canada. The fines that were ultimately paid by several of the participants were increased when the firms tried to impede the investigation.

It was not until July 2001 that fines were announced for the firms involved in the cartel (see EU Commission, IP/01/1010). The largest firms and instigators of the cartel, UCAR International and SGL Carbon, received the highest fines: 50.4 million euro and 80.2 million euro, respectively. The prosecution was assisted by the testimony of Showa Denko of Japan, which acting under the Leniency Notice, received a fine of only 17.4 million euro. The remaining five firms paid fines according to their relative size in the market.

Even though production of grahite electrodes was dispersed across three continents, the industry was nevertheless concentrated, with nearly all of the European market controlled by just eight firms. Graphite electrodes are an indispensable component in the production of steel using electric furnaces—there are no substitutes. In addition, one producer's electrode is largely interchangeable, and this homogeneity permits common pricing practices. As with many of the products already discussed, electrodes are not sold directly to consumers and so their pricing structure is not transparent. The stability and success of the graphite electrodes cartel is not surprising.

Table 5.1 Recent cartels formed in the industrialized world (in violation of antitrust statutes)

Product	*Participants*
Lysine	Archer Daniels Midland, Sewon (S. Korea), Cheil Jedang (S. Korea), Ajinomoto (Japan), Kyowa Hakko Kogyo (Japan)
Bulk Vitamins	BASF (Germany), Hoffman–La Roche (Switzerland), Rhone Poulenc (France), Takeda (Japan), Eisai (Japan), Daiichi Pharmaceuticals (Japan), Chinook (Canada), Lonza A.G. (Switzerland)
Sorbates	Hoescht (Germany), Daicel Chemical (Japan), Nippon Synthetic Chemical ((Japan), Ueno Fine Chemicals (Japan), Chisso (Japan)
Zinc Phosphate	Britannia Alloys and Chemicals LTD (UK), Dr Hans Heubach GmbH & Co. KG (Germany), James M. Brown LTD (UK), Société Nouvelle des Couleurs Zinciques SA (France), Trident Alloys LTD (UK), Waardals Kjemiske Fabrikker A/S (Norway)
Beer	Heineken NV (Netherlands), Heineken Nederland BV (Netherlands), InBev NV and InBev Nederland NV (Netherlands), Grolsch NV (Netherlands), Bavaria NV (Netherlands)
Carbonless Paper	Arjo Wiggins Appleton PLC (UK), Carrs Paper LTD (UK), Mitsubishi HiTech Paper Bielefeld GMbH (Germany), Papierfabrik August Koehler AG (Germany), Zanders Feinpapiere AG (Germany), Bollore SA (France), Papeteries Mougeot SA (France), Distribuidora Vizcainan de Papeles SL (Spain), Papelera Guipuzcoana de Zicunaga SA (Spain), Torraspapel SA (Spain), Sappi Limited (South Africa)
Plasterboard	Société Lafarge (France), BPB LPC (UK), Gebrüder Knauf Westdeutsche Gipswerke KG (Germany), Gyproc Benelux (Belgium)
Graphite Electrodes	SGL Carbon AG (Germany), UCAR International (US), Tokai Carbon Co Ltd. (Japan), Showa Dendo K.K. (Japan), VAW Aluminum AG (Germany), SEC Corporation (Japan), Nippon Carbon Co. Ltd. (Japan), Carbide Graphite Group, Inc (US)
Industrial and Medical Gases	NV Hoek Loos (Netherlands), AGA AB (Sweden), Air Liquide BV (France), Air Products Nederland BV, BOC Group Plc (UK), Messer Nederland BV, Westfalen Gassen Nederland BV
Copper Plumbing Tubes	Boliden AB (Boliden Fabrication AB and Boliden Culvre & Zinc (Sweden), Halcor, S.A. (Greece), HME Nederland BV (Netherlands), IMI plc, IMI Kynoch Ltd. & Yorkshire Copper Tube, Ltd. (UK), KM Europa Metal AG, Trefimetaux SA, Europa Metalli SpA (Germany, Italy and France), Mueller Industries (US, UK, France), Outokumpu Oyj & Outokumpu Copper Products OY (Finland), Wieland Werke AG & Austria Buntmetall AG & Buntmetall Amstetten Ges.m.b.H (Germany)
Soda Ash	ICI (UK) and Solvay (Belgium)
Citric Acid	F. Hoffman–La Roche AG (Switzerland), Archer Daniels Midland (US), Jungbunzlauer AG (Switzerland), Haarmann & Reimer Corp. (US subsidiary of Bayer), Cerestar Bioproducts BV (Netherlands)
Bleaching Chemicals	Solvay (Belgium), Arkema (France), Akzo Nobel (the Netherlands), Kemira (Finland), M Foret (Spain), Snia (Italy), Edison (Italy), Degussa (Germany), L'Air liquide (France)

(*Continued*)

Table 5.1 (*Continued*)

Product	*Participants*
Lifts and Escalators	Kone Group (Belgium, Germany, Luxembourg, the Netherlands), Otis (Belgium, Germany, Luxembourg, the Netherlands), Schindler (Belgium, Germany, Luxembourg, the Netherlands), ThyssenKrupp (Belgium, Germany, Luxembourg, the Netherlands)
Flat Glass	Asahi (Japan), Guardian (US), Pilkington (UK), Saint-Gobain (France)
Gas Insulated Switchgear	ABB (Switzerland), Alston (France), Areva (France), Fuji Electric (Japan), Hitachi (Japan), Japan AE Power Systems, Mitsubishi Electric (Japan), Schneider (France), Siemens (Germany), Siemens (Austria), Toshiba (Japan)
Synthetic Rubber	Bayer (Germany), Tosoh (Japan), DuPont (US), Dow (US), ENI (Italy), Denka (Japan)
DRAM Chips	Elpida (Japan), Infineon (Germany), Hynix (S. Korea), and Samsung (S. Korea)
Marine Hose	Individuals, not firms
Nucleotides (Flavor Enhancer)	Ajinomoto Co. (Japan), Cheil Jedang (South Korea), Daesang Co. (South Korea)
Fasteners)	Prym Group (UK), Coats (Germany), Scovill Group (US), YKK (Japan), A. Raymond SARL (a consortium of 20 firms), Berning & Sohne (Germany
Art Auction Services	Sotheby's (US), Christie's (UK)
Paraffin	Royal Dutch/Shell (UK, the Netherlands), ENI (Italy), Sasol (South Africa), Exxon-Mobil (US), Tudapetrol (Germany), Hansen & Rosenthal (Germany), MOL (Hungary), Total (France), RWE (Germany), Repsol (Spain)
Natural Gas	E.ON AG Ruhrgas (Germany) and GDF Suez SA (France)
Air Passenger/ Freight Cartel	Lufthansa (Germany), Virgin Atlantic (UK), (Partial List) British Air (UK), Korean Airways (S. Korea), Japan Airlines, Air France-KLM (France), Cathay Pacific (Hong Kong), Martinair Holland (the Netherlands), SAS (Denmark, Norway, Sweden)
TFT-LCD Displays	LG Display (S. Korea), Chunghwa Picture Tubes (Taiwan), Sharp Corporation (Japan)
Consumer Credit Services	Visa USA (US), MasterCard (US)

Running concurrently with the European Commission's prosecution of the cartel was a case brought by the US Department of Justice against four corporations and one individual, Robert Hart, for manipulating prices in the graphite electrode market in the US. Four of the firms targeted by the EU Commission also pled guilty to US antitrust charges: UCAR International of the US; Showa Denko Carbon and Tokai Carbon of Japan; and SGL Carbon of Germany (for details on the plea bargain and the subsequent criminal case against Hart, see *U.S. v. Robert Hart*, USDC, Pennsylvania, 99-595). The fines imposed against the Japanese firms were relatively minor ($32.5 million for Showa Denko and $6 million for Tokai Carbon), but UCAR was fined $110 million, and SGL Carbon $135 million. Although the conspiracy in the US involved only four firms (as opposed to eight in the EU case), the corporations controlled over three-quarters of the American market for graphite electrodes. The combined fines imposed by both the EU Commission and the US courts were very large in relation to the size of the electrode market, estimated at $275 million per year in the US, an outcome that should discourage future participation in an illicit agreement.

The Trans-Atlantic Conference Agreement "cartel" (TACA: A Misstep in Antitrust Enforcement)

In 1998, the EU Commission imposed the hefty fine of 273 million euro on the 16 freight carriers that made up the Trans-Atlantic Conference Agreement (TACA). The TACA carriers operated under what amounted to a legal price-fixing agreement. Under this accord (contained in Council Regulation 4056/86), carriers were able to fix both rates and shipping volume between northern Europe and the United States. Although the EU Commission recognized this exemption, it argued that price-fixing on the inland segment of international routes was not covered by 4056/86, and yet shipping firms were setting rates for this component of their business. The Commission further argued that manipulation of pricing on service contracts had occurred.

The EU Commission's action against TACA illustrates what occurs when competition authorities press too hard against minor violations of antitrust exemptions. The members of TACA appealed the Commission's decision to the Court of First Instance, which annulled the fines. The Court indicated that the Commission had acted inappropriately in its evaluation of the evidence of collusion, and had not given the firms a sufficient opportunity to respond to the complaint. The reversal of the ruling was considered a significant blow to the Commission's stature, particularly since it followed a series of defeats in the courts regarding merger rulings. The Court affirmed that some of the practices of TACA were anti-competitive, but concluded that the Commission's violation of procedures warranted dismissing the fines. Jaspers (2004) provides an analysis of the TACA case and offers some insights into the significance of the overturned verdict.

The citric acid cartel

Some corporations have been implicated in multiple collusive schemes. Such is the case with Hoffmann–La Roche, which after being fined for its participation in the bulk vitamin cartel in 1999, was found guilty in 2001 of participating in a worldwide conspiracy to manipulate prices in the citric acid market. Not only did Hoffmann–La Roche take part in the cartel, but together with Archer Daniels Midland of the US acted as a leader of the agreement. As a repeat offender, Hoffmann–La Roche received higher penalties because of its culpability in the earlier case.

Citric acid is used as a flavor enhancer and preservative in the production of beverages and canned fruits. Owing to its stabilizing qualities, citric acid is also an ingredient in the pharmaceutical and cosmetics industries. The citric acid conspiracy began in March 1991, when representatives of Archer Daniels Midland, Haarmann & Reimer Corporation (a US concern), Hoffmann–La Roche, and Switzerland's Jungbunzlauer held a clandestine meeting in Basel. Cerestar Bioproducts (the Netherlands) joined the cartel in the spring of 1992. What followed were numerous conferences, including technical gatherings, labeled "sherpa" meetings, and the more important strategic summits, branded "Masters" meetings. Like most of the collusive agreements already discussed, the five firms did not set the price for citric acid, but instead eliminated normal modes of competition that would put downward pressure on prices. In particular, the participants agreed to price-floors; they also promised to share information, eliminate price discounts, and honor sales quotas (EU Commission, IP/01/1743). Any firm that exceeded its quota was obligated to make payments to the other members, an arrangement that was somewhat unique to this cartel. When Chinese firms began to enter the market for citric acid, largely in response to the increased prices brought about by the cartel, the colluders counter-attacked with selective price cuts.

The investigation of the citric acid cartel began in the US and Canada, with the EU Commission undertaking its own case in 1997. The US prosecution initially centered on the prosecution of ADM, but the conspiracy was so complex that it produced a litany of trials and plea-bargains that dragged on for months. Beginning in August 2006, two Japanese firms, the repeat-offenders, Ajinomoto and Kyowa Hakko Kogyo, entered guilty pleas to conspiracy in the citric acid market and were each fined $10 million. At the same time, Sewon America, Inc. (a subsidiary of the repeat-colluder, Sewon Company, of South Korea) agreed to pay a fine for its participation in the cartel. In October 1996, ADM pleaded guilty to conspiring to manipulate prices in both the lysine and citric acid markets and was fined a collective $100 million. Cheil Jedang (South Korea) admitted to the conspiracy in December of that year, and was fined $1.25 million. Finally, German-based Bayer, through its subsidiary in the US, pleaded guilty in January 1997 to participating in the cartel and was fined $50 million. The EU Commission announced significant fines in December 2001, with cartel managers, Hoffmann–La Roche and ADM, receiving the highest penalties—63.5 million euro and 39.7 million euro, respectively. Cerestar Bioproducts cooperated with the EC's investigation and was ultimately ordered to pay only 170 thousand euro.

As in the other cartels of the food additives industry (lysine, sorbates, and bulk vitamins), the citric acid market is susceptible to collusion. In particular, price manipulation of citric acid can be hidden because of the product's intermediate role in manufacturing. In addition, the industry is highly concentrated. As with the larger food additives sector, the citric acid market does not possess the barriers to entry that will keep out competition in the medium to long term. Indeed, China has emerged as a powerful new source for these commodities, their entry into the market an unintended consequence of the price increases that collusion brings.

The marine hose market

Marine hose is durable rubber tubing used to transfer petroleum from tanker ships to on-shore storage facilities. The hose is crucial to oil extraction and distribution. Hundreds of millions of dollars worth of marine hose are sold annually. On May 2, 2007, eight foreign executives were arrested on bid-rigging charges stemming from an illegal collusive agreement of marine hose. According to a Department of Justice document (US DOJ, December 3, 2007), price-fixing in this sector had been occurring since 1999. Firms in this cartel agreed to:

- not compete for one another's customers;
- submit intentionally high bids as a means of directing sales to certain firms;
- provide extensive customer information to a consultant who acted as cartel manager, overseeing the purchase and distribution of marine hose.

The co-conspirators agreed to utilize code names to conceal their identities. Cartel meetings were generally held overseas (testimony indicated that London and Bangkok were favorite locations). Ultimately, two other participants were indicted, bringing to ten the number of managers charged in the case.

The federal complaint against the marine hose cartel singled out individuals who had directed the Central Selling Point, together with executives from specific firms (Manuli Rubber Industries, Italy; Trelleborg Industries, Sweden; and Bridgestone Corporation, Japan). Ultimately, two executives from Trelleborg pleaded guilty to criminal charges of conspiracy (see DOJ, November 6, 2007).

According to DOJ documents, the firms involved in the marine hose conspiracy used a central selling point to control the distribution and price of their product, in a fashion similar to that of the De Beers diamond cartel. Like most of the goods that have been subject to collusive accords, marine hose is homogeneous, its suppliers are few, and there are no reasonable substitutes. Marine hose is an intermediate good, with final sales to businesses, not consumers.

Despite the extensive criminal charges and numerous convictions that the DOJ has already secured in this case, the difficulties for members of the marine hose cartel are just beginning. In May 2008, the EU Commission announced that it was initiating its own prosecution against a number of European manufacturers of marine hose. This action follows the Commission's raids on the offices of British, French, and Italian producers in the spring of 2007. Firms that have received "objections" from the Commission include Continental (Germany), Dunlop Oil and Marine (UK, but owned by Continental), and the Swedish Trelleborg. In addition, Japan's Fair Trade Commission issued cease and desist orders against the alleged members of the cartel—a sign that Japanese antitrust enforcement may be awakening. The complexity of these interlocking investigations and prosecutions suggests that it may be years before prosecutions of the marine hose cartel run their course.

The food flavoring cartel

The ability of some cartels to fly under the radar of antitrust authorities sometimes owes to the relatively minor role of an input in the production of other products. On August 27, 2001, the US Department of Justice announced guilty pleas by Japan's Ajinomoto Co., Inc., Daesang Japan Inc., and the South Korean Cheil DeJang Corporation for price-fixing of the world nucleotide market. Derived from simple sugars, nucleotides are used to enhance food flavors. Their market is relatively small. Concurrent with the US investigation, the EU Commission brought charges against the aforementioned firms and also implicated Takeda Chemical of Japan. EU authorities concluded that the defendants had manipulated the nucleotides market on the Continent from 1988 to 1998, shutting down only when they became aware of the pending investigation, which started in 1999. Price-fixing in the US nucleotides market took place between 1992 and 1998. The DOJ determined that the Asian companies met regularly to both determine the market price of nucleotides and also allocate the available customers over the three firms. The fines imposed on the cartel members by authorities from both sides of the Atlantic were quite small. Ajinomoto was assessed $6 million by the DOJ and 15.54 million euro by the EU Commission. Cheil Jedang paid a $3 million fine for activities in the US, and 2.74 million euro for its participation in the European cartel. Fines of this size are unlikely to provide adequate deterrence to businesses considering the benefits and risks of collusion.

Something completely different—the art auction cartel

In 2002, the EU Commission announced a "Statement of Objections" on the illicit cooperation between auction houses, Christie's and Sotheby's (EU Commission, IP/02/595). This preliminary step toward an antitrust prosecution detailed cooperative undertakings between Christie's and Sotheby's, specifically: the fixing of commission fees, advances to sellers, and payment conditions. Although there are other auction houses for fine art sales, Christie's and Sotheby's are internationally known establishments vying for the same upper-tier clientele. In effect, this segment of the auction business is duopolistic (the EU Commission estimated the two-firm concentration ratio to be 90 percent), and intense competition had developed between the two houses prior to the beginning of illegal cooperation.

The EU Commission started its investigation in 2000, when Christie's decided to use the Leniency Notice to admit its collusion with Sotheby's. Christie's simultaneously notified both the Commission and the US Department of Justice. The ensuing investigation, which was concluded in the European Union in October 2002 (EU Commission, IP/02/1585), determined that the auction houses had cooperated on pricing for seven years. As part of its findings, the Commission determined that secret meetings had been held in the residences of the firms' CEOs. Because of its cooperation in the investigation, Christie's received full immunity under the Leniency Notice, whereas Sotheby's was fined 20.4 million euro, an amount equal to 6 percent of its annual sales. For its cooperation with investigators, Sotheby's penalty was reduced by 40 percent.

In its independent prosecution of Christie's and Sotheby's, the US DOJ filed a complaint of collusive activities by the firms over the period from 1993 to 1999. In October 2000, the DOJ announced that Sotheby's had agreed to plead guilty to price fixing charges, and would be fined $45 million. Simultaneously, the company's former CEO, Diana Brooks, also pleaded guilty to price-fixing charges. The DOJ determined that Sotheby's and Christie's had engaged in numerous anti-competitive practices, including:

- fixing commissions, which elevated prices in the high-end auction industry;
- publishing rate schedules to affirm compliance with the collusive agreement and exchanging customer information;
- agreeing not to make interest-free loans to those who placed goods on consignment;
- consenting not to make charitable contributions a part of the pricing structure of their firms.

Later criminal prosecutions led to charges and a conviction against Alfred Taubman, the former chairman of Sotheby's. As in the EU investigation, Christie's cooperated with the probe and was not fined. Additional details on the structure and activities of the art auction cartel can be found in Ashenfelter and Graddy (2004).

The collusive agreement reached by Sotheby's and Christie's was different from most cartels because it set fees and conditions of sale rather than fixed prices for their services. Still, the services offered by Sotheby's and Christie's conform in interesting ways to the conditions for successful cartelization of a commodity: it is a homogenous "product," provided by a limited number of producers in a market where entry is difficult since success depends on a business's long-term reputation. Although services such as those offered by E-Bay might be considered substitutes, until recently, purveyors of high-end art did not generally turn to such venues as a viable marketing outlet.

The air passenger and freight cartel

An on-going investigation by the US DOJ and the EU Commission into the pricing and surcharge practices of international airlines has uncovered one of the world's most complex cartels. It is believed that a total of 30 airlines may have colluded in a complex arrangement to boost both fees and surcharges. Unlike the other cartels examined here, both the DOJ and Commission inquiries into the air passenger and freight charges can be described as rolling investigations. Although several firms have admitted guilt and agreed to financial penalties, the prosecution of the cartel will likely continue well into the future.

The recent financial stresses on the major international carriers, particularly the impact of rapidly rising fuel costs, help to explain the rise of collusion in the airline industry. After years of losses, bankruptcies, and forced mergers, airline executives sought relief through coordinated increases in fees and fuel surcharges. With so many participants and an array of pricing mechanism in effect, it is difficult to date the inception of the cartel, but price-fixing was implemented as far back as 2000. The US DOJ has initiated multiple cases against multiple conspirators, and has concluded prosecutions against nine airlines. As of the time of publication, the EU Commission is still in the investigative stage and has conducted raids and notified a number of airlines that they are being scrutinized for participating in the cartel.

The US DOJ's antitrust prosecution of the airline industry began with Lufthansa Airlines' admission of conspiracy to raise fees and charges, expressed in a September 2006 plea deal that called for a fine of $85 million in exchange for conditional immunity against future class-action lawsuits. In August of that year, the DOJ had also accepted an offer of cooperation from Virgin Atlantic Airways, which was granted conditional immunity from fines.

The seriousness with which the DOJ has pursued its agenda with the airline sector is best exemplified by the case it brought against British Airways and Korean Airlines. Virgin reported that it had been colluding with that competitor since 2004. In a plea bargain announced by the DOJ on 1 August 2007, British Airways and Korean Airlines admitted to price-fixing, in violation of the Sherman Act, and agreed to pay criminal fines for colluding. According to the DOJ's media release, the fuel surcharge for a passenger on British Airways in 2004 was approximately 10 dollars per ticket. Two years later, the surcharge had risen to almost $110 per ticket.

At the same time, the fuel surcharge paid by freight shippers rose from four cents per kilogram to 72 cents per kilogram. The DOJ determined that British Airways had participated in the air cargo cartel between March 2002 and February 2006, with consumers ultimately footing the bill for the overcharges on the billions of dollars of goods shipped (US DOJ, press release, August 1, 2007).

It was also established that between August 2004 and February 2006, British Airways had conspired with its competitors to raise fuel surcharges for passengers on its long-haul flights. Korean Airlines was also charged with engaging in collusion in both its air passenger and cargo businesses, from 2000 to 2006. British Airways and Korean Airlines admitted to holding meetings to discuss and set prices, and arranging subsequent gatherings to monitor compliance. Each firm received a fine of $300 million, but no criminal charges were brought against their executives. Only later did the DOJ announce that prior to its arrangement with British Airways, Korean Airlines had been colluding with the Korean carrier, Asiana Airlines (an accord that remained in force from 2000 to 2006). In this lawsuit, Korean Airlines and Asiana Airlines pleaded guilty to price-fixing and were each fined $50 million (US DOJ, press release, April 9, 2009).

Soon after its public declaration of August 2007, the DOJ released a long list of additional alleged conspirators, including Japan Airlines, Air New Zealand, Air France, KLM Royal Dutch Air, Martinair Holland, SAS Cargo Group, Singapore Airlines, Cathay Pacific, and Qantas. Qantas pleaded guilty to conspiracy in November 2007 and was fined $61 million. In April 2008, Japan Airlines, the largest mover of freight between the US and Japan, was fined $110 million for price-fixing. The following month, the DOJ announced that the head of US freight operations for Qantas had received an eight-month sentence and a $21,000 fine for his role in the conspiracy, and five additional employees of the airline were facing charges. In late June 2008, additional guilty pleas were obtained from Air France–KLM (now operating as a single firm following a merger), Cathay Pacific, Martinair Holland, and SAS Cargo Group. The penalties against this group totaled $504 million, with Air France–KLM bearing $350 million of this amount.

To date, the fines imposed by the Department of Justice against the airline sector are approaching $1.5 billion. It is likely that the DOJ will impose additional penalties against the airline industry. The EU Commission's investigation of the airline sector is still in its early stages, but will likely result in separate fines for the firms involved. After both the DOJ and the Commission complete their prosecutions, it is likely that the air passenger and cargo conspiracy will produce fines far beyond those levied in the bulk vitamin case.

The conspiracies among air carriers succeeded in spite of several factors that generally work against successful collusion. First, the product subject to collusion is an intangible rather than a good; freight and passenger traffic is not an intermediate product, so price increases are more apparent to customers. Making the collusion even riskier is the proliferation of consumer watchdog organizations that publicize the pricing practices of the airline industry. Lastly, no other cartel has had so many participants, and therefore, so many possibilities of dissension and confession.

Regional cartels with global participants

The European elevator cartel

At the time it was revealed, the vitamin cartel was considered the most egregious of the collusive agreements, and as such, its participants received the largest fines. In February 2007, the EU Commission announced a new record fine, levied against an international elevator cartel that was operating in Belgium, the Netherlands, Germany, and Luxembourg (European Commission, IP/07/209). The companies involved, Otis (a division of United Technologies) of the US, Schindler of Switzerland, Kone of Finland, and ThyssenKrupp of Germany, were fined a combined 992 million euro ($1.3 billion). The judgment against ThyssenKrupp alone, 480 million euro, reflected both the seriousness of the antitrust violation and the fact that the company was a repeat offender, found culpable in the stainless steel cartel of the 1990s. The elevator companies neither contested the EU Commission's findings nor requested a hearing to address the allegations, but rather acquiesced to the penalties. In this instance, the Leniency Programme did not induce any of the participants to come forward and reveal the existence of the cartel. For their cooperation in the Commission's investigations, however, leniency was granted to Kone, for its activities in Belgium and Luxembourg, and Otis, for its operations in the Netherlands.

Representatives of the elevator cartel took exceptional steps to avoid detection by the authorities. Negotiations were held in restaurants and bars, and phone calls between participants were made using pre-paid cards. That discussions involved top management runs against the typical excuse that "renegade" middle managers are responsible for the collusive behavior. Information exchanged by the conspiratorial companies included pricing strategies, whose aim was to lock in existing market shares. One of the most objectionable aspects of the cartel was the fact that elevator sales include long-term service contracts, some twenty years in duration; in setting its fines, the Commission considered the implications of this extended, dependent relationship between buyer and seller. Ironically, the headquarters of the EU Commission building in Brussels was equipped with elevator equipment installed during the cartel period.

The flat glass cartel

Surprise inspections of glass producers, Asahi (Japan), Guardian (US), Pilkington (UK) and Saint-Gobain (France), were carried out by enforcement officers of the EU Commission in February and March of 2005. The offices of the glass trade group, the European Association of Flat Glass Producers (EAFGP), were also raided. The Commission was acting on its own, without the cooperation of any of the targeted firms. Shortly thereafter, Asahi applied for relief under the Leniency Notice, and its significant assistance to the Commission resulted in a reduction of the fines.

The flat glass cartel controlled the market for plain and specialty glass used in the construction industry. Member firms of the EAFGP produced glass inputs (laminated and basic float, low emission, and mirrored) that were cut for windows, mirrors, and other products. The four cartel members produced 80 percent of flat glass sold in the European market, whose value was estimated at 1.7 billion euro in 2004 (European Commission, P/07/1781). Representatives of the corporations met to share sensitive financial information and establish minimum prices. In addition, a firm designated as the "price leader" was to artificially raise flat glass prices. The EU Commission's investigation established that market manipulation had begun in early 2004. The short tenure of the cartel helps explain why the participants never adopted the secretive techniques (e.g. fictitious names, phony e-mail accounts, etc.) common to collusive agreements. Extreme tactics of duplicity seem to develop when the fear of exposure is sustained over time.

The fines imposed by the EU Commission against the members of the flat glass cartel were substantial. Asashi of Japan had its fine significantly reduced to 85 million euro in exchange for its early cooperation with antitrust authorities. The largest penalty (185 million euro) was paid by the American company Guardian. Total fines paid by the four firms reached 487 million euro—a substantial amount given the short duration of the cartel.

Collusion in the flat glass market was facilitated by the nature of the product. Plate glass is an intermediate good, sold to processors of, among other things, windows, fire-retardant glass, and mirrors. The EU Commission began the antitrust investigation without the aid of a confessor, which suggests that glass processors might have been complaining of unjustified price increases. In the absence of such complaints, the price increases would have been invisible, hidden in the larger costs of home construction and remodeling.

The gas insulated switchgear cartel

The gas insulated switchgear (GIS) is a piece of heavy equipment used to regulate energy flows in electric substations. The eleven major suppliers of GIS to the European market produce similar, if somewhat differentiated, products (see Table 5.1). Electric power utilities search for the insulated switchgear based on price rather than brand. Since the European market has numerous producers and the product is somewhat interchangeable, it is expected that pricing will be competitive. From 1988 to 2004, the industry circumvented price competition by engaging in a number of illegal activities. As in other cartelized markets, separation between the product and the end-consumers of electricity allowed the cartel to operate unnoticed. The higher prices paid by utilities to acquire GIS resulted in higher prices.

The investigation of the switchgear industry began in May 2004, when ABB of Switzerland used the Leniency Notice to reveal the existence of the cartel and apply for immunity. The subsequent investigation revealed that bid-rigging and market exclusion agreements had been in place since 1988. The cartel functioned both by coordinating contract bidding by its members and by establishing minimum bidding prices. Japanese firms in the accord agreed not to sell in Europe, and European companies made a similar commitment to refrain from bidding on contracts in Japan. Global quotas were set so that if a firm secured a contract outside its domestic market, it was counted towards the corporation's allotment. The prohibition on cross-regional sales created highly concentrated oligopoly markets in both Europe and Japan, thereby facilitating cooperation and price-setting.

Although there are times in oligopolistic markets when corporations unknowingly cross the line between tacit cooperation and illegal behavior, the members of the GIS trade association engaged in willful collusion. For example, executives were given code names for communications, and in the final years of the cartel, correspondence was conducted using untraceable e-mail addresses. In fact, cartel "regulations" banned the use of home or office e-mail addresses that could be traced to the individuals involved in the collusion.

The EU Commission concluded its investigation in January 2007, when it announced significant fines for the members of the switchgear cartel. Siemens (Germany), which had acted as the cartel's leader, was ordered to pay 396.6 million euro, one of the highest fines in European antitrust history. The second highest penalty, 118.6 million euro, was imposed on Mitsubishi Electric (Japan). In all, three French, five Japanese, one Austrian, and one German firm were fined a total of 750.7 million euro (EU Commission IP/07/08). Although ABB (Switzerland) was a "repeat offender," its fines, which would otherwise have exceeded 215 million euro, were eliminated under the Leniency Notice. The EU Commission's decision to fine Japanese firms, whose participation in the cartel was based on a promise not to sell their products in Europe, broke new ground in antitrust enforcement, for it was argued that a calculated absence from a market could represent a deliberate restraint of trade. As was the case with many of the previous collusive agreements, the EU Commission actively encouraged firms harmed by the cartel to seek civil penalties.

The synthetic (chloroprene) rubber cartel

As noted in Chapter 3, the market for rubber comprises both the natural product and a synthetic substitute, produced with the raw input of hydrocarbons. One form of synthetic rubber, chloroprene, can withstand significant stress and then revert to its original shape. This durability makes it suitable for use in hoses, power transmission belts, and v-belts. It is also used in the manufacture of diving equipment and shoes.

The cartel for chloroprene rubber operated solely in Europe, with six member firms. No attractive substitutes for chloroprene rubber exist among the other synthetic materials. Once again, chloroprene rubber is an intermediate input and therefore market pricing is not transparent.

In 2002, Bayer (Germany) revealed the existence of the cartel and applied for relief under the Leniency Notice. The EU Commission conducted surprise inspections in March and July of 2003, and soon several participating firms confessed and applied for leniency. Tosoh of Japan was granted a 50 per cent reduction in fines as a second confessor, and DuPont and Dow Chemical, both US firms, were granted penalty reductions of 25 per cent. ENI of Italy and Denka of Japan paid their full penalties. From 1993 to 2002, the cartel utilized standard price-fixing agreements to stabilize synthetic rubber prices, and agreed to share client information and data on market shares.

The imposition of penalties against the members of the chloroprene rubber cartel was complicated by the application of four firms for leniency. In addition, both Bayer and ENI were repeat offenders, and yet because of its role as first confessor, Bayer received complete immunity and the repeal of its fine of 201 million euro. Conversely, owing to previous collusive undertakings, ENI saw its fine increased by 60 per cent, to 132 million euro. In the midst of merger talks at the time of the Commission's ruling, the fines handed to DuPont and Dow are difficult to unravel because market shares were in flux. The former's "direct" fine totaled 59.3 million euro after a reduction of 19.8 million euro, while the "indirect" penalty for Dow was 44.3 million euro after a reduction of 16.2 million euro. Finally, Denka of Japan paid a total of 47 million euro for its role in the cartel. Given that several of the participants are industrial giants, the fines imposed did not inflict significant harm to earnings.

The "Paraffin Mafia"—collusion in the European wax market

This section addresses one of the most ambitious price-fixing agreements ever uncovered. The cartel, widely known as the "Paraffin Mafia," controlled prices for a type of wax used in the manufacture of a wide variety of products. Even for a product as seemingly inessential as wax, the economic consequences of collusion were felt in many industries. Paraffin, in fact, is a crucial input in the manufacture of tires, paper cups and plates, packaging, adhesives, candles, and wax paper. In 2008, it was estimated that annual sales of paraffin in the European market were 500 million euro.

The price-fixing agreements for paraffin were in place from 1992 to 2005. The alleged leader of the "Mafia" was Sasol of South Africa, whose executives denied their alleged role as cartel manager. Nine other firms were implicated in the cartel, including petroleum giants Exxon–Mobil and Royal–Dutch Shell. The agreements reached by the ten firms covered approximately 75 percent of the European paraffin market, a relatively low market concentration for a functioning cartel. In addition to its nickname, "the Paraffin Mafia," the cartel was also known as the "Blauer Salon," the name of a bar in Hamburg where the conspirators held their first meeting. Prices and market shares were established at "conferences" held in hotels throughout Europe.

Royal–Dutch Shell was the first firm to expose the conspiracy. Owing to its participation in the earlier rubber cartel, Shell could have seen its projected fine of 96 million euro raised to 153 million, but as first confessor it received complete immunity. The other repeat offender, ENI of Italy, had previously participated in a price-fixing arrangement in the PVC market and so its fine was raised to 29 million euro. Sasol, the alleged leader of the cartel—a status that currently earns a company a 50 percent increase in fines—received the highest penalty; after a reduction for belated cooperation in the investigation, it was ordered to pay 318 million euro. Total of France was fined 128 million euro. The American firm Exxon–Mobil was handed a penalty of 83 million euro, a fine reduced by 7 percent in recognition of the small part the firm played in the investigation. The remaining five firms received penalties ranging from 12 million to 37 million euro (for a list of the conspirators, see Table 5.1). The fines imposed by the EU Commission on the paraffin cartel reached 650 million euro, the fourth largest aggregate penalty ever imposed for a collusive accord in Europe. The harshness of the fines reflects new EU Commission guidelines that increase penalties by 100 percent for each year the cartel is in operation.[2] These hefty penalties reflect the Commission's frustration with the persistence of collusion. As antitrust authorities in Europe and the US seek to establish monetary damages large enough to deter price-fixing, it is likely firms will pay a higher price for collusion.

The US DRAM conspiracy

The market for DRAM (Dynamic Random Access Memory) chips has posed special problems for regulators since the 1980s, when the product came to be regarded as yet another commodity in computer manufacturing. The ascent of the next generation of chips, based on RISC (Reduced Instruction Computing) technology, forced DRAM producers to market their device as a homogeneous product, with one manufacturer's output a near perfect substitute for another's. In an anti-dumping case pursued by the Reagan Administration in 1985, significant fines were imposed under the competition rules of the General Agreement on Tariffs and Trade (GATT). US manufacturers initiated the complaint through the DOJ in response to a flood of below-cost chips into the US market. By September 1986, an agreement had been reached between Japan and the US to eliminate the dumping of DRAMs, and the formal GATT complaint was withdrawn. The persistence of excess capacity in the industry, and the relatively low rate of return available on DRAM sales, made future attempts at market manipulation inevitable.

In 2006, the DOJ announced that Japan's Elpida Memory (a spin-off of Hitachi Ltd. and NEC) had pleaded guilty to charges of price-fixing in the global computer chip sector, and the company was fined $84 million. Elpida was the fourth company to plead guilty to collusion in the DRAM market. Infineon Technologies of Germany, which admitted to the conspiracy in October 2004, was fined $160 million. This was followed by guilty pleas from the South Korean firms, Hynix Semiconductor, in May 2005, and Samsung Semiconductor, in November of that year. These admissions led to fines of $185 million for Hynix and $300 million for Samsung. According to DOJ documents (US DOJ, press release, 2006), the four firms had negotiated agreements to set prices for major computer and server manufacturers in the US, including Dell Inc., Compaq Computer Co., Hewlett-Packard Co., Apple Computer, Inc., International Business Machines Co., Gateway, Inc., and Sun Microsystems. Nearly every US firm that produced personal computers and servers was affected. The two-count felony indictment against Elpida and its co-conspirators in 2006 alleged that the companies met to discuss marketing strategies for their chips and to establish pricing guidelines for the DRAM market. The cartel members had also agreed to exchange future information on sales to ensure that the agreement remained in force. In addition to price-fixing, Elpida was also charged with bid-rigging in a chip sale to Sun Microsystems. By January 2006, fines for the DRAM cartel totaled over $700 million, and still the investigation remained open. As part of its guilty plea, Elpida agreed to cooperate with the DOJ in its continuing investigation of the computer chip market. Beyond the large fines imposed on the cartel's members, several individuals were charged with criminal activity, including four executives of Infineon, who entered guilty pleas in December 2004, and were sentenced to short jail terms and also ordered to pay significant fines. Additional prosecutions in the DRAM sector are likely, especially since individual states (e.g. New York) have opened their own antitrust investigations.

The DRAM market conforms well to the conditions necessary for collusion. First, the chips are homogeneous across manufacturers, especially since the 1980s, when they became a commodity product. Even with the inflated prices that collusion produces, DRAMS were still more desirable processors than their substitute, the more expensive RISC. Finally, as rates of return in the DRAM market have fallen, industry concentration has risen, so that the four firms prosecuted for collusion by the DOJ represented nearly all the DRAM production sold in the US.

The fasteners cartel

During the last quarter of the twentieth century, a series of parallel cartels formed in the market for fasteners—zippers, snap buttons, and rivets, together with the machinery that affixes these devices to products. The first cartel, formed in 1977, included the Prym Group, from the UK, and Coats, from Germany. The EU Commission took notice of a second cartel that operated from 1991 to 2001. Joining the Prym Group and Coats corporations in this later collusive accord were the Scovill Group (US), YKK (Japan), A Raymond S.A.R.L. (a network of companies operating in over 20 countries), and Berning & Sohne (Germany). In a move that portends a change in the Commission's attitude towards trade associations, the German industry group Fachverband Verbindungs-und Befestigungstechnik was also fined a symbolic 1,000 euro. This iteration of the cartel involved coordinated price increases only (EU Commission, IP/07/1362). Functioning as a cartel within a cartel, Prym Group and YKK raised their cooperation to a higher level between 1999 and 2003, when the two firms allocated customers and fixed prices by product and sales region.

Once the EU Commission began its investigation, the cartel members became compliant. The first to come forward with information on the cartel, the Prym Group, received partial immunity under the Leniency Notice and reduced fines of 40.6 million euro. Owing to their delayed cooperation with authorities, YKK and Coats paid stiffer fines, of 150.3 million euro and 122.4 million euro, respectively. The other members of the cartel received only minor fines.

In considering the conditions for successful collusion, the fasteners' cartel presents an exception to the rule that products subject to price-fixing be homogeneous. It was only in the final phase of the cartel's history, when Prym Group and YKK were holding separate negotiations, that uniform pricing of specific products was attempted. The fasteners industry is not highly concentrated, another factor working against fruitful cartelization. In the end, it was market segmentation rather than price controls that secured the cooperation needed to maintain collusion for over 20 years. With their dominant market position, the six members of the fasteners cartel saw their collusive agreement flourish even without broad participation in the sector.

Cartelization of the TFT-LCD display panel industry

Soon after the liquid crystal display (LCD) panel was patented in Taiwan in 1996, it became the industry standard, supplanting the bulky cathode ray tubes in screen technology. By 2006, annual sales of LCD panels had reached an estimated $70 billion. The industry is highly concentrated, with only a few firms producing most of the output. Of these, LG Display Co., Ltd. (South Korea), Chunghwa Picture Tubes Ltd. (Taiwan), and Sharp Corporation (Japan) formed a cartel in 2001. The interconnectedness of the sector is apparent from a reading of the US DOJ's complaint, in which the subsidiaries of LG Display were identified as LG Philips LCD Co. (a joint venture with Philips Electronics and LG Electronics) and LG

Display America, a California-based affiliate (see US DOJ, press release, November 12, 2008). The DOJ concentrated its investigation specifically on the market for TFT–LCD (Thin-Film Transistor–Liquid Crystal Display) panels. Although production of the TFT–LCD panels is technologically advanced, none of the producers could claim to have achieved a breakthrough that would differentiate their product from those sold by competitors. The computer, television, and cell phone manufacturers regarded TFT–LCD panels as a homogeneous product.

Although the TFT–LCD industry was initially profitable, excess capacity and falling demand resulted in weak financial performance for the three firms involved in the conspiracy. By 2001, these producers were searching for a means of securing higher prices. According to the US DOJ, LG Display and Chunghwa Picture Tube initiated the cartel. In the course of meetings held in the US, Taiwan, and South Korea, cartel members set prices TFT–LCD panels and agreed to monitor compliance by exchanging sales data. The DOJ named Dell Inc. and Apple Computer as the primary customers of the cartel's TFT–LCD panels. In addition, large panels were supplied to television manufacturers, and smaller panels were furnished to cell phone manufacturers, including Motorola. During the course of its investigation, the DOJ served subpoenas on smaller firms, but these manufacturers were eventually cleared. The TFT–LCD cartel operated for only five years. It is unclear from the documents how the conspiracy was uncovered. No announcement of leniency was made for any of the indicted firms. In November 2008, the first phase of the DOJ's case was completed and Sharp, LG Display, and Chunghwa Picture Tube pleaded guilty to antitrust charges and agreed to pay significant monetary penalties. Due to its complex involvement through various subsidiaries, LG Display was identified as the primary offender, and ordered to pay \$400 million in fines, the second highest monetary penalty ever imposed by the DOJ in an antitrust prosecution. Sharp and Chunghwa were fined \$120 million and \$65 million, respectively. The \$585 million in penalties imposed on the TFT–LCD cartel was one of the largest settlements ever for a collusive agreement. The members of this cartel still face an uncertain future, as the EU Commission opened a parallel investigation into the TFT–LCD industry that has yet to produce indictments.

Regional cartels

Collusion in Europe's zinc phosphate market

Assuming a relatively small niche in the specialty metals market, zinc phosphate is widely used in the manufacture of anti-corrosive paints. Beginning in March 1994, six firms—Britannia Alloys and Chemicals Ltd. (UK), Heubach GmbH and Co. (Germany), James Brown Ltd. (UK), Nouvelle des Couleurs Zinciques S.A. (France), Trident Alloys Ltd. (UK), and Waardals

Kjemiske Fabrikker A/S (Norway)—forged a collusive agreement in this market. In a meeting held at a hotel at Heathrow Airport, the participants divvied up the British, French, German, and Scandinavian markets. At least 15 additional meetings were held to establish recommended minimum prices. Although the market for zinc phosphate is not large, the six firms controlled nearly 90 percent of output in the countries where their cartel was in force. Unlike many previous collusive accords, there was no confessor to this price-fixing arrangement. As soon as EU regulators uncovered the agreement, all six firms were fined. The relatively modest penalties doled out (Britannia received the highest fine of only 3.37 million euro), were in consideration of both the annual sales of the firms and the overall size of the market.

The success and longevity of the zinc phosphate cartel were due to market characteristics that made collusion possible. With high industry concentration, the six firms could easily orchestrate price and supply controls. Although some variations existed in the processing of zinc phosphate across firms, final-users regarded the product as homogeneous. As with many of the products discussed above, zinc phosphate is not marketed directly to consumers, and prices are therefore hidden.

Carbonless paper

Carbonless paper is chemically treated with micro-encapsulated dye that breaks on contact to create printed material. In December 2001, the EU Commission imposed significant fines on ten companies for engaging in market-sharing and price-fixing agreements in the carbonless paper industry (For a list of firms, see Table 5.1). The collusive agreements were negotiated and maintained through the trade association, Association of European Manufacturers of Carbonless Paper. The number of firms involved and the geographic expanse of participation made this an unusual cartel. The fines imposed ranged from 1.54 million euro to 184.27 million euro, and involved companies in six countries (European Commission IP/01/1892). Only the prosecution of the vitamin cartel yielded higher penalties.

The cartel for carbonless paper began in 1992. According to papers filed by the EU Commission, the cartel's members held five meetings between September 1993 and February 1995 at hotels in Paris and Frankfurt. At these "general meetings," sales quotas were established, target prices were set, and monitoring systems were devised (European Commission IP/01/1892). During its short tenure, the carbonless paper cartel controlled some 90 percent of the European market, whose annual sales averaged 850 million euro. The Commission began its investigation of the cartel in fall of 1996 when Sappi Limited of South Africa utilized the leniency clause to admit its participation in the cartel. In 1999, the French firm Mougeot also began cooperating with the Commission's investigation in an attempt to escape fines. Ultimately, Sappi avoided penalties for its participation in the agreements, but Mougeot paid a reduced fine due to its late "confession."

The carbonless paper cartel was relatively short-lived—three years—so its success in manipulating the market is somewhat surprising. With production diffuse, the cartel members placed special emphasis on pricing compliance during its meetings. The colluding firms also needed to coordinate their operations with non-European companies entering the market. Working in favor of the cartel was the homogeneity of the product, and also the lack of acceptable substitutes. Although the barriers to entry are not insurmountable, establishing a niche in the market requires huge capital outlays and a multi-year business plan, a time commitment perhaps longer than the lifespan of the cartel itself. The most serious challenge to maintaining a viable cartel in this paper sector was the number of participants in the agreement. Although the cartel had no cheaters, the number of colluders raised the likelihood that one of the firms might decide to "come clean," an option that Sappi eventually exercised.

The European plasterboard cartel

In early 1992, executives from BPB LPC of the United Kingdom and Gebrüder Knauf Westdeutsche Gipswerke KG of Germany met in London to discuss ways to stop an ongoing price war in the plasterboard business. The initial agreement that came from this meeting covered plasterboard sales in the United Kingdom, France, Germany, and the Benelux nations. Price monitoring systems were set up to ensure compliance with the agreement. By mid-June, a third manufacturer, Société LaFarge of France, was drawn into the cartel. Gyproc Benelex SA/NV of Belgium joined the agreement in 1996. The members of the cartel exchanged financial information, including sales volumes and upcoming price increases. At a meeting in Versailles in 1996, the cartel participants discussed how to avoid an imminent price war in Germany, and between 1996 and 1998, the firms were able to raise prices in that market. Subsequent meetings of lower level executives were held in the shadow of trade association gatherings in which further agreements were forged to stabilize and increase prices in various European markets.

The plasterboard sector conforms in most ways to the conditions for cartelization. The product is homogeneous, and the four firms in the conspiracy controlled 80 percent of the European market (European Commission, IP/02/1744). As with many of the cartels discussed here, the product is primarily an intermediate good for the construction industry. One of the more interesting aspects of the plasterboard cartel is the lack of a "confession" under the Leniency Programme. The EU Commission began its investigation of the industry in 1998 by conducting on-site inspections of several company offices. In 1999 and 2000, the Commission requested information on the companies' pricing and marketing practices. Facing heavy fines, BPB began cooperating with authorities in 1999, and Gyproc Benelex followed in 2000. The Commission completed its investigation in November 2002 and fines were levied on the corporations involved (see Table 5.1). LaFarge and BPB paid the highest penalties, 249.6 million euro and 138.6 million euro, respectively—fines that would have been lower had the firms not pleaded guilty in 1994 to other price-fixing arrangements (LaFarge for its role in a cement cartel, and a subsidiary of BPB for its part in a cartonboard cartel).

Collusion in the copper plumbing tubes market

In January 2001, the multinational firm Mueller Industries Inc. informed the EU Commission that it had colluded with seven other firms to control prices for copper tubing in the European market. One of the most enduring of the collusive agreements uncovered by the Commission, the cartel manipulated prices for 13 years (1988 to 2001). The cartel's founding firms were KM Europa Metal AG (Germany, Italy and France) and Boliden Group (Sweden). Five additional companies joined the accord in 1989. Mueller (US, UK, France) only began its participation in 1997, but this lack of seniority did not prevent the company from being the first to disclose the price-fixing arrangement to the EU Commission in exchange for relief from fines. The members of the copper plumbing tubes cartel acted out their collusion almost as fictional narrative, using code names and private addresses, employing a "secret information exchange system," and sometimes meeting in airport lounges to set market prices and shares (EU Commission, IP/04/1065). With the exception of Mueller, which was exempted from penalties under the Leniency Notice, the firms in the cartel paid significant fines. For their cooperation in the investigation, four firms received some relief in penalties: KM Europa was fined 67.08 million euro, Outokumpu (Finland) paid 36.14 million euro, Weiland (Austria) was levied 27.84 million euro, and Halcor S.A. (Greece) was ordered to pay 9.16 million euro. Outokumpu's total fine would have been lower had it not been caught colluding in the stainless steel cartel in the 1990s.

The industry for copper plumbing tubes was ideally suited to cartelization. As in the industrial and medical gases cartel discussed below, the market for copper plumbing tubes cartel is small enough (total Eurozone sales in 2000 were 1.15 billion euro) for price increases to go unnoticed by regulators. The high concentration ratio in the industry, coupled with the lack of a substitute product, also made collusion feasible. Copper tubing is considered homogeneous by end-users, so agreeing upon a common price is simple. The product is seldom sold directly to consumers, so the market can be manipulated through minute price increases, hidden within the larger construction costs of new homes and commercial space. Without the confession of Mueller Industries, the cartel could well have persisted for a considerable period of time.

The soda ash cartel

The soda ash cartel, which operated in the European Community in the 1980s, affected a small but essential market. Soda ash is a critical input in the manufacture of glass. Due to the diminutive size of the market in Europe, glass manufacturers typically had supply contracts with one of the two producers of soda ash. The collusion that took place in this market is unusual both in that it involved a duopoly, and also that an unconventional pricing structure insured captured markets. The British firm ICI and the Belgian Company Solvay carved up the European market by using so-called "top slice" rebates; businesses received a certain quantity of soda ash at a conventional price, but purchases over that threshold were heavily discounted. The most cost-effective option for a glass producer was to order everything from one company, as split orders negated the discount. Finally, in order to ensure that no competition took place (e.g. glass firms playing ICI off Solvay, or vice versa), discounts were kept secret until the time of purchase. With the profit margins built into the first or "conventional" part of the sale, this discount system ensured that both firms in the duopoly remained in the black. Competitors could not enter the market unless they immediately established a scale of production to rival that of ICI and Solvay, a volume of sales that would permit a two-tier pricing structure. Any attempt to skim off a small proportion of sales would force a new entrant into competition with the "top slice" rebates—an unwinnable proposition. In 1990, the Commission found both firms in violation of Article 82. Solvay was fined 20 million euro and ICI 10 million euro. The EU Commission defends these penalties as being substantial for this market. The management of both Solvay and ICI vehemently denied any wrongdoing, perhaps believing that the peculiar pricing mechanism they had employed was not collusive. After a decade of appeals, the fines imposed by the Commission were upheld by the European Court of Justice. The primary lesson learned from the soda ash cartel is that "innovative" pricing to segment markets is illegal. Not a quick learner, Solvay soon found itself caught up in the prosecution of the bleaching chemicals cartel.

The bleaching chemicals cartel

Among other industrial agents, the bleaching chemicals industry produces two relatively simple products: hydrogen peroxide and its derivative, perborate. Hydrogen peroxide is a bleaching agent utilized in the textile and wood pulp industries, and is used as a disinfectant, notably in the treatment of sewage. Hydrogen peroxide acts as the base compound in the production of other cleaning agents, notably, perborate. Perborate, in turn, is the active ingredient in a number of cleaning products, including detergents. Production of bleaching chemicals is diffuse, with a significant number of firms producing both products. Total sales of peroxide and perborate were estimated at 470 million euro in 2006 (EU Commission, IP/06/560).

The European market for bleaching chemicals comprises nine firms of varying sizes. In December 2002, the German firm Degussa approached the EU Commission to admit the existence of the cartel and apply for leniency, a request that was complicated by the corporation's culpability earlier that year in a prosecution of the animal feed cartel, for which it received a fine of 91 million euro. Once the bleaching chemicals cartel was exposed, several of the participants hurried to confess. As a result, some of these late confessors received a reduction of fines. One of the more peculiar aspects of the case was the ruling against L'Air Liquide (France); the firm could not be fined because it had exited the market in 1998 and the Commission's right to impose fines had expired.

The cartel for bleaching agents began in August 1997 when firms met and agreed to fix prices. Three months later, the cartel's members met in a Brussels restaurant to assess their new pricing structure and implement further price increases. A subsequent meeting, held in early 1998, was conducted to measure compliance with the price agreements. The consortium functioned as a stable cartel until Degussa stepped forward to confess.

The fines imposed on the cartel members ranged from substantial to silly. Solvay (Belgium) received the highest fine, approximately 167 million euro, a penalty that reflects a 10 percent reduction for the firm's belated cooperation. France's Arkema was next, with an assessment of 78.7 million euro (reduced 30 percent from the original fine). Edison/ex Ausimont of Italy was penalized 58 million euro, while Kemira of Finland was ordered to pay 33 million euro. Akzo Nobel (the Netherlands) paid only 25.2 million euro after a 40 percent reduction for the firm's assistance in the investigation. FMC Foret Corporation (Spain) was ordered to pay 25 million euro, and and Snia/Caffaro of Italy paid only 1.1 million euro. As first confessor, Degussa escaped any penalties. Conversely, the amounts paid by Solvay and Edison ex Ausimont had been increased over the original assessments because of their status as repeat offenders.

The bleaching chemicals cartel provides an instance in which the Leniency Notice produced a confessor that took EU authorities by surprise. The executives at Degussa must have realized that the sheer number of firms in the cartel made detection more likely, either by way of a confession or the carelessness of one of the participants. The company was already facing fines for its participation in the collusive accord for animal feed. If Degussa had not ratted out the bleaching chemicals cartel, the price-fixing arrangement could have persisted for many years, as the market fulfills many of the characteristics necessary for cartelization (see Table 5.2).

Market segmentation in the natural gas sector

In 1975, Ruhrgas AG (Germany) and Gaz De France (GDF; from France) decided to construct the MEGAL pipeline to route gas from Russia to both German and French markets. The firms agreed in writing to sell gas only in

Table 5.2 Collusion, the recent European experience

Industry	*Number of firms*	*Date*	*Geography*	*Violations of assumptions?*
Lysine	5	1992	International	Barriers to entry weak
Bulk Vitamins	6	1989	International	Too many firms
Zinc Phosphate	6	1994	Europe	Barriers to entry weak
Beer	6	1996	Europe	Not an intermediate product, not homogeneous, barriers to entry weak
Carbonless Paper	11	1992	Europe	Too many firms, barriers to entry weak
Plasterboard	4	1992	Europe	Barriers to entry weak
Stainless Steel Tubes	8	1990	Europe	Too many firms
Graphite Electrodes	8	1992	International	Too many firms
Nucleotides	4	1989	International	None
Fasteners	6	1977	International	Barriers to entry weak
Art Auction Services	2	1995	International	Not an intermediate industry
Paraffin	10	1992	Europe	Too many firms, barriers to entry weak
Air Freight	At least 9	2000	International	Too many firms
Industrial/ medical Gases	7	1989	Netherlands	None
Copper Plumbing Tubes	12	1988	Europe	Too many firms
Soda Ash	2	1980s	Europe	Barriers to entry weak
Citric Acid	5	1991	International	None
Flat Glass	4	2004	International	Barriers to entry weak
Gas Insulated Switchgear	10	1988	International	Too many firms
Synthetic Rubber	6	1993	International	None

their home markets. At the time the deal was signed, GDF benefitted from a legal monopoly covering the import of natural gas into France, an arrangement that persisted until August 2000. Ruhrgas enjoyed a similar regional monopoly within its district until 1998, when such "demarcation agreements" were declared illegal. Despite changes instituted by the EU to outlaw such monopolies (August 2000 under the Directive 98/30/EC), the two firms persisted in maintaining the prohibition of cross-border sales that had been in place since 1975. The EU Commission began investigating the market in 2006 by conducing surprise inspections of both firms, and in June 2008 delivered "Statement of Objections" to the companies. Neither firm took advantage of the Leniency Notice, presumably because they had waited too long and their cooperation would have provided little material benefit to the investigation. The companies eventually named in the Commission's charges were larger corporations, formed through mergers: E.ON acquired Ruhrgas in 2003 to become known as E.ON Ruhrgas, and GDF merged with Suez to form GDF Suez SA in 2008.

By maintaining the agreement of 1975 after the markets had been deregulated, E.ON Ruhrgas and GDF Suez SA were openly violating antitrust statutes. As noted by the EU Commission, both parties declared in 2004 that they had "long regarded the letters [of their original agreement] as null and void" (EU Commission, IP/09/1099, July 2009), yet neither firm made any attempt to market gas into the other's territory. It was not until September 2005 that the firms made any effort to sell across one another's borders. At the completion of the Commission's investigation, significant fines were imposed on both firms. Recognizing the equal roles played the corporations, the same penalty was imposed on each firm: 553 million euro. The length and audacity of the natural gas conspiracy contributed to the magnitude of the fines, the second highest ever imposed by the Commission.

Exceptions to the rule—localized cartels

Industrial and medical gases—the Netherlands

Compared to other collusive agreements of the past twenty years, the cartel that manipulated prices for industrial and medical gases in the Netherlands appears quaint. In this case, seven relatively small firms colluded in a minor market niche of a single country, and the fines imposed by the European antitrust authorities were some of the smallest ever recorded (see Table 5.1). The cartelized products included acetylene and argon (inputs for metal fabrication), as well as oxygen, nitrogen, and carbon dioxide (used in the medical field).

Cooperative arrangements among producers began in 1989 and remained in place for just two years. The agreements were reinstated in 1993 and persisted until 1997. Unlike cartels discussed earlier in this chapter, two firms participated in the industrial and medical gases cartel only briefly during the first phase of price-fixing: Westfalen Gassen Nederland BV from March

1994 through December 1995; and BOC Group PLC from June 1994 until December 1995. Whether this defection owed to the threat of possible sanctions from the EU Commission or a desire to honorably compete with rival firms, is not entirely clear. The Commission found both firms to be only "passive" participants in the agreement, and the small fines they received reflects their half-hearted commitment (BOC Group received a penalty of 1.17 million euro, Westfalen Gassen, 0.43 million euro).

The members of the cartel agreed to implement price increases and respect price floors. In addition, the participants promised not to contact one another's existing customers and to established industry standards for the delivery and rental of gas cylinders. The corporate representatives met regularly, although they did not seem to skulk around like members of some of the other European cartels. The EU Commission imposed fines on the seven firms in July 2002 (EU Commission, IP/01/1139), with NV Hoek Loos receiving the largest penalty, 12.6 million euro. Two firms, AGA AB and Air Products Nederland BV, were each granted a 25 percent reduction in fines in exchange for their cooperation in the investigation.

The small number of firms in the industrial and medical gases market, coupled with the invisibility of sales, made cartelization relatively easy. Although, the cost of entry into this market would have been minimal, the strong customer relationships common to this sector could be expected to impede start-up firms. Businesses using these products would nevertheless assume a homogeneous product, so a uniform pricing structure could be easily constructed. The relatively small contribution to total input costs that these gases represented to end-users explains the longevity of the cartel as well as the very low fines imposed by the EC. The impact of the price increases on the bottom-line of a dentistry practice would be minor, so why complain? It is possible that cartels of this type can remain invisible for an extended period.

The Dutch Beer Cartel

The Dutch Beer Cartel differs from most collusive agreements uncovered in recent years in that the product is not an intermediate good. Between roughly 1996 and 1999 (the dates remain uncertain), the Netherlandish firms, Heineken, Grolsch, InBev and Bavaria met to divvy up the Dutch market and elevate prices. The EU Commission found that high-ranking executives were present at these conferences (so-called "agenda meetings" or "sliding scale meetings") indicating that it was not rogue managers who had pursued the agreements.

Since prices were raised at the consumer level—at supermarkets, restaurants, and hotels—collusion was more apparent to regulators. In April 2007, the European Commission announced stiff penalties against three firms: Heineken was fined nearly 220 million euro; Grolsch, 31.7 million euro; and Bavaria, 22.9 million euro. The fourth participant, InBev, escaped penalties by providing information on the cartel under the EU Commission's Leniency Programme (in the absence of cooperation, InBev's fine would have been 84.4 million euro). (Parenthetically, a beer cartel had formed in Belgium between 1993 and 1996. Instigated by Danone, under its subsidiary Alken-Maes, with the participation of InterBrew, Danone was ordered to pay a fine of 44 million euro.)

The Beer Cartel is unusual not only because it impacted prices at the consumer level, but also because the products under collusion were not strictly homogeneous. Brand loyalty on the part of consumers, together with the producers' assumption that their beer was superior in flavor to that of their competition, may have complicated pricing negotiations amongst the cartel members. The corollary in international commodity markets would be coffee, whose pricing is complicated by significant quality differentials. The longevity of the beer cartel suggests that potential sources of friction must have been addressed at the early "agenda meetings."

Exclusionary agreements—Visa, MasterCard, and the US credit card business

Visa and MasterCard are the most widely used bank-issued consumer credit cards in the world. The brands are essentially owned and managed by the thousands of banks that issue the cards (in 2000, approximately 14,000 banks issued Visa cards, and 20,000 banks issued MasterCards). Many banks belonged to both networks, issuing accounts under both the Visa and MasterCard logos. These same institutions agreed not to issue American Express or Discover Cards (what the DOJ terms the "exclusionary rule"). In the initial cases brought against Visa and Mastercard in the District Court of the Southern District of New York (163 F. Supp.2d 322 and 183 F. Supp.2d 613), it was alleged that the exclusionary rule was illegal under the Sherman Act, as it effectively stifled competition by restricting the number of competing cards issued by banking institutions.

The Court of Appeals for the Second District had difficulty sorting through a business structure to determine liability. Visa USA and MasterCard are open joint ventures—clearinghouses, in a sense—and as such, the labels are owned and operated by the banking institutions that issue these cards to the public. As noted, many banks issue cards through both networks, indicating a significant degree of common interest across the two consortia. Over-arching organizations, Visa USA and MasterCard are operated as non-profits that collect fees and assume responsibility for payment defaults. In contrast, Discover and American Express are organized as profit-making entities: in particular, they deal directly with consumers, rather than operating through a clearinghouse. In 1995, American Express changed its business model so that banks could also issue cards with its logo. While this program was highly successful outside the US, the exclusionary rule in force in the US deterred any bank from issuing the

American Express card, since such a move would force it to abandon both the Visa and MasterCard labels. The court rejected Visa's assertion that their particular exclusionary agreement was legal, and further ruled that both the Visa and MasterCard arrangements were illegal (an affirmation of the verdict reached in the Second District).

The illicit activities undertaken by Visa and MasterCard were a crime of exclusion more than collusion. Had Visa International implemented an exclusionary agreement of this kind on its own, the DOJ would probably have pursued it as an illegal restraint of trade. The combination of both Visa and MasterCard pursuing such a policy, however, suggested to authorities that the two entities were acting in concert to secure market share and prevent American Express and Discover from obtaining additional customers. Unlike other cartel cases, there was no attempt by the corporations to increase prices (i.e. fees), segment markets, or exclude new members (provided the issuing bank carried the Visa or MasterCard labels). The credit and issuers functioned as a cartel by preventing the entry of new providers to the system.

Unlike many of the cartels discussed here, the prosecution of Visa and MasterCard did not end with the decision of the Appellate Court. As noted, both the US DOJ and the European Commission actively encourage firms wronged by a cartel to seek redress through the civil courts. This provides yet another incentive for firms to avoid cartelization. The cost of exposure includes the fines (and jail time) imposed by the appropriate enforcement agency, as well as potentially unlimited civil fines. The number of instances in which businesses harmed by collusive practices have followed the advice of the DOJ and the Commission to a successful conclusion is few. In the case of MasterCard and Visa case, however, the successful prosecution of the two companies was followed by an equally successful civil action by Discover Financial Services. Although the 2004 lawsuit floundered for over four years, Visa and MasterCard tentatively reached a settlement with Discover in October 2008, in which Visa agreed to pay Discover fines of $1.9 billion, with MasterCard responsible for the remaining $900 million of the penalty. In conjunction with the actions of the US courts, the antitrust prosecution made the Visa and MasterCard scheme a very costly business decision.

Collusion among colleges and universities—fixing financial aid

There is some debate as to whether collaboration between admissions officers at various elite colleges and universities was a case of bad judgment or intentional collusion. In August 1989, the Department of Justice began investigating tuition and financial aid practices at a number of colleges and universities. Eventually, 57 schools (the so-called Overlap Group) came under scrutiny for sharing information on applicants and jointly setting tuition and financial aid awards. Ultimately, the DOJ decided to confine its prosecution to the eight Ivy League schools, and the Massachusetts

Institute of Technology (MIT). In its formal complaint of May 1991, the DOJ charged the colleges' admissions officers with sharing the financial data of prospective students for the purpose of constructing matching financial aid packages (*U.S. v. Brown University*, Civil Action 91-CV-3274 (1993)). The price-fixing deception had relieved the colleges and universities of the messy competition for students that arises when the privacy of admission packages is honored. The Ivy Leagues settled the complaint the very day of the filing by signing a consent decree that disallowed the sharing of financial aid information for admitted students. MIT refused to sign the decree, which triggered a federal lawsuit that found against the school in September 1992. MIT promised an appeal of the decision to the Third Circuit Court. In December 1993, however, an agreement was worked out between the DOJ and MIT that permitted limited sharing of financial aid practices, but forbade the revealing of specific financial aid packages offered to students.

Colleges and universities have shared information about tuition and room-and-board charges for decades. Strategically, institutions need to position themselves against competitors of similar reputation and size, at least within the region from which applications are drawn. Between 1950 and 1990, some schools began exchanging information on financial aid, essentially revealing the tuition discount applied to accepted students (Morrison, 1992: 810). This cooperation evolved into the sharing of entire financial aid packages, a practice equivalent to a business revealing its marketing strategy, with the expectation that its competitors will match those practices. The system clearly crossed the line into illegality when the schools began to openly coordinate financial aid offers.

As noted by Morrison (1992), this price-fixing arrangement differed from "classic" collusion in a critical way: the vast majority of colleges and universities remained outside the cartel. Morrison (1992: 811) argued that the Ivies were able to cooperate with one another because the "product" they offer (higher education) is highly differentiated. It is the nature of the tiered system of higher education that the Ivy League schools insulate themselves academically from lower-ranked schools, but the hierarchy is financial as well. Students applying to the elite schools will compare tuition among the Ivies, so admissions officers can ignore the fee structures of other institutions. The regional nature of college applications further reinforced the admissions officers' resolve to keep their information-sharing between themselves, for they knew that most students from the Northeast and mid-Atlantic regions seeking admission to the Ivies or to MIT would not extend their search to other geographic areas of the country.

Was the cooperation between these schools price-fixing? Shepherd (1995) believed it was, and agreed with the DOJ's challenge of the pricing practices of the Ivies and the broader Overlap Group. Certainly, the price-fixing arrangement pursued by the schools took a different form than any other cartel discussed here. Firms have managed to reinvent the cartel model a number of times, whether it was the soda ash arrangement that used volume discounts as a means of preventing competition, or the yet-to-be-discussed pricing strategies of professional organizations that effectively fix fees (see Chapter 6). The method used by institutions of higher education to set aid packages is so specific to the college and university market that it is unlikely another sector of the economy could use it as a model. This antitrust case illustrates how wily authorities must be if they are to overcome the innovative accords that develop to lessen competition.

Cartel investigations currently underway

In February 2008 it was announced that EU authorities had begun an investigation of the chocolate market. The European investigation followed a Canadian inquiry into the pricing practices of Hershey, Mars, Cadbury, and Nestlé, an investigation that involved dawn raids at the offices of the candy makers in Canada. As of the time of publication, the US is still examining the pricing policies of Mars, but has not yet scrutinized the practices of the European producers. In addition, over four dozen civil actions alleging price-fixing in the chocolate business have been filed in the United States. Antitrust authorities in Germany raided the offices of major international candy manufacturers Nestlé, Kraft, and Mars, and one of their domestic producers, Ritter Sport, has also been targeted.

The characteristics of the chocolate market are somewhat conducive to collusion. The market is highly concentrated, and brand loyalty (achieved at least partly through advertising) is strong enough to provide a meaningful barrier to entry. The major difficulty for producers is the high degree of product differentiation and the challenge of establishing uniform prices across so many dissimilar items. Unlike so many of the collusive agreements that have surfaced in Europe during the recent cartel period, chocolate is a retail product, and the visibility of price increases heightens the risk of exposure to authorities. The manufacturers most likely took the gamble because collusion promised them relief from the constant price pressure they have faced in recent years. It has yet to be determined if the rising price of chocolate owes more to collusion or rather the interdependency of an oligopolistic market.

Despite the global stretch of recent cartelization, occasional domestic price-fixing agreements emerge. On September 24, 2008, the Humane Society of the US filed a complaint with the FTC contending that egg producers were conspiring to set prices. Four days later, a class-action lawsuit alleging price-fixing was filed against the three largest industry trade groups and 13 of the biggest egg producers. An unexpected plaintiff in an antitrust case, the Humane Society challenged the certification system that producers used to promote their eggs as the product of humanely treated hens. The Humane Society's lawsuit alleged that the United Egg Producers' certified logo, UEP, was a ruse, for in enforcing its so-called "animal husbandry guidelines" (e.g. marginally increasing the size of cages, which reduced the number of hens on a given farm) the association was interested only in reducing total egg production. The true purpose of the labeling, the suit contended, was to reduce output and elevate egg prices. The DOJ has opened a preliminary investigation into the allegations of price-fixing in the egg sector.

The egg industry is an unusual subject for cartelization. There are many producers and the barriers to entry are weak. Yet, consumers regard an egg imprinted with the UEP label a homogeneous product. Additionally, the fragility and limited shelf-life of eggs shields the sector from international competition. In the alleged price-fixing of the egg industry, the standard approach of setting price targets would not have worked. Consumers would have reacted to the higher prices by cutting consumption, thereby leaving producers with an excess supply of a perishable good. The trade associations adopted an approach used by international commodity cartels: collectively cut production until prices rise. As alleged in the lawsuit, egg prices rose 45 percent between August 2007 and March 2008. The suspected collusion in the egg industry provides another example of price-fixing in consumption goods.

Summarizing the recent cartel experience

The analysis of these 26 prosecuted arrangements, together with the numerous pending investigations, provides an overview of the structure and management of industrial cartels in the period after 1990. A number of inferences can be drawn regarding both the type of industry susceptible to cartelization, and the means used to initiate and maintain these agreements. Such information can be of assistance to antitrust authorities as they continue to look for early signs of collusion.

With the exceptions of the cartels for beer, art auctions, and carbonless paper, all of the collusive arrangements presented in Table 5.2 handled intermediate goods. Cartels are less likely to be discovered when consumers are only indirectly impacted by price-fixing. The feasibility of managing prices in the absence of retail sales was demonstrated by the 16-year run of price manipulation in the gas-insulated switchgear market.

It has been widely assumed that only industries with a limited number of firms can undergo successful cartelization. But a review of Table 5.2 shows that only 11 of the 20 cartels listed have six or fewer firms (six being the number arbitrarily chosen here to indicate optimal concentration). The difficulty of policing large collusive arrangements explains the increased activity of trade associations, under whose aegis corporate managers can gather without raising the suspicion of antitrust agencies.

A more thorough look at the cartels presented in Table 5.2 indicates that few of these collusive agreements conform to all of the conditions for cartelization. In addition to the cumbersome membership rolls of nearly half the cartels, many of the industries represented are characterized by weak barriers to entry. In fact, this sample supports the notion that cartelization arises primarily in established, older industries; perhaps as a response to declining profitability (this was the case with zinc phosphate, carbonless paper, steel tubes, paraffin, soda ash and flat glass sectors).

The collusive agreements under consideration also provide some support for the efficacy of the Leniency Notice. As discussed above, in nearly half of the cases under review here, the EU Commission was approached early in its investigation by a member of the cartel who was anxious to come clean. In the sorbates and carbonless paper industries, the Commission's investigations began with confessions. Although the Leniency Notice is an imperfect instrument for encouraging confessions (see Bloom, 2006), there is presently no better way of breaking the ranks of cartels.

One of the recent trends in the literature has been to utilize price data as a means of detecting operating cartels, a process that is complicated when an intermediate product is sold through a bidding process whose outcome is known only to the parties involved. The market characteristics examined in Chapter 2 provide a starting point for developing more sophisticated models of cartel detection.

Using samples to determine the population of colluding firms

The capture–recapture model detailed in Chapter 2 can be used to estimate the total population of colluding firms. This procedure, whose methodology is derived from environmental biology, is fraught with problems. It assumes, for example, that like fish, recaptured (i.e. re-exposed) firms are typical of the population as a whole. As when measuring other illegal populations, partial information may be superior to none at all. The repeated utilization of capture–recapture techniques on different samples (varied by date, for example) would provide an estimate of the prevalence of collusion. Equally important, this model could be applied to estimate the incidence of collusion by industrial sector. This clarity would come at the cost of a significant reduction in the sample available for analysis.

It is impractical to apply the capture–recapture model to the entire sample of firms that have been caught engaging in price-fixing, as variations in market conditions and legal environments would corrupt the results. Instead, the model will shed light on a well-defined sample of cartel participants uncovered during a defined period of time (specifically, those exposed in the European Union, as presented in Table 5.2). Of the 123 firms involved in these collusive agreements, ten participated in a second price-fixing agreement during the specified period. If one defines the components of the Capture–Recapture model as:

C_1 = Total # of colluding firms
c_1 = Total firms exposed, period 1
c_2 = Firms charged in second round
c_2^* = Number of those that are repeat offenders

Then:

$$c_2^*/c_1 = c_2/C_1.$$

From above:

$$10/53 = 80/C_1$$

If this methodology is correct, then only 18.9 percent of colluding firms are exposed and the total number of businesses engaged in collusion over the period can be estimated at 423. This number is wholly consistent with other estimates of the hidden population of cartels. Previous estimates of the exposure rate of cartels (see Zimmerman and Connor, 2005) suggest that only 10 to 35 percent of colluding firms are ever revealed.

Comparing the four cartel periods of cartelization

One of the most intriguing aspects of the cartel periods discussed here is the heterogeneity of the four phases of cartelization: in terms of pricing mechanisms, policing, the scope of antitrust enforcement, and product coverage. Prior to the passage of the Sherman Act in 1891, firms colluded openly with impunity. After 1891, collusion in the US and Europe became clandestine at the very time international cartels were becoming more common. Antitrust enforcement was weak and firms secured cooperation through such tactics such as interlocking boards. In the third phase of collusion, international commodity cartels, represented by developing nations, worked in full view of DOJ and EU officials. With no need to conceal their activities, the participants in these arrangements employed various means to control prices, including buffer stocks and export-and-production controls. Even with all available tools for manipulating prices at their disposal, however, the commodity cartels were rarely successful in the long-term. In the fourth and current cartel period, aggressive antitrust enforcement has altered both the mechanisms of collusion and the products involved. In particular, all but two of the cartels discussed in this chapter involve intermediate products whose prices not apparent to the final purchaser. In addition, cartel participants turned to simple, "invisible" means of managing prices, such as bid-rigging, price minimums, and partitioning of sales. While these methods are unlikely to produce the "monopoly" rates of return of true collusion, they substantially reduce the probability that the illegal activity will be uncovered. Given the collective legalistic fixation of the developed world, the breadth and scope of collusion being pursued today is ironic.

Conclusion

The establishment of collusive agreements in an era of significant antitrust penalties has led to forms of cartelization that differ markedly from earlier price-fixing arrangements. As the narrative of cartel formation in the US and Europe demonstrates, collusion is alive and well in the industrialized economies. Despite a ratcheting up of enforcement and penalties, new cartels continue to form, particularly in businesses that sell intermediate products. The extent of the cartelized industries uncovered—from food additives to construction supplies, from financial products to even auction services—is staggering. In July 2009, for example, the EU Commission levied total fines of 61 million euro against eight Western and Eastern European producers of calcium carbide: small market, small fines, but evidence of the continued pressure that antitrust authorities are exerting. The US Department of Justice and the EU Commission are committing ever greater resources and more innovative investigative tools to combat the invidious and persistent collusion that undermines their free markets.

6 Regulatory reform

The exposure of so many collusive agreements within the major industrialized economies since 1990 suggests that antitrust policy and enforcement need further reform. As discussed in Chapter 5, most of the cartelized industries from this period manufacture or sell intermediate products. Consequently, both the end-user and the consumer are harmed by higher prices. Elevated fines and even jail time have neither extinguished the drive of some firms to collude nor ameliorated the economic damages of price-fixing. Although the EU Commission encourages those harmed by cartels to seek monetary compensation, litigation is an expensive and inefficient way to redress economic losses.

Even amidst the calls for more heavy-handed competition policy in recent years, some economists have expressed concerns that antitrust intervention can adversely impact the natural cycle of oligopolistic markets. Ridding markets of collusion ensures lower prices in the short term, but may lead to mergers or business failures that are anti-competitive in the long run. When Archer Daniels Midland entered the lysine market to compete with established Chinese producers, overproduction yielded significantly lower prices in the near term, and the participants soon turned to cartelization. In the absence of collusion, increased market concentration in the lysine sector was inevitable. Certainly one cannot espouse price-fixing as a means of stabilizing markets besieged by competitive pressures, yet the long-run outcome of forceful antitrust policy may, paradoxically, be significantly higher prices for consumers.

This chapter examines how both proposed and implemented changes in antitrust policies can be counter-productive to the goal of maintaining competitive markets. A number of scholars have argued against the use of any antitrust enforcement measures, contending that anti-cartel and merger policies can inhibit competitive forces and even increase the likelihood of bankruptcy. The role of trade associations will also be considered, particularly with regard to how competition policy can more effectively address the information-sharing that forms an inevitable part of industry gatherings.

The case for and against global enforcement

As detailed in Chapter 4, the globalization of collusion has produced significant jurisdictional problems for antitrust authorities. Corporations collude more often in nations and regional markets whose laws are less onerous. It can be said, for example, that the absence of jail sentences for price-fixing in Europe has resulted in more cartel activity there than in the US, where criminal penalties are common. In addition, lack of coordination between national competition agencies results in less effective parallel prosecutions for the same crime.

Joint competition policy was part of the agenda in the post-war negotiations that led up to the signing of the original GATT accord in 1947. This accord called for the creation of a super-national body, the International Trade Organization (ITO), to oversee the elimination of tariffs and the promotion of measures friendly to free trade. Negotiators eventually approved the ITO, but the US Congress considered the proposed organization to be excessively intrusive and refused to ratify the pact, adopting instead the less comprehensive trade provisions of the GATT. While the GATT framework has served as a powerful tool for reducing tariffs and other trade barriers, nothing in the document addresses competition policy.

The debate about internationalization of anti-cartel prosecutions continues to this day. In the US, the argument is cloaked in the language of "federalism," with the jurisdictional debate focused on whether states or the federal government should bear the responsibility for prosecuting collusion. In the European Union, individual countries maintain sovereign competition authorities despite the presence of the EU Commission (for an early meditation on the problem of overlapping authorities within the European Community, see Buxbaum (1964)). Internal instances of collusion are addressed by national authorities, but the EU Commission may also intervene (see, for example, the narrative of the medical gases cartel in the Netherlands, discussed in Chapter 5). Current European competition policies do not clearly articulate the jurisdictional hierarchies of country versus region. As detailed by Klevorick and Sykes in their analysis of the *Empagran* case (2007), the designation of judicial authority is sometimes left to case law to establish. It can be argued that unified jurisdiction at the international level regularizes prosecutions and extends the reach of antitrust policy. Still, authors such as Epstein and Greve (2004), considered the development of integrated international competition policy an unlikely proposition.

A forceful statement of the case for global antitrust enforcement was advanced by Guzman (2004), who argued that the current system of competing antitrust agencies is costly both in terms of corporate compliance to sometimes conflicting statutes and also in terms of court expenses. On the problems associated with jurisdictional competition, see also Kerber and Budzinski (2004). Guzman (2004: 114–17) proposed various levels of cooperation for authorities and concluded that all held the promise of efficiency and cost savings. Conversely, Stephen (2004) provided an overview of the arguments against greater cooperation, and posited that it would be impossible to create an international body that produces optimal outcomes for all cooperating states (Stephen, 2004: 78).

Any attempt to unify antitrust enforcement would have to address the universalizing of penalties for collusion. As noted in Chapter 1, the disparities in antitrust response are exemplified by the US DOJ's decision to imprison corporate executives for collusion whereas the European Commission relies on fines alone; as well as the stunning laxity with which Japan has enforced its competition law. Given the differing views of price-fixing in each nation and region, it is unlikely that the industrialized world can reach a consensus on suitable punishments for price-fixing.

As an alternative to the intergovernmental discussions detailed in Chapter 4, it has been suggested that global antitrust policy be pursued through the World Trade Organization (WTO). As cartelization has become firmly entwined in international trade, the WTO seems a logical place to address antitrust practices. Gerber (2007) outlined the potential for inclusion of competition law within the WTO framework and considered the issues that are preventing the development of such a policy. Bhattacharjea (2006) discussed the WTO's role in framing of competition policy from the perspective of the developing world, whose concerns include the restrictive effects of antitrust enforcement and anti-dumping policies on emerging economies. Sweeney (2007) further elaborated on the debate surrounding export cartels and noted that the importing nations have the most to lose under an intergovernmental regime.

Antitrust enforcement and the potential for unintended outcomes

The goal of anti-cartel enforcement is fairer markets with lower prices and more choices for end-users and consumers. But if strict antitrust measures drive some firms to merge or exit the sector altogether, the resulting increase in market concentration will lead to higher prices, an unintended consequence. Figure 6.1 illustrates the challenge of determining the appropriate levels for penalties in antitrust prosecutions. A policy advocating lax enforcement with modest penalties produces the undesirable outcome presented in Panel A. When participants in a cartel feel little pressure from antitrust authorities, potential penalties for collusion may be regarded as a mere stumbling block in the drive to manipulate the market and achieve higher rates of return. The situation is more complex when strict antitrust enforcement is practiced (Panel B). In this scenario, the greater probability of detection, coupled with higher sanctions, may lead to the oligopolistic equilibrium described in Chapter 2. Although end-users pay lower prices than they would under collusion, there is a greater likelihood that one or

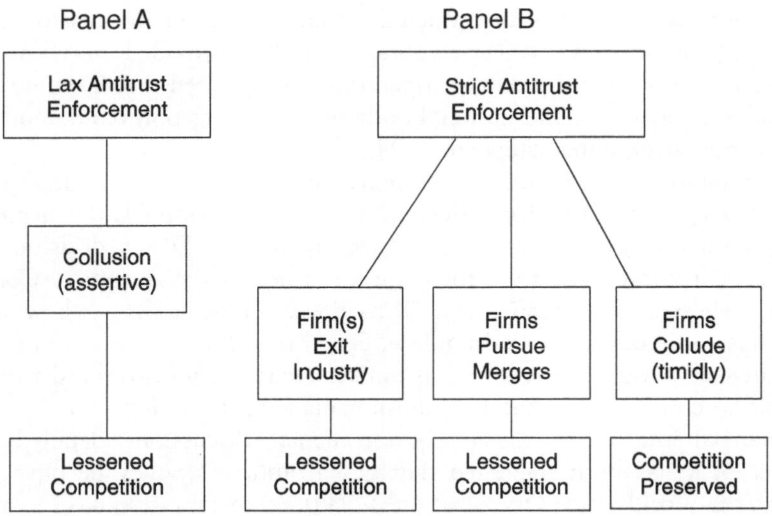

Figure 6.1 Competition effects of lax and strict antitrust policy.

more producers will depart from the industry, thereby raising market concentration.[1] If firms successfully collude, price increases are likely to be suppressed so as to avoid detection. Firms will pursue cartelization techniques such as price floors rather than more visible measures such as market segmentation. If the cartel is uncovered and significant penalties are imposed, there is the potential for greater market concentration if firms are driven into bankruptcy or resort to mergers.

The issue of "ability to pay" is now being raised by firms penalized in cartel prosecutions. In Europe and Japan, where fines are de facto the only penalty available to regulators, there has been a drive for higher fines (to a cap of 10 percent of annual sales in the EU's competition law). Such draconian penalties can bankrupt a firm, thereby leaving the market less competitive than it was under collusion. In its release, "The Bankruptcy Wildcard in Cartel Cases", the Centre for Competition Policy (CCP) in the UK argued that some corporations are resorting to provisions of the developing Financial Constraints Discount Criteria to threaten insolvency when faced with the EU Commission's anti-competition fines (Stephan, A., CCP, 2006). The author noted that the EU's policy objective of protecting employment may make the Commission more amenable to negotiating with a firms that appears to be at financial risk.[2] Craycraft et al. (1997) provided a counterargument to the "ability to pay" gambit. In their analysis of 386 instances of price-fixing, the authors concluded that few of the fines imposed were significant enough to jeopardize the solvency of the penalized firms.

Any attempt to measure the economic impacts of cartelization versus the higher prices that arise from merger and increased concentration is complicated by the dearth of pricing data. Nearly all the cartels discussed in

Chapter 5 involve intermediate businesses whose charges are not market prices but rather price quotes known only to the buyer and seller. Since they can serve as a form of signaling in a collusive agreement, even published prices are suspect.

Evenett et al. (2001) examined cartels and their antitrust response in the 1990s and noted the unanticipated durability of these collusive agreements. The authors argued that aggressive cartel enforcement is counterproductive if firms respond to the stricter regulatory environment by taking other paths to lessen competition (e.g. mergers). Motta and Polo (2003) considered the unintended outcomes of leniency programs, as when firms build a leniency discount for their confession into their cost-and-benefit analysis of cartelization; they concluded that the price of extending leniency is justified by the information that confessions yield.

The prospect that competition might be lessened as a consequence of over-reaching antitrust policy explains the new emphasis that agencies, particularly the US DOJ, have placed on prosecuting individuals. The EU Commission and Japan's antitrust authorities, on the other hand, have demonstrated an aversion to these criminal penalties, particularly judgments that include jail time. The plethora of collusive agreements uncovered in the last ten years suggests that the penalties for corporate managers may need to be ratcheted up even further.

Securing competition: the integration of antitrust initiatives and merger policy

Anti-cartel policy needs to be part of a broader pro-competitive strategy that includes guidelines for corporate mergers. Firms seeking to mollify competition can consider acquiring rival companies (see Chapter 1 for a detailed look at the FTC's role in overseeing mergers). If antitrust policy is sufficiently lax in regard to mergers and acquisitions, then consolidation offers a simple way to circumvent anti-cartel laws. The impact of mergers on end-users is the same as that of price-fixing: a tendency toward an approximation of monopoly pricing.

As detailed by Fox (1997), antitrust authorities in the European Union have tended to view mergers and acquisitions with much less suspicion than their counterparts in the United States. One of the early goals of European economic integration was the rationalization of markets—consolidation within the small countries with indigenous, inefficient firms (Bermann et al., 1993). Following integration, the EU's relatively relaxed merger policy allowed larger corporations, with lower per-unit costs, to develop and compete in global markets. As noted by Fox (1997: 348), mergers and acquisitions are viewed in Europe as a means of increasing the degree of integration between countries.

Europe's relatively benign outlook on market concentration stands in contrast to merger policy in the US, where antitrust authorities treat mergers of all kinds—vertical, horizontal, and conglomerate—as potential impediments to competition. Section 7 of the Clayton Act (see Appendix 1.2 for text of the Act) stated:

> No person engaged in commerce or in any activity affecting commerce shall acquire, directly or indirectly, the whole or any part of the stock or other share capital and no person subject to the jurisdiction of the Federal Trade Commission shall acquire the whole or any part of the assets of another person engaged also in commerce or in any activity affecting commerce, where in any line of commerce or in any activity affecting commerce in any section of the country, the effect of such acquisition may be substantially to lessen competition, or to create monopoly.

The Clayton Act granted agencies broad authority to oppose mergers of all kinds. While the FTC is especially wary of horizontal mergers, it also frowns on vertical mergers by which businesses acquire their suppliers. Conglomerate mergers are the least likely to draw the attention of the FTC.

Corporations that are in a "competitive dance of death," struggling to survive the vagaries of ceaseless price-cutting, may consider either collusion or mergers as attractive means of achieving stability. Antitrust agencies in the US and abroad must recognize that if strident competition policy regarding collusion is coupled with rigid treatment of mergers and acquisitions, some weakened corporations will be forced into bankruptcy.

Recent cartels and the "ability to pay"

If the "law of unintended consequences" is alive and well in the antitrust arena, then it may be desirable to consider alternatives to the current trend toward ever-tougher enforcement. In this regard, one thinks of the US DOJ's machinations in the "inability to pay" ruling in the DRAM market, and the EU Commission's Financial Constraints Discount Criteria.[3] The ad hoc application of these provisions means that some firms will benefit from an agency ruling while others are penalized. This inequity of punishments may owe to characteristics of the market prior to cartelization, and certainly members of a long-established industry that decides to initiate a collusive agreement should receive the harshest treatment in the courts. Businesses facing a calamity as a result of the entry of competitors or other fundamental changes in the market, however, may need to be granted some level of clemency if the desire is to maintain competition rather than crush the offender. Stephan (2006) noted that the EU Commission considers the financial constraints that face corporations and acknowledges the possibility that their fines might drive a faltering business into bankruptcy. Conversely, Craycraft et al. (1997) examined nearly 400 price-fixing cases and concluded that nearly all the firms could pay the fines that had been imposed.

Examples of cartels formed in response to competitive pressures

The lysine cartel was in force from 1992 to 1995. The conspiracy ended in 1996 when Ajinomoto informed the EU Commission of its involvement in the cartel. The profitability of the lysine market was undermined by the entry of ADM in the early 1990s. In January 1991, the price of lysine stood at approximately $1.40 per pound in the European market, a little less than that in the United States. Collusion began after mid-1992, when the price of lysine fell to less than $0.90 cents per pound. As noted in Chapter 4, after the cartel formed, prices firmed to just over $1.15 per pound, but then fell once again to the lows of June 1992. Once cooperation between all companies was in place, however, the price of lysine rose to the level that had prevailed prior to ADM's entry into the market.

A nearly identical situation occurred in the citric acid market when Cargill entered production in 1990. Citric acid prices fell as a result of the enhanced competition, although not as dramatically (at least in percentage terms) as that in the lysine market. In 1990, the spot price for citric acid was approximately $0.72 per pound. By 1991, with Cargill now a significant supplier to the market, prices dropped as low as $0.61 per pound, a decline of over 15 percent. The cartel began in March 1991, and although it took some time to pull a sufficient number of producers into the agreement, by the spring of 1992, prices had risen to over $0.70 per pound. The cartel managed to push prices to a high of $0.81 per pound in the summer of 1994. Cooperation ceased when it became apparent that the cartel would be uncovered as a consequence of the DOJ's parallel investigations into other food additives sectors.

As discussed in Chapter 5, one of the longest-lasting cartels was the conspiracy in the DRAM chip market. The near-perfect interchangeability of these bulk chips, regardless of manufacturer, made competition in this industry fierce and profits elusive. In the early 1980s, ten firms participated in the market. Product development costs were extremely high and remained so because of the cost of continual innovation. Nine US firms, including chip-making giant Intel, exited the market in the 1980s and 1990s due to poor profits. By the late 1990s, the remaining five producers turned to collusion to bolster their flagging operations. Despite illicit cooperation between producers, prices continued to soften, which led to more aggressive collusive tactics, including mutual production cuts to eliminate persistent over-supply. When the cartel unraveled in 2004–5, it was regarded as one of the most extensive conspiracies ever uncovered.

The graphite electrodes industry provides yet another example of economic circumstances driving an industry to cartelization. As noted by Grout and Sonderegger (2005), this market was in a state of perpetual over-production and weakening prices. When the cartel formed in 1992, the member firms faced increased concentration, excess capacity, and industry restructuring (Grout and Sonderegger, 2005: 8). In addition to the graphite electrodes industry, the authors pointed to the citric acid, soda ash, bulk vitamins, and plasterboard cartels as good examples of collusion that had been spawned by "intense competition."

The cases mentioned above illustrate the potential connection between increased competition, falling prices, and subsequent collusion. When industries are in the grips of destructive competition, executives may consider cartelization the only way to prevent business failure. The imposition of a fine on a failing corporation may be counterproductive to the goal of maintaining competitive markets.

That these oligopolistic industries produce a homogeneous intermediate input rather than a final product makes collusion all the more likely. These producers face intense competition that is likely to keep costs low, and since prices charged are generally unknown, competitors cannot adequately assess where their product stands in the market. Cartelization therefore becomes an avenue that both promises higher prices and also lowers risk by making price information transparent to members of the accord. Nearly all the price-fixing agreements uncovered in recent years have involved these perpetually unstable intermediate markets.

An argument can be made for departing from strident anti-cartel policies of the last two decades in those cases in which corporations—facing unanticipated competitive pressures from the elimination of trade barriers or the entry of a new producer—find themselves in imminent danger of collapse. Rather than see the flailing business exit the industry or merge with another firm for survival, a better course may be to provide the firm breathing room to adjust to the new competitive forces. If corporations knew such a path were available, they might pursue a legal route to restoring profitability, rather than skulking around airport lobbies devising price-fixing schemes. For the makers of the intermediate products discussed above, medium-term protection from competition might have meant the difference between adjusting to new market pressures and resorting to collusion or industry departure.

With cartelization now a truly global phenomenon, the most straightforward means of implementing such a reform would be through short-term tariff protection—an approach that would require a unified effort by competition authorities and the WTO. The goal would be to preserve competition whenever possible. Certainly, antitrust agencies would need to be prepared for a flood of firms seeking shelter from competition as merely a form of sustained protectionism. A possible model for temporary abeyance of competition onslaught can be seen in the protection extended to Harley-Davidson in the 1980s, when the company struggled to compete with Japanese imports. Six years of tariff protection enabled the firm to remain in business and ultimately emerge as a healthy competitor in the high end of the market. In fact, the company's restructuring was so successful that it petitioned the US government to remove the tariffs one year ahead of schedule. In the limited number of instances in which otherwise sound firms are reacting poorly to new competitive pressures beyond their control, intervention of this sort may prevent a corporation from exiting the market and lessening competition and product choice in that industry. For most sectors, the length of time needed to get a suffering company back on its feet would not be as long as the five years that Harley-Davidson required, because the speed of transition is generally faster.

Leniency programs—is further reform necessary?

The evolution of leniency policy in the US and the EU has increased the probability that individuals will expose collusion to avoid prosecution. Leniency policies are now more universal and countries like the US are experimenting with programs such as the "Leniency Plus," which provides a form of blanket immunity when multiple cartels are involved. In addition, as criminal prosecutions are pursued against individuals, leniency has been extended to include relief from jail sentences. As described in Chapter 2, the underlying problem with leniency programs is that the profit-maximizing strategy of any firm is to collude and then be the first to step forward with a confession. As noted by several authors, this reversal is comparable to the prisoner's dilemma: does one admit guilt to avoid prosecution, or remain quiet in the belief that no other perpetrators will speak up? The difference between leniency policy and a criminal prosecution, however, is that the first confessor to collusion is usually offered complete amnesty, a reality that makes both collusion and confession attractive propositions.

Trade associations

One of the most complex issues to be addressed in any reform of competition policy is the role that trade associations play in nurturing collusion. Industry gatherings provide a perfect venue for competitors to exchange information, meet suppliers, and discuss marketing strategies. As discussed in Chapter 5, conversations within these associations can veer from the legal to the illicit quite easily. Corporate executives are frequently unaware of what constitutes illegal activity, and may inadvertently engage in collusive activities. Trade associations foster an exchange of information that promotes the adoption of best practices. Antitrust authorities hesitate to place limitations on such networking franchises. A possible means of addressing the potential problems of trade associations would be to mandate competition policy education as part of the organization's charter.

The widespread practice of trade associations publishing quoted prices for intermediate inputs is usually anti-competitive in intent. Most prices for primary inputs are internal quotes privy only to seller and buyer. When the sorbate producer association began posting prices in the *Chemical Market Reporter*, for example, the figures can only be construed as signals for other competitors. How else can it be explained that the industry maintained a unified price structure? Banning the release of such information in trade journals may be a necessary first step in curbing the use of signaling.

What do competition authorities do with cartel fines?

A review of the cartel prosecutions in Chapter 5 shows that, even when adjusted for inflation, monetary penalties imposed on firms for antitrust violations have climbed steeply in recent years. The monies that the US DOJ collects are relegated to victims' compensation funds. Although the DOJ has required restitution in some of its cartel prosecutions, in general firms and individuals harmed by collusion are not compensated. Given that the overwhelming majority of collusive agreements manipulate prices in intermediate markets, it is downstream firms and consumers that are most likely to be harmed. When the EU Commission collects fines under negotiated settlements, the money goes into the EU's general treasury. Businesses harmed by cartelization are encouraged to seek compensation through civil courts, an expensive and time-consuming path not usually taken. Distribution of fines to those harmed should be considered by competition authorities.

The case against antitrust

This chapter concludes with an examination of arguments put forth against antitrust action to dismantle cartels. These provocative assertions generally fall into the following categories, namely the beliefs that:

- anti-cartel policy is ineffective and randomly enforced;
- antitrust actions do not necessarily result in more competitive markets;
- US legislative efforts to increase market access are more effective than legal maneuvers undertaken by the Executive Branch and the DOJ.

Phillips (1959) provided a convincing argument for supporting some degree of collusion in circumstances in which competition is better fostered through cooperation. In *U.S. v. Trans-Missouri Freight Association* (166 U.S. 290 (1897)), one of the earliest prosecutions of a cartel, the "conspirators" actions had been deemed reasonable by two lower courts and a four-vote minority of the Supreme Court. The Court's majority, however, ruled that any cartel is, by definition, illegal (the so-called *per se* rule). A similar decision was reached in *U.S. v. Joint Traffic Association* (171 U.S. 505 (1898)). In both instances, large shippers were using their market power to force rate reductions. Common pricing appeared to these corporations to be the only means of securing adequate returns to stave off bankruptcy. The Court, in ruling against collusion, was not ruling in favor of continued competition. Dewey (1961) presented a different argument against early applications of anti-cartel laws, deriding the practice of pursuing large price-fixing agreements while small, but more numerous, violators were left to collude with impunity. According to the author:

> In legal theory virtually all cartels—unless explicitly sanctioned—are criminal conspiracies. In practice, gentlemen's agreements are so ubiquitous that they cannot be suppressed; and state governments seldom bother to prosecute even open conspiracies under their little "Sherman Acts."
>
> Dewey, 1961, p. 256

Dewey argued that antitrust authority was undermined by the flagrant and widespread disregard for competition policy.

In his comprehensive attack on the entire antitrust "enterprise," Armentano (1986) asserted that anti-cartel enforcement has too often targeted industries that are no more constricted than other oligopolistic markets. Consistent with Leach's argument below, Armentano noted that substantial efficiency gains are possible when price-fixing agreements achieve significant risk-reduction. Bowden (2005) described antitrust policy as a "war" against contracts, the author contending that contracts, the fundamental right of those engaged in business, were now under the purview of competition authorities. Perhaps even more forcefully, Binswanger (2005) and Hull (2005) regarded antitrust action against a firm as a penalty for success, and cited as proof of their assertions the cases involving Intel and Microsoft.

In their examination of antitrust policy, Moran and Novak (2009) detailed the negative outcomes—in particular, the increased concentration of markets—that may arise when governments act against cartels. The authors noted that owing to their inherent instability, cartels cannot fully exercise their powers, and so price increases are kept in check. In his analysis of a number of cartels (including those of petroleum refining and cardboard), Sproul (1993) suggested that prices rose after the demise of price-fixing agreements. This thesis supports earlier work by Newmark (1988), who determined that collusive agreements in Seattle's bread market did not raise prices. Leach (1994) attacked the fundamental assumption that collusion is always detrimental. To his mind, price-fixing eliminates substantial uncertainty and allows firms to plan appropriately for future demand. Using the South African cement industry as a case study, Leach noted that pressures from both cheap imports and more expensive domestic substitutes not only prevented the cartel from abusing consumers, but also eliminated concerns about highly variable prices.

What can one discern from these strident attacks on antitrust in general and the anti-cartel actions of competition authorities in particular? Abandoning enforcement would seem to be folly, permitting both the destabilization of markets and the outright abuse of consumers. Perhaps the healthy skepticism expressed by these scholars could form the basis of an alternative approach to certain specific cases of antitrust infringement. Industries facing new market pressures beyond their control could apply for price supports to sustain a reasonable rate of return until markets improved. One of the vexing problems with this isolated use of protectionist measures is how competition authorities would select winners and losers.

Conclusion

This chapter has detailed some of the major developments in anti-cartel enforcement since 1980. Antitrust doctrine has become more global in reach, with agencies in the US and the EU working toward greater cooperation. The OECD's efforts to define best practices, both in the investigative and penalty phases of enforcement, have enabled the DOJ and the EU Commission to more aggressively fight cartels. Despite some coordination of competition policies, however, cartel inquiries typically involve parallel investigations and prosecutions, a process that multiplies the number of work hours devoted to a case and increases the investigative costs for all agencies involved. To date, the DOJ and the European Commission have not jointly prosecuted a single cartel. It would be beneficial to markets if nations integrated their investigatory arms. An example of this unified response to suspected collusion was seen in 2003, when the US and Canada undertook a joint inquiry into the Canada-based sulfuric acid producers, Falconbridge and Noranda, whose price-fixing had impacted US firms. Utilizing the Mutual Legal Assistance Treaty, the DOJ requested proprietary data on the colluders, and the Canadian authorities then raided the offices of the firms in fulfillment of this entreaty. While recognizing the intricacies of national laws regarding privacy clauses, it is clear that such cross-national investigations could empower antitrust enforcement at the international level.

In addition to investigative disparities, the US and the EU hold dissimilar philosophies on judgments and penalties for collusion. In particular, the US has pursued an aggressive program of levying criminal penalties and even jail time for corporate managers found culpable for orchestrating collusive accords. According to the OECD report of 2005, executives "repeatedly offered to pay high financial fines if they could avoid jail time" (OECD 2005: 27). On the human level, collusion is less attractive for a firm active in US markets than it is abroad. A manager considering collusion in an international market might be wise to limit the price-fixing operation to Europe; or perhaps Japan, where lax competition policy has allowed cartels to operate more or less freely since World War II. Interestingly, the Australian government is reforming its competition policy to include criminal penalties (Competition Policy Reform Act 1995, No. 88[4]). Similar moves by other nations would make collusion within the industrialized world far less attractive. A simple means of increasing the pressure on cartels would be to achieve some symmetry between expected sanctions in different markets. The troubling reality, however, is that new cartels continue to be exposed at an alarming rate, particularly in the European Union.

The leniency programs enacted in both the US and the EU have helped bring to light a significant number of price-fixing agreements. The tinkering that is being done to these successful leniency provisions (as in the US DOJ's *Leniency Plus*, which offers complete amnesty in exchange for confessions) is intended to further incentivize firms to confess their transgressions. As noted in Chapter 2, the drawback to leniency offers is that firms can reap the benefits of collusion, and then confess to the price-fixing for immunity from prosecution. Still, the carrot approach of leniency programs has proven effective when fines have not.

Open, unfettered collusion has not been practiced in the US since the late nineteenth century. The Sherman and Clayton Acts have provided the template for antitrust policy and allowed the Department of Justice to aggressively address the problem of cartelization. Article 81 and Article 82 form the basis of the European Union's antitrust regime, which is similar to the US system in its objectives and enforcement.

The early twentieth century brought increased international competition. Cartels operating in the industrialized world in the 1920s and 1930s experimented with interlocking boards and export control agreements as a means of colluding without the appearance of price-fixing. In the post-war world, with tariff rates back to levels similar to those of the late 1800s, cartels were again primarily intra-national in their scope. The international commodity agreements of this period represented a new twist on collusion—producers in the developing world could cooperate openly, and without fear of any consequences. Raw material exporters experimented with export and production controls, price targets, common levies, and buffer stocks. Although there are identifiable periods during which most of these cartels managed to impact prices, ultimately, market forces overwhelmed market management, and commodity cartels were largely abandoned.

The recent wave of collusion in the US and Europe since 1980 has taken place in an environment of dramatically lower tariff rates. Businesses once shielded from real competitive forces can find themselves struggling to adjust to fierce competition. At the same time, aggressive antitrust policy in the US and Europe has made price-fixing far riskier. Corporations that produce intermediate products have been especially likely to assume the dangers of collusion, since the odds of detection are measurably lower in industries in which final prices are not transparent. The seemingly endless stream of cartels uncovered in Europe beginning in the 1980s suggests an antitrust system in need of fresh strategies for investigation and prosecution.

Notes

1 The regulatory environment—antitrust law and enforcement in the US and the EU

1 *Conseil de la Concurrence*, Procedural Notice, April 17, 2007, "Relating to the French Leniency Program." Although there are some minor differences, the 2007 Notice contains provisions very similar to those established under EU regulations.
2 This is the act that created the FTC: "An Act To Create a Federal Trade Commission, to define its powers and duties, and for other purposes," September 26, 1914.

2 Oligopoly markets, collusion, and the operation of cartels

1 Although the action taken by UNCTAD appears to be revolutionary, the proclamation followed upon approximately ten years of experimentation with cartel price-management by the developing world, commencing with OPEC in 1969. In addition, despite the rhetoric, commodity prices had begun to increase significantly in the early 1970s. Consequently, the impact of the *Integrated Programme for Commodities* was mostly political.
2 As will be demonstrated in Chapter 5, most recent collusive agreements in Europe and the US amount to unenforceable (since they are illegal) agreements to partition markets and maintain minimum selling prices. Although this is the most common form that cartels take in the industrialized world, it does not represent a formal cartel mechanism. The major reason for this divergence in practices is the types of markets that have recently been subject to collusion; intermediate goods not for final consumption. As market prices do not exist, firms are unable to apply the mechanisms that were common practice for the international cartels.
3 De Beers' hold on the market is now rapidly diminishing, due to significant overproduction, and the inability of De Beers to buy and stockpile sufficient quantities of diamonds. In addition, by 2005 artificial diamonds that were virtually identical to mined stones were entering the market, presumably ending the remaining power of De Beers to set prices.
4 The list of markets where this outcome can be observed is extensive, and includes the soft-drink industry (Coke and Pepsi), the fast-food burger sector (McDonalds and Burger King), and the commercial jet aircraft industry (Boeing and Airbus).

3 The historical background

1 Natural rubber competes directly with synthetic rubber for most industrial uses. Automobile tires, however, must be made of natural rubber, as tires made from synthetics wear poorly.

4 Globalization and corporate collusion

1 The discussion will be confined to the cartels that operated globally under the threat of antitrust enforcement. While the commodity cartels of the 1980s were, by definition, global in nature, their structure and behavior was not determined by the need to avoid prosecution.
2 One of the peculiarities here is the plasterboard cartel, which operated in only six nations. In addition, the elevator accord operated in only four countries. In the latter case, the specificity of the product to an individual job may have made a European-wide agreement difficult to negotiate. Given the characteristics of plasterboard, the cartel for this product would have been expected to cover more of the continental market.
3 Document #C (98)35).

5 Collusion in the industrialized world—the structure of the recent US and European experience

1 See EU Commission, "Commission Fines Four Companies in Sorbates Cartel a Total of 138.4 EUR million," Brussels, October 2, 2003. A similar, if smaller probe also took place in North America against sorbate producers.
2 If one does a simple calculation of the penalties based on sales, the fines appear quite dramatic. Using the Commission's figure of 500 million euro as the annual sales of paraffin, a fine amounting to 10 percent of sales over 13 years would equal the total fines imposed—considered by the EU as the upper limit of antitrust penalties. Yet, sales of that magnitude were for the current year only and presumably exceeded sales of prior years. In addition, the cartel controlled only 75 percent of the market. These fines must be regarded as significant penalties from an EU Commission exhausted with continual antitrust violations.

6 Regulatory reform

1 A reasonable example of this is the US airline industry, which exhibits highly interdependent pricing. As a result of the 2007–8 rise in fuel costs, the airlines as a whole generated enormous losses, and some consolidation of the industry occurred.
2 The example given by Stephan is the German firm SGL Carbon, which was found to have participated in three different cartels since 2001. The corporation asserted that it was unable to pay the fines imposed by the Commission, and still stay in business. SGL Carbon was granted a 33 percent reduction in each of the fines.
3 The DOJ reduced the fine imposed upon Hynix in the DRAM conspiracy, and allowed the firm to pay over an extended period (five years).
4 Full title: "An Act to amend the Trade Practices Act 1974 and the Prices Surveillance Act 1983, and for Related Purposes."

References

Adams, W. (1951) "The Aluminum Case: Legal Victory—Economic Defeat," *American Economic Review*, 41: 915–22.

Armentano, D. (1986) *Antitrust Policy: The Case for Repeal*, Washington, D.C., Cato Institute.

Ashenfelter, O. and Graddy, K. (2004) "Anatomy of the Rise and Fall of a Price-Fixing Conspiracy: Auctions at Sotheby's and Christie's," National Bureau of Economic Research, working paper.

Baker, W. and Faulkner, R. (1993) "The Social Organization of Conspiracy: Illegal Networks in the Heavy Equipment Industry," *American Sociological Review*, 58: 837–60.

Barbezat, D. (1989) "Cooperation and Rivalry in the International Steel Cartel, 1926–1933," *Journal of Economic History*, 49: 435–47.

Barbezat, D. (1991) "A Price for Every Product, Every Place: The International Steel Cartel, 1933–39," *Business History*, 33: 68–86.

Bergenstock, D.J., Deily, M.E. and Taylor, L.W. (2006) "A Cartel's Response to Cheating: An Empirical Investigation of the De Beers Diamond Empire," *Southern Economic Journal*, 73: 173–89.

Bermann, G., Geobel, R., Davey, W. and Fox, E. (1993) *Cases and Materials on European Community Law*, Minneapolis, West Publishing.

Bhattacharjea, A. (2006) "The Case for a Multilateral Agreement on Competition Policy: A Developing Country Perspective," *Journal of International Economic Law*, 9: 293–323.

Binder, J. (1988) "The Sherman Antitrust Act and the Railroad Cartels," *Journal of Law and Economics*, 31: 443–68.

Binswanger, H. (2005) "Antitrust: 'Free Competition' at Gunpoint," in Hall, G. (ed.), *The Abolition of Antitrust*, New Brunswick, N.J., Transaction Publishers.

Bloom, M. (2006) "Despite Its Success, The EC Leniency Program Faces Great Challenges," EU Competition Law and Policy Workshop/Proceedings, European University Workshop.

Blum, V., Steinat, N. and Veltine, M. (2008) "On the Rationale of Leniency Programs: A Game Theoretical Analysis," *European Journal of Law and Economics*, 25: 209–29.

Bolotova, Y. (2009) "Cartel Overcharges: An Empirical Analysis," *Journal of Economic Behavior and Organization*, 70: 321–41.

Bolotova, Y., Connor, J. and Miller, D. (2009) "Factors Influencing the Magnitude of Cartel Overcharges," *Journal of Competition Law and Economics*, 5: 361–81.

Bond, E. (2004) "Antitrust Policy in Open Economies: Price Fixing and International Cartels," in Choi, E. and Hartigan, J., (eds.) *Handbook of International Trade, Volume II*, Blackwell.

Bowden, T. (2005) "Antitrust: The War Against Contracts," in Hall, G. (ed.) *The Abolition of Antitrust*, New Brunswick, N.J., Transaction Publishers.

Burger, K. and Smit, H. (1990) "Long-term and Short-term Analysis of the Natural Rubber Market," Weltwirtschaftliches Archives, 125: 718–47.

Buxbaum, H. (2004) "National Courts, Global Cartels: F. Hoffman–LaRouche Ltd. v. Empagran S.A. (U.S. Supreme Court 2004)," *German Law Journal*, 5: 1,095–1,106.

Buxbaum, R. (1964) "Incomplete Federalism: Jurisdiction over Antitrust Matters in the European Economic Community," *California Law Review*, 52: 56–94.

Cason, T. (1994) "The Impact of Information Sharing Opportunities on Market Outcomes: An Experimental Study," *Southern Economic Journal*, 61: 18–39.

Clarke, J. and Evenett, S. (2003) "The Deterrent Effects of National Anticartel Laws: Evidence from the International Vitamins Cartel," *Antitrust Bulletin*, 48: 689–726.

Coate, M. (2005) "Empirical Analysis of Merger Enforcement Under the 1992 Merger Guidelines," *Review of Industrial Organizations*, 27: 279–301.

Combe, E., Monnier, C. and Legal, R. (2008) "Cartels, the Probability of Getting Caught in the European Union," *Bruges European Economic Research Papers*, #12.

Connor, J. (1997) "The Global Lysine Price-Fixing Conspiracy of 1992–1995," *Review of Agricultural Economics*, 19: 158–74.

Connor, J. (2001) "Our Customers are our Enemies," *Review of Industrial Organizations*, 18: 5–21.

Connor, J. (2002) "The Food and Agricultural Global Cartels of the 1990s: Overview and Update," Working Paper Series #02-4, Purdue University, Department of Agricultural Economics.

Connor, J. (2005), Price-Fixing Overcharges: Legal and Economic Evidence, Staff Paper # 04-17, Purdue University.

Connor, J. (2006) "The Effectiveness of Antitrust Sanctions on Modern International Cartels," *Journal of Industry, Competition and Trade*, 6: 195–223.

Connor, J. (2007) *Global Price Fixing*, 2nd Edition, New York, Springer.

Connor, J. and Lande, R. (2007) "Cartel Overcharges and Optimal Cartel Fines," Working Paper, available at SSRN.

Craycraft, C., Craycraft, J. and Gallo, J. (1997) "Antitrust Sanctions and the Firm's Ability to Pay," *Review of Industrial Organizations*, 12: 171–83.

Cyrenne, P. (1999) "On Antitrust Enforcement and the Deterrence of Collusive Behaviour," *Review of Industrial Organizations*, 14: 257–72.

Dewey, D. (1961) "Mergers and Cartels: Some Reservations about Policy," *American Economic Review*, 51: 255–62.

Dick, A. (1992a) "Are Export Cartels Efficiency-Enhancing or Monopoly-Promoting?," *Research in law and Economics*, 15: 89–127.

Dick, A. (1992b) "The Competitive Consequences of Japan's Export Cartel Associations," *Journal of the Japanese and International Economies*, 6: 275–98.

Dick, A. (1993) "Japanese Antitrust: Reconciling Theory and Evidence," *Contemporary Policy Issues*, 11: 50–61.

EU Commission (2003) "Commission Fines Four Companies in Sorbates Cartel a Total of 138.4 EUR million," Brussels, October 2.

Epstein, R. and Greve, M. (2004) "The Intractable Problem of Antitrust Jurisdiction," in Epstein, R. and Greve, M. (eds.) *Competition Laws in Conflict: Antitrust Jurisdiction in the Global Economy*, Washington D.C., AEI Press.

Evenett, S., Levenstein, M. and Suslow, V. (2001) "International Cartel Enforcement: Lessons from the 1990s," *World Economy*, 24: 1,221–45.

Feldenkirchen, Wilfried (1992) "Competition Policy in Germany," *Business and Economic History*, 21: 257–69.

First, H. (1986) "Japan's Antitrust Policy: Impact on Import Competition," in Pugel, T. and Hawkins, R. (eds.) *Fragile Interdependence*, Lexington, MA, Lexington Books.

Fox, E. (1997) "US and EU Competition Law: A Comparison," in Richardson, J. and Graham, E. (eds.) *Global Competition* Policy, Washington, D.C., Peterson Institute.

Fry, J. (2001) "Struggling to Teethe: Japan's Antitrust Enforcement Regime," *Law and Policy in International Business*, 32: 825–57.

Gal-Or, E. (1985) "Information Sharing in Oligopoly," *Econometrica*, 53: 329–43.

Gerber, D. (2007) "Competition Law and the WTO: Rethinking the Relationship," *Journal of International Economic Law*, 10: 707–24.

Gilbert, C. (1987) "International Commodity Agreements: Design and Performance," *World Development*, 15: 591–616.

Gilbert, C. (1996) "International Commodity Agreements: An Obituary Notice," *World Development*, 24: 1–19.

Goodwin, G. and Mayall, J. (1980) *A New International Commodity Regime*, New York, St. Martin's Press.

Green, E. and Porter, R. (1984), "Non-cooperative Collusion Under Imperfect Price Information," Econometrica, 52, 87–100.

Griffin, J. and Xiong, W. (1997) "The Incentive to Cheat: An Empirical Analysis of OPEC," *Journal of Law and Economics*, 40: 289–316.

Grout, P. and Sonderegger, S. (2005) "Predicting Cartels," University of Bristol, Working Paper.

Gupta, Bishnupriya (2001) "The International Tea Cartel During the Great Depression," 1929–33, *Journal of Economic History*, 61: 144–59.

Guzman, A. (2004) "The Case for International Antitrust," in Epstein, R. and Greve, M. (eds.) *Competition Law in Conflict*, Washington, D.C., AEI Press.

Hadley, Eleanor (1970) *Antitrust in Japan*, Princeton, NJ, Princeton University Press.

Haley, J. (2001) *Antitrust in Germany and Japan: The First Fifty Years, 1947–1998*, Seattle, University of Washington Press.

Han, M., Schinkel, M. and Tuinstra, J. (2008) "The Overcharge as a Measure for Antitrust Damages," Amsterdam Center for Law and Economics, Working Paper #2008-08.

Harris, S. and Goldman, C. (2001) *Competition Law Outside the United States*, Illinois, American Bar Association.

Hay, G. and Kelley, D. (1974) "An Empirical Survey of Price Fixing Conspiracies," *Journal of Law and Economics*, 17: 13–38.

Heidenhain, M., Satzky, H. and Stadler, C. (1999) *German Antitrust Law* (5th Edition), Huntington, NY, Juris Publishing.

Hermann, R., Burger, K. and Smit, H. (1993), *International Commodity Policy: A Quantitative Analysis*, Routledge, London.

Hess, Glenn (2000), "Worldwide Sorbates Cartel used CMR to Fix Prices in US for 17 years," *Chemical Market Reporter*, October 30, Vol. 258.

Hillman, J. (1988) "Malaysia and the International Tin Cartel," *Modern Asia Studies*, 22: 237–61.

Hillman, J. (1997), "The Impact of the International Tin Restrictions on the Return to Equity of Tin Mining Companies, 1927–39," *Business History*, 39: 65–80.

Hilton, G. (1966), "The Consistency of the Interstate Commerce Act," *Journal of Law and Economics*, 9, 87–111.

Holloway, S. (1988) *The Aluminum Multinationals and the Bauxite Cartel*, New York, St. Martin's Press.

Hovenkamp (2005) *The Antitrust Enterprise: Principle and Execution*, Cambridge, MA, Harvard University Press.

Hull, G., (2005) "Antitrust is Immoral," in Hull, G. (ed.) *Antitrust Policy: The Case for Repeal*, New Brunswick, NJ, Transactions Publishers.

Inoue, A. (2007) *Japanese Antitrust Law Manual*, Netherlands: Kluwer Law International.

International Monetary Fund (various dates), *International Financial Statistics*, Washington, D.C.

Ito, T. and Maruyama, M. (1990) "Is the Japanese Distribution System Really Inefficient?," National Bureau of Economic Research, Working Paper #3306.

Jandl, M. (2004) "The Estimation of Illegal Migration in Europe," *Migration Studies*, 61: 141–55.

Jaspers, M. (2004) "The TACA Judgment: Lessons Learnt and the Way Forward," *Competition Policy Newsletter*, 1: 34–9.

Jones, C. (1990) "OPEC Behavior under Falling Oil Prices: Implications for Cartel Stability," *Energy Journal*, 11: 117–29.

Kerber, W. and Budzinski, O. (2004) "Competition of Competition Laws: Mission Impossible?" in Epstein, R. and Greve, M. (eds.) *Competition Laws in Conflict*, Washington D.C., AEI Press.

Kirby, A. (1988) "Trade Associations as Information Exchange Mechanisms," *Rand Journal of Economics*, 19: 138–46.

Kleit, A. (2005) *Antitrust and Competition Policy*, Edward Elgar.

Klevorick, A. and Sykes, A. (2007) "United States Courts and the Optimal Deterrence of International Cartels: A Welfarist Perspective on *Empagran*," *Journal of Competition Law and Economics*, 3: 309–33.

Landes, W. (1983) "Optimal Sanctions for Antitrust Violations," *University of Chicago Law Review*, 50: 652–78.

Langenfeld, J. and Silvia, L. (2004) "Federal Trade Commission Horizontal Restraint Cases: An Update," *Antitrust Bulletin*, 49: 521–91.

Leach, D. (1994) "The South African Cement Cartel: A Critique of Fourie and Smith," *South African Journal of Economics*, 62: 156–68.

Lean, D., Ogur, J. and Rogers, R.(1985) "Does Collusion Pay ... Does Antitrust Work?" *Southern Economic Journal*, 51: 828–41.

LeClair, M. (2000) *International Commodity Markets and the Role of Cartels*, New York, M.E. Sharpe.

Levenstein, M. and Suslow, V. (2006) "What Determines Cartel Success," *Journal of Economic Literature*, 44: 43–95.

Lyons, B. (2004) "Reform of European Merger Policy," *Review of International Economics*, 12: 246–61.

Mahler, V. (1984) "The Political Economy of North–South Commodity Bargaining: The Case of the International Sugar Agreement," *International Organization*, 38; 709–31.

Marquez, J. (1994) "Life Expectancy of International Cartels: An Empirical Analysis," *Review of Industrial Organization*, 9: 331–41.

Marshall, R. Marx, L. and Raiff, M. (2007) "Cartel Price Announcements: The Vitamins Industry," *International Journal of Industrial Organization*, 26: 762–802.

McMahon, G. (1987) "Do Small Countries Benefit from International Commodity Agreements? The Case of Coffee and Kenya," *Economic Development and Cultural Change*, 35: 409–23.

Miller, L., Schnaars, S. and Vaccaro, V. (1993) "The Provocative Practice of Price Signaling: Collusion Versus Cooperation," *Business Horizons*, 36: 59–65.

Moran, A. and Novak, J. (2009) "The Adverse Effects of Government Action Against Cartels," Institute of Public Affairs.

Morrison, R. (1992) "Price Fixing among Elite Colleges and Universities," *University of Chicago Law Review*, 59: 807–35.

Motta, M. (2004), Competition Policy: Theory and Practice, Cambridge, UK, Cambridge University Press.

Motta, M. and Polo, M. (2003) "Leniency Programs and Cartel Prosecution," *International Journal of Industrial Organization*, 21: 347–79.

Nakazawa, T. and Weiss, L. (1989) "The Legal Cartels of Japan," *Antitrust Bulletin*, 34: 641–53

Nash (1950) "Equilibrium Points in *n*-person Games," *Proceedings of the National Academy of Sciences*, 36: 48–49.

Newmark, G. (1988) "Does Horizontal Price Fixing Raise Price? A Look at the Bakers of Washington Case," *Journal of Law and Economics*, 31: 469–84.

Nicolaïdis, K. and Vernon, R. (1997), Competition Policy and Trade Policy in the European Union, in *Global Competition Policy*, Graham, E. and Richardson, J. (eds.), Washington, D.C., Institute for International Economics.

Nieberding, J. (2006), "Estimating Overcharges in Antitrust Cases Using a Reduced Form Approach: Methods and Issues," *Journal of Applied Economics*, 9, 361–80.

Normann, H. and Tan, E. (2005) "The Effects of Cartel Policy: Evidence from the German Power-Cable Industry," Royal Holloway College, London, Working Paper.

Organization for Economic Cooperation and Development (1998) "Recommendations of the Council Concerning Effective Action Against Hard Core Cartels," Paris, OECD.

Organization for Economic Cooperation and Development (2002), "Fighting Hard-Core Cartels: Harm, Effective Sanctions and Leniency Programs," Paris, OECD.

Organization for Economic Cooperation and Development (OECD) (2003) "Hard Core Cartels: Recent Progress and Challenges Ahead," Paris, OECD.

Organization for Economic Cooperation and Development (OECD) (2003b), "Germany—The Role of Competition Policy in Regulatory Reform," Paris, OECD.

Organization for Economic Cooperation and Development (2005) "Third Report on the Implementation of the 1998 Recommendations," Paris, OECD.

Peterson, R. (1998) "An Assessment of the Accuracy of Independent Retailer Judgment of the Legality of Selected Commercial Practices," *Journal of Business and Economic Perspectives*, 14: 32–41.

Peterson, R. (2001) "Small Retailer and Service Company Accuracy in Evaluating the Legality of Specified Practices," *Journal of Small Business Management*, 39: 312–19.

Phillips, A. (1959) "A Critique of United States Experience with Price-Fixing Agreements and the Per Se Rule," *Journal of Industrial Economics*, 8: 13–32.

Pindyck, R. (1977) "Cartel Pricing and the Structure of the World Bauxite Market," *The Bell Journal of Economics*, 8: 343–60.

Porter, R. (1983) "Optimal Cartel Trigger Price Strategies," *Journal of Economic Theory*, 29: 313–38.

Ramseyer, J. (1985) "The Costs of the Consensual Myth: Antitrust Enforcement and Institutional Barriers to Litigation in Japan," *Yale Law Journal*, 94: 604–45.

Rill, J. and Chambers, C. (1997) "Antitrust Enforcement and Non-Enforcement as a Barrier to Import in the Japanese Automobile Industry," *Empirica*, 24: 108–35

Rothstein. R. (1979) *Global Bargaining: UNCTAD and the Quest for a New International Economic Order*, Princeton, Princeton University Press.

Schaede, U. (2000) *Cooperative Capitalism: Self-Regulation, Trade Associations, and the Antimonopoly Law in Japan*, New York, Oxford University Press.

Shapiro, C. (1986) "Exchange of Cost Information in Oligopoly," *Review of Economic Studies*, 53: 433–46.

Shepherd, G. (1995) "Overlap and Antitrust: Fixing Prices in a Smoke-Filled Classroom," *Antitrust Bulletin*, 40: 859–884.

Spar, D. (1994) *The Cooperative Edge*, Ithaca, Cornell University Press.

Sproul, M., (1993) "Antitrust and Prices," *Journal of Political Economy*, 101: 741–54.

Stephan, A. (2005) "An Empirical Assessment of the 1996 Leniency Notice," Centre for Competition Policy Working Paper # 05-10.

Stephan, A. (2006) "The Bankruptcy Wildcard in Cartel Cases," Centre for Competition Policy Working Paper #06-5.

Stephen, P. (2004), *Against International Cooperation*, in Epstein, R. and Greve, M. (eds.), Competition Law in Conflict, Washington, D.C., AEI Press.

Stigler, G. (1964) "A Theory of Oligopoly," *Journal of Political Economy*, 72: 44–61.

Stocking, G. and Watkins, M. (1991) *Cartels in Action: Case Studies in International Business Diplomacy*, Buffalo, NY, Business Enterprise Reprint Series.

Suzumura, K. (1997) "Formal and Informal Measures for controlling Competition in Japan: Institutional Overview and Theoretical Evaluation," in Graham, E. and Richardson, J., (eds.), *Global Competition Policy*, Washington, D.C., Institute for International Economics.

Sweeney, B. (2007) "Export Cartels: Is there a Need for a Global Rules," *Journal of International Economic Law*, 10: 87–115.

Sweezey, P. (1939) "Demand Under Conditions of Oligopoly," *Journal of Political Economy*, 4: 568–73.

Tilley, D. and Khaerunisa, I. (1996) "Impact of International Coffee Agreement Abandonment on Indonesia Coffee Prices," *Agribusiness*, 12: 157–66.

Upham, F. (1987) *Law and Social Change in Postwar Japan*, Cambridge, MA, Harvard University Press.

U.S. Bureau of the Census, *Historical Statistics of the U.S.*, Washington D.C., U.S. Government Printing Office.

U.S. Department of Justice (DOJ) (1999), "F. Hoffman–La Roche and BASF agree to Pay Record Criminal Fines for Participating in International Vitamin Cartel," press release, May 20.

U.S. Department of Justice (DOJ) (2006) "Japanese Company Agrees To Plead Guilty To Participating In DRAM Price-Fixing Conspiracy," press release, January 30.

US Department of Justice (DOJ) (2006) "Seven Steps to Better Cartel Enforcement," text of presentation to the 11th Annual Competition Law & Policy Workshop, EU Institute, Florence, Italy.

U.S. Department of Justice (DOJ) (2007) "British Airways Plc And Korean Air Lines Co. Ltd. Agree To Plead Guilty And Pay Criminal Fines Totaling $600 Million For Fixing Prices On Passenger and Cargo Flights," press release, August 1.

U.S. Department of Justice (DOJ) (2007), "Two Executives of French Manufacturer of Marine Hose Agree to Plead Guilty to Participating in Worldwide Bid-Rigging Conspiracy," press release, November 6.

U.S. Department of Justice (DOJ) (2007), "Three United Kingdom Nationals Charged with Participating in Worldwide Bid-Rigging Conspiracy in the Marine Hose Industry," press release, December 3.

US Department of Justice (DOJ) (2008) "LG, Sharp, Chunghwa Agree to Plead Guilty, Pay Total of $585 Million in Fines for Participating in LCD Price-Fixing Conspiracies", press release, November 12.

U.S. Department of Justice (DOJ) (2009) "Three International Airline Companies Agree to Plead Guilty to Price Fixing on Air Cargo Shipments," press release, April 9.

Van Groenendaal, W. and Vingerhoets, J. (1995) "Can international commodity agreements work?" Journal of Policy Modeling, vol. 17, 257–78.

Verouden, V., Bengtsson, C. and Albaek, C. (2004) "The Draft EU Notice on Horizontal Mergers: A Further Step Towards Convergence," *Antitrust Bulletin*, 49: 243–85.

Wells, W. (2002) *Antitrust and the Formation of the Postwar World*, New York, Columbia University Press.

White, L. (2001) "Lysine and Price Fixing: How Long? How Severe?," *Review of Industrial Organizations*, 18: 23–31.

Wilk, K. (1939) "The International Sugar Regime," *American Political Science Review*, 33: 871–73.

Wils, W.P. (2006) "Optimal Antitrust Fines: Theory and Practice," *World Competition*, 29: 183–208.

Wood, D. (2004), "Cooperation and Convergence in International Antitrust: Why the Light is Still Yellow," in Epstein, R. and Greve, M. (eds.), Competition Law in Conflict, Washington, DC, AEI Press.

World Bank (various dates) *World Development Index*, Washington D.C., World Bank.

Zane (2003) "The Price Fixer's Dilemma: Applying Game Theory to the Decision of Whether to Plead Guilty to Antitrust Crimes," *Antitrust Bulletin*, 48: 1–31.

Zimmerman, E. (1964) "The Federal Trade Commission and Mergers," *Columbia Law Review*, 64: 500–23.

Zimmerman, J. and Connor, J. (2005), "Determinants of Cartel Duration: A Cross-Sectional Study of Modern Private International Cartels," Department of Agricultural Economics, Purdue University, Working Paper.

Case references

Addyston Pipe and Steel Co. v. U.S., 175 U.S. 211 (1899).
Brown Shoe v. U.S., 370 U.S. 294 (1962)
Catalano, Inc. v. Target Sales, Inc., 446 U.S. 643 (1980)
F. Hoffman–La Roche v. Empagran, S.A., 542 U.S. 155 (2004)
Fairdale Farms v. Yankee Milk, 635 F.2d 1037 (1980)
Goldfarb et ux v. Virginia State Bar et al., 421 U.S. 773 (1975)
Hartford Fire Insurance v. California, 509 SC 764 (1993)
Japan v. Idemitsu Kosan K.K., 985 Hanrei Jiho 3 Tokyo High Ct. (1980)
Japan v. Sekiyu Renmei, 983 Hanrei jiho 22 Tokyo High Ct. (1980)
Maryland and Virginia Milk Producers v. U.S., 362 U.S. 458 (1960)
Mitsubishi Building Maintenance Case Mitsubishibiltechnoservice 41 SINKETUSHU 46, FTC (1994)
National Society of Professional Engineers v. U.S., 435 U.S. 679 (1978)
Pillsbury Inc. v. FTC, 354 F.2d 952 (1966)
Swift & Co. v. U.S., Sup Ct. 196 U.S., 375 (1906)
Toshiba Chemical Company v. JFTC, 906 HANREITIMES 136 Tokyo High Ct. (1995)
U.S. v. Alcoa, 91 F. Supp. 333 SDNY (1950)
U.S. v. American Tobacco Company, 221 U.S. 106 (1911)
U.S. v. Appalachian Coal, 288 U.S. 344 (1933)
U.S. v. Borden, 308 U.S. 188 (1939)
U.S. v. Brown University, Civil Action 91-CV-3274 (1993)
U.S. v. Container Corporation of America, 393 U.S. 333 (1969)
U.S. v. E.I. DuPont de Nemours and Company, 351 U.S. 377 (1956)
U.S. v. Ian P. Norris, Criminal No.: 03-632 (2003)
U.S. v. Joint Traffic Association, 171 U.S. 505 (1898)
U.S. v. Robert Hart, USDC Pennsylvania, 99-595 (1999)
U.S. v. Trans-Missouri Freight Association, 166 U.S. 290 (1897)
U.S. v. U.S. Steel, 251 U.S. 417 (1920)

Index